Short Stories From The Neighborhood

A Collection of Nostalgic Writers From Carbondale, IL

Compiled and Edited

by Robert Pankey, Ed.D.

DEDICATION

This book is dedicated to all those people who have grown up in small towns across America. Their successes, fears, hopes, mistakes, loves and joys were parallel to the writers in this short story book. The following stories were written by ex-students of Carbondale, Illinois public schools, and Carbondale Community High School. We are thankful to these writers for their creative contributions to the memorable experiences from the past.

INDEX

ACKNOWLEDGMENTS

Congratulation and much appreciation goes to all the people who created their personal stories for this book. The future proceeds from the sales of this short story book will be going to help the programs at Carbondale Community High School (CCHS). I found that there were resounding commonalities in the writers desires, friendships, heart aches, aspirations, hopes and love of life when they were growing up. Thank you all for your effort! I appreciate the help from H.B. Koplowitz who gave me advice and a second set of eyes on the editing of this book. I would also like to give a big thanks to my writing coach, Ms. Sara Eyestone, curator of the Art Collections at La Posada de Santa Fe. Through Sara's summer workshops sprang the idea of taking on this project. Lastly, I want to thank Jill Pankey, my better half, for her patience and support when I was spending endless hours in front of the computer, compiling and editing the stories that came in during the summer of 2019. May everyone find enjoyment in reading these personal short stories and recall what a blessing it was to have grown up in Carbondale.

JR. HIGH SCHOOL BULLIES COME IN ALL SHAPES AND SIZES

by Mel Hughlett

In Fall of 1959 Television was in black & white and so was everything else in America. I began kindergarten that year in a proud racially segregated K-12 system known as Attucks School. My Building Accommodated K-8 and just to the east of it on the same grounds stood the very proud Attucks High school.

Together those buildings seemed to personify the best a community could offer. Teachers and instructors that inspired and aspired, programs in art, music and drama that turned a community out to watch and marvel and feared Basketball & Baseball teams that made a community so proud. The historic Mascot was the iconic Bluebird and a little neighborhood boy in those days would live for the day that he himself could pour into one of those uniforms and I was no exception.

By fall of 1965 all that remained of that school was K-6th due to legislated school integration and I was a 6th grader, big kid, budding ball player and looked up to on that campus. I adored that school, its halls, it memories and its pride and purpose. Part of that included the fact that I would tend to see my teachers at Church, the park, Grocery stores and at community events. The rod of correction was always nearby and it seemed so with the cooperation of our parents.

They exuded love and care and over the years I have taken great pride in the fact that I was the last athlete competing that ever wore a Bluebird jersey in competition. In any event, in fall of 1966 I was registered in Lincoln Jr High, a PWS (predominantly white school) on the SE side of the community where the environment was radically different if not borderline hostile. Add to this my being assigned to the homeroom of a maniacal militarized man who seemed to think his point was made clearer at decibel levels that would get most folks tossed from civilized places and things would only get worse.

This man was a bully, boisterous, bigoted and racially resentful. It turns out that I was his appx height and more physical than he and a few of the darling little white girls in class were attracted to me and it wouldn't help in his eyes. He taunted me, screamed at me, attempted to intimidate me, told me that my aspirations were unrealistic, placed me at the back of the class and isolated me.

Many of the rules & regulations this school fostered in its orientation were foreign to many of us Attucks transfers such as certain shoes being barred in class, certain hairstyles prohibited, no chewing gum or cough drops in class, no standing in Hallways during lunch and no food or drinks in the Gym during anytime. So the atmosphere seemed hostile & detached compared to my previous understanding of school and I was unable to feel inspired or even respected inside these walls. As a youngster of that period you were perhaps unable to fully articulate your impression but emotionally you sensed a disconnect directly.

The most definitive moment for me happened during my final year at that school (8th grade). The aforementioned maniacally loud & hostile teacher also served as Gym monitor during lunch. On one particularly cold winter day my friends and I had arrived back at campus with cold drinks in our hands and decided to get warm in the gym while waiting for class bell. My friends, per policy dumped their drinks prior to entering. I did not. Sort of forgot. in any event, the gym crowd was always segregated and I sat several rows up in the 'black' section as I slurped on my drink.

Mr. Loud came quickly and asked if I had a drink to which I said yes. He told me to put it in the dumpster which sat close to the door on the first level. I immediately asked a friend of mine down on that level to take the drink and dump it. This somehow aggravated Mr. Loud and he went into a very gruffly loud 'I TOLD YOU TO DUMP IT, NOT HIM, YOU GET DOWN HERE NOW'! at once all the resentment I held towards him from the previous year came rushing back to me and by now I am even taller than he and quite a bit more physical and very sure of my boxing and wrestling skills. I took two bleachers and jumped all the way down to the floor in front of him and began threatening his health and I meant every last bit of it. The 'white' side of the gym erupted into applause and the fear in his eyes was palpable and he began to wilt asking the other kids not to get involved and trying to suddenly de-escalate the matter. As I look back, that moment was pivotal and could have gone so terribly wrong. District 95 knew who, what and how this man was yet they allowed him to work with children. Impressionable youth which suggest that they tacitly approved of his conduct and they knew he bullied and screamed at kids while forcing them to keep military style cadence in a walk to the library and bathrooms.

Had this man attempted to manhandle me that day I would have been forced to harm him severely which may have been the last thing I ever did as a free citizen. As I write this I realize that I could only now be getting released from incarceration if at all. That is simply how much I resented that God awful human. Fortunately, he backed off and I was able to get my parents, Big Roosevelt and Ms. Pauline to intervene and prevent further issue. In the meanwhile In the meanwhile, Big Roosevelt made a few things very clear to Mr. Loud about how he'd prepared me to respect authority but maintain my own dignity.

What I resent most, to this day, was that the methods Administrator's used in in choosing educators obviously did not consider temperament, leadership and effective soft skills. That oversight could have caused a kid, like myself, to be sent to an adult reformatory and changed my history forever. Mercy!

MIDLAND HILLS

By Dr. Bob Pankey, Ed.D.

Midland Hills was a country club unlike the typical ones you might see in *Golf Digest* magazine. Instead of a 50-meter swimming pool, the country club had a lake. The lake was full of the clearest water and largest bluegills I have ever seen.

The Huffman family owned a little log cabin at Midland Hills where they spent their summer weekends. It had a tin roof that carried the most peaceful sounds when it rained. At one end of the cabin, there was a big rock fireplace, just right for roasting marshmallows on a chilly night. Usually in the summer, our family would visit the Huffman's cabin, and there was little need for a fire, just an occasional playful swim in the lake to cool off. The worst thing about that cabin was the bathroom. Actually, I guess one would call it an outhouse. It was a tiny little shack to the north of the cabin, and when the wind was blowing from the north, you could hardly stand to be downwind.

The Pankeys, my family, the Huffmans, and the Hall family were best of friends during those summer weekends. They would gather their kids up on weekends and take them to the cabin to get away from the heat and boredom from sitting around their houses in Carbondale.

The wives would cook all day and tell stories and complain about their old husbands. Helen Huffman, in her tube-top that was two sizes too small, would be cooking with one hand and holding her cigarette with the other. Mary Pankey continually washed the dishes and carried on about the cliffs being too dangerous to jump off of, and Mary Hall would sit at the kitchen table and oversee Mary and Helen's work, giving her input when needed.

The men would sit out on the porch in the back of the cabin, drink beer, and tell lies about how big the fish were that they caught in the lake that day. They fished from small boats and canoes, occasionally tipping them over when they stood up too fast. As night fell, I could hear my dad and the other men having contests over who could "break wind" the loudest.

Between the families there were five boys and two girls, all of whom were excellent swimmers. During those hot summer days we would cross the lake to the beach two or three times just to see who was around, and we would play all day in the sun. We were innocent and happy, and the days and evenings would seemingly last forever. My skin would turn as golden brown as the leaves on an oak tree in the fall, and Mom would claim that I must have gotten mixed up at the hospital when they were handing out babies because I looked so different from my fair-skinned brothers. At night the moon would reflect off the lake and strike us full in the face. Some nights we would all sit around the boat dock and laugh and shout and feel carefree. Those days and nights were truly some of the best of my childhood life.

Time went on, like it always does, and our families grew apart. A few years later, my father passed away. At his funeral, Peaches Hall, my dad's best friend, walked with me away from the grave site, and I remember telling him that I missed the good times that we had at Midland Hills together. Peaches looked at me and said that he did too and assured me that we would all get together again and there would be other good times. But we never did. Those warm summer days that lasted forever were gone, and I still miss them now and then.

Last week I was sitting in a lawn chair at a condominium complex at Padre Island, Texas with Dave Bacharach, Jim Woosley, and our wives watching our children play in the sand and surf. The setting was a world away from that which I grew up with in Southern Illinois. While I was basking in the sun watching the waves come in off the beach, it occurred to me that the day had lasted forever. We were all sitting around drinking beer, bragging about fishing, and, yes, having contests. These folks were my best friends, and they were as much fun as the kids I once played with at Midland Hills. The nice thing about being out with friends and the ones we love is that it sometimes brings back those earlier times when laughing was second nature and time would stand still. Being with my wife and our friends last weekend reminded me of the times when I was a kid, playing in the sun as if the day would never end. It was a weekend that reminded me of the days gone by, and I came to realize that Peaches was right that there would be other good times like those at Midland Hills.

CHICKEN HAWKINS AND THE ICE BALL

By Larry Eastwood

One thing we can count on in life is that as we grow older we reflect more on memories that tend to define us as people, Shakespeare referred to as players on a stage. None more so than those events experienced when we were young and shared with friends.

I am about to recant such a tale that attempts to pay tribute to a fallen classmate and charter member of the "Gang." This is not a story of fiction. There is no changing of names to protect the innocent. The following is a true account of what occurred in late February, 1968 as witnessed by Terry Etherton and myself. However I must digress. I have always enjoyed a good story, be it told in books, music, or film. I have particularly admired people who could tell a good tale, especially a person who adds more than just words, but enhances and embellishes the story like an actor on stage. Dick LeFevre was a consummate story teller. In fact, our visits over the years, which happened to be our class reunions consisted of him regaling us with elementary, junior high, and high school stories with uncanny detail and minutiae. I believe it was his way of expressing how much those days meant to him and how much he cared for us.

He and I would always end up saying after a good "cackle session," how we were glad to be part of a close class and how we were fortunate to be surrounded by funny people. Now I know most of it was off color and low brow, but I don't think it was ever conceived to be hurtful even though we could have cast off some of the nicknames. The hell of it is,

LeFevre came up with the majority of those monikers that we still use. He passed them out like John Belushi's character Bluto in Animal House. Okay, so what about my story?

My tale begins in homeroom one morning when the" Avacado" asked me if I wanted to walk with him downtown during lunch to make a deposit at a local S & L. No doubt those funds and the miracle of compound interest were the monetary foundation for the renowned Etherton Galleries in Tucson. So anyway, fourth hour lunch rolls around and the "Umphigan" spots us not entering the cafeteria, " Where do you knob knosters think you're going?"

" We're going to walk downtown so the " Goose" can make a deposit.", I said, "Not without me, but let's haul ass or the Ol' Maid will report me tardy to Ol' Man Diamond."

We jumped off N. Springer on to W. Main and headed east toward downtown. Soon we arrived at Main and University in front of the First Baptist Church, calmly waiting for the light to change. I watched from the corner of my right eye, a figure running obliquely to our direction. This apparition stopped not ten feet in front and slightly to the right of us and hurled with all its might a snowball. The menacing projectile sailed harmlessly over our heads and for what seemed like centuries, eons of time; we stared at one another incredulous, dumbfounded. I shook off the shock and screamed, " That's, Chicken Hawkins"!

Well C.H. didn't stop and apologize. He took off as fast as his terrorist little legs would allow heading east, laughing as he stole glances over his left shoulder. Our only choice of retaliatory ordnance happened to be dirty, slushy snow near the curb.
The Oaf spread both of his arms and shouted, " Stand back!"
He squatted down and quickly rolled a one pound round of grape shot and dipped it in a mud puddle to compact the deadly sphere. By this time the dastardly perpetrator had passed the United Methodist Church in full stride. Time stood still as my mind's eye saw in perfect Sports Center slow motion, the Umph hurl that ice clad sabot toward our attacker. I thought of a warm, sunny afternoon in Pittsburgh's old Forbes Field and Roberto Clemente unleashing that cannon of an arm, throwing a frozen rope from deep in right field, gunning down a speedy Maury Wills trying to score from third base.

The three of us watched as the paths of the ice ball and our target converged. The only outcome is obvious at this point. The falling howitzer shell and the back of Chicken Hawkins' noggin fused together,

as if in a shower of dirty slush and pink mist Marine Snipers see in a
clean head shot. C. H. sprawled on the sidewalk before he could reach
the safety of a left turn on N. Illinois Avenue.
There you have it. On that day in that moment, this Main Street, USA
was safe from terrorism. Good triUMPHED over evil. Where did this
evil come from you might ask? Steven Hawkins wasn't raised to be bad.
As a matter of fact he is a pious, Christian family man living in Paducah.
He works in purchasing for a successful electrical supply house. I had
occasion to do business with him at the store five or six years ago.
Nothing was said of the incident, but you could not cut the tension in the
room with a 10" Rambo army survival knife with serrated edge. John
Richard LeFevre, Jr. would relay this saga as I have described not in
words on a page but more like an actor in a one act play. He would write
the script, play all the parts, supply all the dialogue in whatever accent or
inflection appropriate, and create the art work.

I want to bring attention to his drawing skills because his penchant
for cartoons always brought me to my knees. I want to bring particular
homage to two examples. The first one he drew when both of us had
American History in summer school. My teacher was Norman Findley
and he had Mrs. Friedline ("Teddy, Teddy Roosevelt was a good man!")
The classes met in the new Learning Center divided by a sliding
partition. We both sat in the back. One morning I saw a folded piece of
paper moving slowly my way on the floor. I reached down and opened it.
I stopped breathing and bit down on the inside of my cheeks trying not to
howl in fits of laughter. He had made a holiday greeting card with two
happy swine going at it hoggy style. The caption read: YOUR
CHRISTMAS HAM IS BEING MADE TO ORDER

The second one is a classic and has the dubious honor of getting the
" Slob" a visit to see Gerald Cuendet. It was a picture of a quizzical
Waldo Crane staring at a vending machine labeled: RENT A MOM. I
knowingly have strayed from the point of this story, but my intent is to
bring out the essence of the man by illustrating some of his many talents.
There are hundreds of good examples. This tale is my favorite. It's a
good story by itself, but it has a deeper meaning to me.

Back in 1982, Mrs. Agly (Joyce Eastwood) and myself along with
our two sons, Brent and Steve were in Carbondale visiting her mom and
dad. Dr. LeFeev was just beginning his practice in Topeka, KS. He was
in town also staying with Mr. & Mrs. "Smiles". They had built a new
home on top of Snyder Hill, directly across from Roy Bain. Richard
called and said come over, so we did. Mrs. LeFevre
was the only other family member there. Well we began reminiscing and
I brought up the Chicken Hawkins story. The Oaf's eyes lit up and he

8

began moving living room furniture. Pretty soon I could tell my sons were getting absorbed after showing mild amusement at first. Then all of us were into it watching him act out all the scenes until the denouement when Hawkins and the ice ball collided. He went down and slid halfway into the kitchen. We all hooted and clapped. Mrs. LeFevre looked at Dick and said, "Richard, you're a Doctor now; you shouldn't act this way!" " It's what happened, Mom." It did indeed. Joyce and the boys were treated to a man of the theater.

EVERYTHING I NEEDED TO KNOW I LEARNED IN LITTLE LEAGUE

On Christmas Day, 1956 I received one of my most cherished gifts. Little did I know this present would spark a lifelong love of the sport of baseball. It was a Rawlings Stan Musial three fingered fielders mitt, so named because your middle and ring fingers fit neatly in one of the glove's leather appendages. Also I knew the following spring I would turn six years of age and I could play Little League.

Moving forward over six decades, I have realized that children playing team sports allows them to learn many of the lessons that help shape character such as comradery, sportsmanship, and teamwork. Upon reflection sports also give us subliminal messages that shape us in how we perceive others sometimes who are different from us. Although never conscious of the physical differences of people at six years old, I did learn a valuable lesson soon before and after I enjoyed my first boys of summer experience.

During the previous winter I practiced the time honored ritual of breaking in my new glove which entailed some glove oil rubbed into the palm of the mitt then placing a baseball honorably in the pocket and wrapping the leather fingers tightly around it with a big rubber band. This was done religiously each evening.

Finally the day arrived two weeks before school was let out for the summer. I was assigned to the Jets in the Atom League. I remember when the coaches had us gather around the bench for passing out our new shirts and hats. These tee shirts were royal blue with scarlet lettering. The hats were a matching blue with a beautiful upper case red colored J on the crown. That was all we got for uniforms but it was grand and we were all so proud. To complement our attire we wore blue jeans that were cuffed at least six inches and high topped tennis shoes. The parks department in our town provided the fields and were designated B,C and D diamonds. "A" diamond was reserved for the big kids. Neither of these grand venues had grass infields. There was just lots and lots of dust. The kind that would get all over you and invariably fill our jean cuffs to the point of weighing us down when we ran the bases and stern warnings from our moms to turn down those cuffs before we even thought of coming indoors.

The Jets were coached by Chester " Sport" Greer and Larry Doyle, Coach Doyle was a jovial sort and was a local radio personality. He also walked with a pronounced limp that made him seem slightly mysterious. I had been selected by Coach Doyle to be the opening day starting pitcher not because I could bring the heat or after setting the batter up with the fastball, I could send him to the bench with a wicked Uncle Charlie. No it was simple. I could put the ball over the plate. This is a significant attribute, since anyone ever witnessing a Little League game can say how an endless parade of walks makes the contest even more boring.

Coach Doyle was going to warm me up. He went over to the equipment bag and pulled out one dozen brand new baseballs. He removed one from a small box and handed to me. I marveled at its feel and even the smell of the horse hide. We walked off the distance from home plate to the mound along the first base line close to our bench. Coach Doyle crouched down bending his right knee and sliding his left leg out straight on the ground. He gave me a target and I let it fly. I do not know if I was nervous or the new ball was slick, but that pitch went down and way to his left. What happened next was pure amazement. The ball hit his leg and went over my head in a line drive striving for altitude. The sound was an unmistakable crack of the bat as when a bolt of white ash squarely meets a baseball. We all stood there with our mouths wide open. He laughed and stood up. He pulled his pant leg up and there before us was a wooden leg. We had never seen one.

The impact of that moment was better illuminated at the end of the season. The coaches and their wives invited us to picnic at one of our local lakes. We were going to swim prior to eating and as we walked in the sand toward the water, Coach Doyle was on the dock and began to undress. When he got down to his trunks, he began to undo the straps that firmly held the prosthesis to what was left of his leg. It had been amputated at mid- thigh. He laid the object of our attention beside his clothes and began to hop all the way down the dock and dove cleanly in that blue water. He came up and started swimming magnificently toward the middle of the lake. Nothing I have ever witnessed was more purely athletic. It was like Johnny Weissmuller as Tarzan swung out of the jungle into that river to save Jane. He swam fast and with purpose.

The words handicapped or disabled never occurred to us. He was a hero to me then and still to this day.

THE GANGS OF CARBONDALE

By Glen Freeberg

The Owls were one of the most notorious gangs of street toughs that pillaged and terrorized the Southwest region of Carbondale Illinois during the late 1950's. Most reputable historians consider the "Owls" as the most ruthless and violent of the many bird youth gangs of the period – rivaled only by the "Bats" - or perhaps the "Wrens" - for savagery and bloodlust.

The picture above was taken after they were captured and arrested by undercover agents posing as gang members (back row). First row: Terry "Someday I'll open an art gallery and pick up chicks like a mega-magnet" Etherton, Michael "I've got a bad attitude now and I am still going to have a bad attitude throughout high school so bite me authority-breath" Given, John "Cherry Popping" Chaney, Unknown Thug, Unknown Thug, John "Take No Jesus Kool-Aid" Rist, Unknown Thug, Bob "Amway Bad Boy" Westberg?, Unknown Thug, Glen "I seek only to add some measure of grace to the universe" Freeberg. Second row: Gary "I think my name was" Hanebrink, Unknown Thug, Bob "I'm going to outgrow my aviary gang ways throw 33 touchdown passes in my senior year and go on to become a Renaissance Man" Pankey, Unknown Thug. Third row: Federal Undercover Agents (names withheld by request).

As Mike Given noted, the Owls were indeed the most notorious of the 1950s "bird gangs" that laid waste to all other 8 year old gangs in many rumbles at the now defunct Oakland ball field. With some archival research, I was able to pin down the identities of a few who were listed here as "unidentified." Between "Jesus Juice" Rist and "Skinny" Westberg, is Tom "Watch Me Pick My Nose in Centerfield" Aunie. Between Westberg and "Dynamite" Freeberg is Mike "I'll Swing at the First Three Pitches So The Ball Won't Hit Me" Gholson. At the end of the second row, next to "Pink Nose Toes" Pankey is David "I Like to Scratch My Junk and Chase Butterflies in Left Field" Hileman.

As is obvious from this picture, the feds thought they had contained the Carbondale gang problem, but they were sadly mistaken. The Given family, after the disgrace and shame brought on by this bust, was forced to move across the border to the Notorious North Side, where the next year Given hooked up with some of the worst 9 year old Original Gangstas the city has ever seen: Johnny "June Bug" Tucker, Doug "My Dad is a Jeweler and I Wear a Rolex While Catching" McNeil, Mike "Li'l Hippie" Dillow, and Steve "Donkey" Ragsdale. This group terrorized the city for years, under various designations and incarnations: the Bees, the Pros, and the Bears, until once again, the Given family was forced to flee, this time returning to the secure confines of the Southwest.

It was here that Given met Lawrence "Loonies" Lutz. The two of them then formed the heart of what was to be the most feared and respected of all Cdale gangs, The South Side Studs (A.K.A. the Rod Lane Gang). Other pretenders to the throne included The East Side Rangers, The Country Cousins, The Gang, and The Ulies. But The S.S.S. controlled most of the hot chicks and the distribution and consumption of Old Milwaukee and Busch Bavarian beer on weekend nights in the city.

They dominated their turf, which included Teen Town, The McDonald's parking lot, and the "lover's lane" at Evergreen Park.

They had alliances with other "affiliates" who moved back and forth between gangs, such as Glen "I'm Not Really a Ulie" Freeberg, Bob "Strieg Sweets" Striegel, and Larry "Agly-Bagly" Eastwood.

There are rumors to this day that Lutz became the head of an international online gambling ring and that Steve Jobs was actually Michael Given, but unfortunately, no one knows the true answer to the question: "Whatever became of the old Carbondale gangs?"

Larry Eastwood indicated that his indoctrination to " Gangdom " began in the hallowed recesses of GCCGS Giant City Consolidated Grade School with Vic " Tiefer" Tiller, Rusty " Krusty " Kracht, Dave " The Mad " King, and David " Snakeman " Whitacre. We rode pre-mountain bikes to Little Grassy and Devils Kitchen Lakes and terrorized locals in the summers and snapped training bras in class during the winter months. Our moniker proclaimed by " Snakeman " Whitacre was " The Ophiologists " I know what you must be thinking, did those guys go around studying "The Oaf? " No indeed not? Our colors were a mixture of copperhead bronze and timber rattler brown and proudly displayed on our P.N. Hirsch and Rector Bros. vinyl jackets.

Initiations into our gang were rich with ritualism and grandeur. Novices were made to stand in a circle around a fire late night on top of " The Cliffs " at Devils Kitchen. They were then instructed to yell out the names of all the girl classmates they wanted to " get with" right there on the rocks. I happened to re-live those moments years later with Barbara Yow. "The Oph's" dissolved in the fall of 1965 when we moved to CCHS and as my good friend " Sebnn Lebnn " Given said I found I could move freely about inside the hierarchy of " The Gang ", " The Rod Laners," The Country Cousins," " The Ulies, but not so much " The East Side Rangers," because " Big Lahh " (Les Taylor) wanted to shoot me.

CATHY FRAILEY'S BIG BIRTHDAY TRUCK AND OTHER FREEDOM VEHICLES

By Anne Cochran

World standards are such that I will say I'm lucky enough to recall some pretty remarkable celebrations of my own birthdays over my lifetime, especially since I've lived in Los Angeles for my entire adult life. The general culture of LA delivers a certain state/style of living that brings forth specific sorts of cultural perks and oddities to enjoy within the birthday celebration arena. For example, over these many years I've birthday'ed in a movie-lot commissary; on a famous film producer's yacht in Cannes; up and down the California coastline in breathtaking homes and on the rocks of Big Sur; in St. Tropez and Manhattan and in Barcelona and deep Provence; under a palapa in San Felipe with warm water lapping at my toes while sleeping; in the center of an entire population of teenaged well-wishers and teachers within a school I founded; on top of a desolate Yosemite mountain next to a clear bass lake after a days-long vertical backpacking trip; in God-only-knows-what number of stylish Hollywood eateries that continually open and close; and on edgy backyard terraces of people types in Bel Air and Beverly Hills of various levels of celebrityhood who've come and gone throughout my life. I list these encounters not to brag, but because I want to highlight the fact that one little birthday celebration in my little Southern Illinois hometown is something much more than a faint blip on one's birthday radar in a sea of flashier such versions. In fact, I want you to know that my absolute favorite celebration of all birthday celebrations took place four nights before my 15th birthday on Friday, September 12, 1969 in Carbondale, Illinois.

This 15th-birthday observance began in the tiny childhood home I shared with my widowed mama at 1208 W. Freeman. Mom threw together a last-minute dinner and birthday cake for my closest girl buddies and me, counting Gail Evers and Cathy Frailey from the Class of '71; and my '72 buddies, who included Leigh Richardson and Patty Dugas, Cathy Ehrenfreund, Nancy Gass, maybe Bev Henderson; guessing Susan Le?er and Carla Ott from '73; perhaps several others. Then all of us happily hurried out the door together and headed over to Bleyer Field to hang together and watch that night's CCHS Terriers football game. In fact, judging from the early-in-the-season date, I'm thinking it might've been the year's opening game, so everyone was sure to attend. Some of us were dating Terrier varsity team players and were looking forward to Homecoming in October, so the night promised lots of late-'60's small-town magic and school-yard romance.

A quick side trip up front…throughout the preceding summer and early fall of my sophomore year at CCHS, Cathy Frailey, Gail Evers and I were Three Musketeers of sorts. Turning from 14 to 15 during that specific time window, I was thrilled to be running around with two "older girls." Cathy had just acquired her driver's license, and her folks were astonishingly nice about letting her drive the wheels o? their cars. She was a big-personality, fun-loving speed demon and it was a gas to be a passenger in whatever machine she was driving. She came alive behind the wheel and pushed the envelope just enough to make things exciting…and I've never met anyone since that time who lit up in quite that same way by merely sliding through a driver's-side front door and into an awaiting driver's seat.

Back to the anticipated September 12 football evening…Cathy drove her dad's giant old stake bed truck to my house and then to the game — you know, one of those three-on-a-tree, manual-shift hauling trucks with a loud engine, open trailer and enclosed front cab. Cathy, Gail and I climbed into the cab and everyone else crawled into the open back…and o? we went, hollering and bouncing into the fall night air. No one mentioned seat belts, wrecks, cops, helmets, cracked heads, death…fun, freedom and adventure firmly dominated the evening's agenda.

After the game, all kinds of school friends joined us, girls and boys from all classes. Hell, I'm pretty sure 30 or 35 kids piled into the back of that behemoth of a sinister- looking vehicle and we held onto each other as we tore o? into the dark night. And we frolicked, laughed and rocked all over Southern Illinois…sped up and down country roads and hills, out onto Highways 51 and 127 and 13, back and forth from McDonalds to Italian Village to McDonalds to Italian Village, through SIU and around to Campus Beach, out to the Crab Orchard spillway. The trip was fast and endless, we barked out current hit songs at the tops of our lungs…"Green River" by Credence Clearwater Revival (Gail's fave). "Honky Tonk Women," "Sugar, Sugar," "Build Me Up Buttercup." Everyone contributed their quarters and dimes to 32-cents-per-gallon gasoline refills at the Clark gas station — we must've pit-stopped there a half-dozen times. My boy buddies cussed like sailors and smoked cigs, throwing back their heads in unabashed laughter at their own newly acquired daringness and freedom.

No Hollywood-sort-of-sunshine-lit birthday with lofty trimmings since that time has ever, ever come close to matching this Carbondale-located memory. I can still feel the wind blowing in my face as I leaned out over the truck's cab from the trailer's front, arms in the air, head tilted upward at the stars, howling like a wolf. I can still see, smell, taste the green Sassafras trees on the sides of the roads. It was exactly like some sort of adolescent scene from a John Hughes movie…I doubt he could've choreographed a more visual or slice-of-life one.

Freedom. Unblushing, innocent freedom. Trust. Truth. Straightforward, not-even-a- little-complex friendship. Casting one's fate to the wind. And OH — so fearless! How often do such simple joys and opportunities ever truly come along in one's life? I don't experience them now. Responsibilities are weighty, at times unbearably sobering, limitations abound as one ages, yes? I don't think my own LA-raised adult children probably know exactly what that sort of adolescent freedom felt like. Their generation was Managed with a capital M — preened, prodded, marketed, directed, Looked After.

Over the following couple of years after that teenager's dream-come-true-of-a-night on the town and countryside, I constantly drove my friends around Carbondale and rode in their cars as a sort of unspoken group-sanctioned pledge to living together inside a snapshot of freedom at its best. Myriad quick decisions were mine to be made with surprisingly few parent-mandated parameters.

I remember Michael Crenshaw zipping over to my house in his two-seater, army-green MGB and how we'd tear all over Little Grassy and Devil's Kitchen Lakes' roads, hair flying in the breeze while holding our best attempts at philosophical discussions and together we consoled and mourned lost high school loves. Two years older, he was one of my favorite buddies during those springtime months. I was broken hearted when he totaled the MGB. He quickly replaced it with a big-engined, sandy-colored Pontiac convertible. Plenty cool for sure, but not quite the same deliverer of the Sunday-afternoon, scenes-from-Makanda magic as the departed MGB. Mike joined the service right after high school, learned to pilot planes, moved onto another life experience somewhere far away, and those salad days were over.

I joyfully jaunted out into the local hinterlands with Mike Milligan in his blue Torino as he delivered newspapers in dewy-dark morning hours to local country folk in and around De Soto and south 51 in the other direction. One-hit-wonder Mungo Jerry's "In The Summertime" song blared out into the sweet countryside air's stillness from his eight-track car stereo.

Bob Crowell was the pinnacle of my 15-year-old love life — my sun rose and set around his swingy blonde bangs and blue eyes. He let me drive his family's blue Chevy Station wagon before I was ready, and I nearly crashed it into a mailbox on Emerald Lane when I flew around the corner from Chautauqua Road. I didn't yet comprehend how to finesse braking while turning, so I just went for broke and flew. He grabbed the wheel and we narrowly missed disaster. During that phase, Bob, Mike Byrne, Patty Dugas and I developed an odd kid-like and pointless propensity for stealing road signs of any sort. No activity was more thrilling or satisfying while riding around in a car. Bob's father found our booty hidden away in one of the Crowell's outbuildings on their property and Bob correctly caught hell.

Months later, Bob's dad traded in the blue station wagon for a shiny new silver Nova that he allowed Bob to use in order to transport himself and sister Kathy to school from out where they lived near Eckerd's farm and Midland Inn. So on one dull morning at the start of a day in the CCHS parking lot, Bob, Mike Byrne and I stood around at 7:30 am craving an impulsive adventure, so we skipped school and drove two hours over to the Illinois State line, crossed the Mississippi River bridge and into the outskirts of St. Louis. The problem was we hadn't really thought things through thus we weren't too sure what to actually do there upon arrival. We had a quick burger at Lambert Field's co?ee shop and watched planes land for a few minutes, then silently and nervously drove home in order to arrive back in the CCHS parking lot by the school day's end. After all, Bob was expected to drive sister Kathy home from school and he wasn't supposed to be fooling around in that way with the family's new car. Of course, I ran my big fat mouth to my friends, so my mother heard from Shirley Russell's mom that I'd "skipped school with two older boys and crossed the state line" and she became hysterical. Her Roaring '20s-fueled imagination ran the gamut of underage drinking to various forms of illicit sex and general sleaziness. I might as well have been caught turning tricks in a roadhouse bar and smuggling contraband. She couldn't comprehend the overriding innocence that prevailed in the making of that snap decision. We were very good kids who were merely playing within the concept of experiencing that same old pull of a mischief-loving freedom Siren.

Nick Fink came home from boarding school and showed up in my Freeman Street driveway in his dad's collector-worthy Morgan with its leather-strapped hood, yet another spectacular army-green two-seater that I never wanted to exit. It was an exotic, raw, smart ride for certain...never did it again. A couple of years later, so many of us were sad as Nick tragically died when he rolled the family station wagon out on Old Crab Orchard road, no doubt carried away by that special taste of youthfully wild freedom gleaned from being placed in a driver's seat.

Tom Pankey blew his brother Denny's yellow Corvette Sting Ray into same 1208 W. Freeman driveway — now that one was a proper carriage for any Sun-In-bleached, Baby Oil-tanned teenaged girl — easily one of the most memorable car rides of my life. I think of that moment every single time I see an old Corvette rolling down an LA freeway.

The next summer, I felt free as a bird as I rode around Carbondale in then-boyfriend Scott Ottesen's red Ford Fairlane convertible. I felt like high school royalty. He also had usage of his father's Diesel-burning, smoke-stacked semi-truck cab without any trailer attached to the back, one that must've pulled the family business' for-sale-on-a-lot mobile homes.

Charlie Scott ran his mama's Oldsmobile all over town with my as-yet-unknown-future- husband Chuck's huge 4x12'" Sunn speaker cabinet wired up to the car's eight-track stereo, blasting teeth-rattling Jimi Hendrix all over the steamy summer landscape. I sat in the lone leftover spot next to the blaring speaker in the rear while Gail Evers and Christine Winemiller sat and laughed and flirted and charmed Charlie on the long bench seat in the front. The bulky Sunn speaker and I were unhappy, awkward travel companions. I felt like a chump, an unwilling third wheel — arms tightly folded across my chest, lower lip thrust outward, silently glaring out the window as we flew down Glenview Drive to blasted-out "Foxy Lady."

During the spring of that sophomore year, Krista Erickson and I tooled around town with Leigh Richardson in her white Mustang as all three of us wore our new and trashy blonde pageboy wigs with our noses pointed skyward. "Hey, YO, the WIG Club!!!," Mike "Tag" Vanhorn good-naturedly hollered at us as we pulled into the Moo 'N Cackle next to his famous metallic-gold, four-door ride. We were serious about selling our new looks as smart blonde sophisticates in sunglasses and Tag righteously wasn't having it.

On one lazy and boring Saturday afternoon, Scott Voigt livened up things for his passengers by jauntily steering his boxy old white Toyota through the CCHS student parking lot — wantonly bouncing across the grass in front of the so-called Learning Center, down the narrow shaded sidewalk of campus' '60s section and through the entire length of the walkway overhangs, across the expansive lawn in front of Bowen Gym and out onto High Street up to the Oakland Avenue stop sign, all in about 15 seconds' flat. Months later, Scott drove us to Murphysboro in a borrowed shiny-red Lemans convertible for me to side sit on its lowered cloth top and rear fender in the Apple Festival Parade as a queen candidate. I parade-waved my white-gloved hand at everyone who lined the route. Scott wore a gray suit and solemnly, o?cially stared face-forward as though he was mandated with the guarding of a princess. I certainly didn't come anywhere close to being crowned the Apple Festival Queen (oh boy, that lesson taught me a lot about political maneuvering!), but we still felt pretty darned uptown and Hollywood on that warm fall afternoon.

I remember riding in Bob Caraway's fast GTO out on the four-lane highway near the Sav-Mart…a formidable ride stu?ed full of kids who'd lost their judgment, including me. I was uneasily perched on the front console. We hit 140 MPH in nothing flat. Lucky we're here to look back and tell of it.

And we used to race out to some hilly gravel roads near the SIU farms with Norman North and Phil Renfro, maybe Scott Taylor was along. The hills were so steep and we drove so fast that when we crested the top of any given one, we'd just full-on fly. I swear. Airborne every time. The sheer in-one's-face madness of it blew us into maniacal fits of laughter. I have no doubt in my mind that teenagers are inherently scary little beings. And my poor mama's Buick! She was always mad when I brought her car home with mud caked all over the bottom — if only the Buick's undercarriage could talk. I'd still be grounded to this day.

Some of the vehicles in which we experienced our shared Carbondale life traveled on water, the most memorable one being what I called "The Jerry Summers Houseboat." A bunch of those guys were industrious indeed — acquiring crude building materials through nefarious means so it was rumored, and building a big-old tank of a heavy floating plywood shack on pontoons with sliding-glass doors — and they launched it onto Crab Orchard Lake. Their raw and collective ingenuity was impressive. The floating rust-brown shack was a wild-ass-looking thing of a backwater-sort of beauty and I never had so much fun in my life, and felt a kinship to every single kid who floated on the lake with me in that questionable vessel. Sometimes they pulled us behind the boat in big black inner tubes. Jerry and company understood the concept of having fun every bit as much as did Cathy Frailey. One time the Crab Orchard police force (hmmm…what, the Coast Guard? Lake Authority? State Wildlife Fish and Games?) pulled up and requested to come aboard to count passengers and life vests. We had far too few and didn't want to be fined or even worse — barred from future summer fun, so as they entered the front sliders, we one-by-one dropped o? the back in as organized of a military-style procedure as any frogman team — but it was improvised. We quietly swam underneath the boat and lined up in the airspace between the pontoons until they were satisfied with our safety provisions and left us.

And speaking of all of us doing every single bit of socializing while perched on top of wheels…some of us even lived on them in the form of renting mobile homes!
Accordingly, this CCHS Class of '72' girl graduated a year early with the Class of '71 as did buddies Leigh and Krista, and enrolled at SIU in the fall. One night at a party out at

Charlie Scott's rented mobile home near The Gardens Restaurant, I struck up a conversation at the kitchen table with one young Chuck Cochran, CCHS Class of '70. Although we'd been acquainted for years, I'd never known him well prior to this moment, and he was dusting himself o? from the demise of a long-term romance with my buddy Krista. I immediately took a liking to him, thought he was smart and interesting, a potential kindred spirit. He seemed so di?erent from everyone else — even though "everyone else" was dear to me. I don't exactly know how to explain it, but I judged him to be substantially gifted in the heart-and-brains departments. He seemed to be intensely interested in virtually everything. Before I left Charlie's party with my friends, I said to him "Why don't you stop by The Squire Shop at Murdale tomorrow night before we close? I'm working as a gift wrapper and I can sell you a pair of jeans for cheap. It'll be Christmas Eve, you know, so we'll close a little early — don't be late."

Sure enough, around ten minutes prior to quitting time, Chuck strolled through the door and and bought two pairs of six-dollar jeans he didn't want. Shop owner Mr. Haege was happy with the unexpected last-second sale. Chuck walked me to my car in the snowfall. I said "Hey, there's another party out at Charlie's on Christmas night. Why don't you come?"

And once again, sure enough, when I drove my girl pals out to Charlie's soirée on Christmas night in Mom's muddy-yellow Buick Le

Sabre — on the floor in Charlie's trailer already sat Chuck Cochran, patiently awaiting my arrival. I noted that he proved to be dependable, a man of his word. Alas, Karen Stephens got to him first. I could swear she seemed to intuit my intention, wished to spar with me for sport and swooped down into place next to him, charming him with conversation she'd refined during her initial college semester at SMU in Dallas. I felt defeated, sad and disappointed. Nevertheless, I called up my courage, strolled over to the two of them and addressed Chuck, looking him squarely in the eyes. "Some of us are driving into town — there's another party at the Delta Chi House on Main Street. Maybe I'll see you there…" I tossed my hair at Karen, shot her my best stink eye, and out the door I flounced with my group…and when I turned the big Buick's ignition switch, my five girlfriends cried out in laughing, good-natured unison "ANNE'S PISSED!"

Please indulge this side trip before we press on…I was pretty sure something remarkable was happening to me, but I couldn't quite place it. Things were suddenly so di?erently skewed, I felt so alien to myself, traveling out of my own physical self and mind. Throughout my little-town life, I'd nurtured high-handed, unreasonable ambitions to the point where my Mom tended to address me as "Miss Astor." I guess I was just hardwired that way. My mom's dream for me was that I'd learn shorthand and typing at SIU, become a secretary, moved to St. Louis, get a job at McDonnell-Douglas, and become her idea of a Career Gal, sitting tall in a trim business suit — seated in front of an IBM Selectric typewriter, taking clerical orders from the man in an o?ce. I didn't look down my nose at Carbondale — I was way too self-e?acing and insecure for such an attitude to secure a foothold. But I did indeed possess a lifelong deep-seated notion that I belonged somewhere else. My own early-life ambition was that I'd get rich on my own because I just would, move to New York, and live in one of those serene and divine Eames or Schindler or Breuer houses featured in the home magazines I studied when Mom took me with her to Maudie's Beauty Shop in Mound City. I was self- tutored by the architectural photos in House Beautiful, and developed my own aesthetic at that point of origin. The structures were sleek, dreamy, spare, sophisticated. Oh, how I wanted that life! I cut out Sears Catalogue paper dolls who I placed in those houses in my mind's eye. They were little extensions of me, I thought. I also wanted to "su?er" in New York City for a bit, live in a ladies' boarding house while becoming a television soap opera star, making my Mom proud when I would finally appear on "As The World Turns" while she knitted in her tv-viewing chair and bragged to her Bridge-playing friends. I also read in Look Magazine about how graduating from Syracuse University (instead of my fated SIU destination) would be a smart college path to choose if I could only figure it out on my own, allegedly creating a straight line for me into executive ranks of the film and tv and theatre worlds where I would surely become a lady boss type sporting a sti?-blonde briefcase at CBS Rockefeller Center in NYC, grouchily flying around the country on a TWA jet, striking terror in the worker bees' hearts at CBS' station a?liates. I would run things. And I certainly wouldn't fall in love and get married until I was, oh…30..or some such old age. I would be Powerful. Smart. Independent. RICH. Ambition and fantasy drove me to push forward in school every single day without much desired e?ort and passion for it — just get the hell outa there, wrap it up, don't try too hard — just check the boxes…get going already! I carefully pondered and sorted out my future plans as I drove alone through chilly Carbondale streets in the Buick.

But wait, now…back here on Planet Earth…here at only 17 — I'd just met one Chuck Cochran. I couldn't believe this abrupt turn of events and best-laid plans, but I was dramatically learning a little something about Love. I was riveted by its very nature and how it rapidly derails carefully crafted plans o? the tracks and into oblivion.

So back to the story narrative…on that Christmas night of '71, my friends and I entered the big old beautiful Delta Chi house, snow falling on the front lawn of this formerly glorious and stately home of Carbondale's prominent Stotlar family with its worn-yet- beautiful dark woodwork everywhere plus a couple of giant lit-up Christmas trees. All of the older Carbondale kids who'd gone away to college were home for the holidays and were present in full force at this particular party. It was festive, old-fashioned, scene-from-a-movie-like, so incredibly nice, so upbeat, so much fun. There was music, even singing of carols as I think I can recall. Yet another John Hughes scene.

And then…and then…a dude from the past Carbondale's situated social and athletic life, as I knew it, brightly smiled at me.

Hmmm. Bob Pankey.

HUH?

I was astonished, even a tad terrified. I judged him to be way, way beyond my social station and grasp, someone I regarded as living a charmed life — certainly one that was clearly more impressive and full of realistic possibilities than mine. He was three years' my senior and attending college at U of Missouri. Why was he paying so much direct attention to little-nobody me, someone at whom he'd surely laugh in learning about her secret fantasy world that was not-so-much unlike Walter Mitty's? Did he even know my name prior to this Christmas night? He quickly proved to be so, so nice…well turned out, clearly smart, focused, very handsome, a young man of the world who presented to me as being resolutely placed on an ever-upward-moving path. I kept turning around, searching for the true target of his apparent interest. Wasn't he probably addressing some other girl who was standing behind me? Wasn't I just mistaken and confused?

No..it was me.

Then Bob Pankey asked me if I'd like to leave the party for a while and drive around Carbondale and just talk…you know, take the University Avenue run, Italian Village, McDonalds. We did and we had a lovely time. But what on earth could he possibly want from me? My attitude was a cautious one as two years' back, I'd had a brief September-to-October romance with his younger brother Tom that didn't end well once the '69 Homecoming came and went, so I was gun shy of taking up with yet another, even-more-high-profile member of the revered Pankey clan — scared of being hurt again by a romantic matching that was over my head. But Bob proved to be a very good guy, a gentleman in every way — a straight shooter, developing sophisticate and interesting to boot — far surpassing his stereotypical athlete-star persona. He asked me out on a date for the upcoming '71 New Year's Eve while he self-assuredly steered us around Carbondale in his car, holding a surprising, more-than-decent conversation with me. Of course I said yes to the date request while my head spun o? my shoulders.

When Bob and I arrived back at the Delta Chi house, the party was rocking out on all three floors. When we walked downstairs to the basement-level gathering, over on the three-seater overstuffed sofa sat — yes again, sure enough — Mr. Chuck Cochran, patiently awaiting my arrival.

My 17-year-old self instantly knew I was about to make the most important decision of my life as I gingerly perched between my two Christmas suitors. I looked to my left. I looked to my right. Which one should I pick? What's the correct decision? Any girl in town would've shouted through a megaphone "PICK. BOB. PANKEY. — YOU ABSOLUTE IMBECILE!" Seated on my right was Bob Pankey…such a shiny-townie celebrity in my mind's eye that it was hard to imagine he'd remember me once he went back to college. But then here was Chuck Cochran on my left…with his earnest tone and way of speaking, his desire to hold endless conversation about seemingly everything under the sun, his intense and probing brown eyes, a gifted and passionate guitar player (I was a dyed-in-the-wool rocker by my very nature which helped along the decision and not so much a sports fan), wearing that loony Afro that ballooned out over his brow line.

It was crystal clear to me at that very second like a sharp knock on the head I'd already fallen seriously in love with Chuck in spite of Carbondale's prized young man being attentively parked on my right side — and nothing would ever be the same again.

We rode around in Chuck's family's vehicles — his stripped-down brown Nova with ugly green Chuck-installed household carpet, his mom's flashy two-toned Monte Carlo, his housepainter Dad's white Ford Econoline van with the engine butting up in the middle of the front cab. We analyzed everything within sight and mind. We learned about each other and life as we drove Carbondale's streets and countryside. We turned crazy donuts in the ice on the frozen parking lot in his amateur-paint-jobbed, metallic blue, tandem-wheeled Stepvan — recently retired as a Carbondale UPS truck and now loaded to the ceiling with heavy black rock band equipment. He'd hand-painted his band's Payge III logo with bright-white lettering on the Stepvan's side using an overhead projector in his mama's driveway during midnight hours on Canterbury Street.

Chuck craved Freedom and Truth. I sought Truth and Freedom.

I kept my New Year's Eve date with Bob. After all, it was just too soon for me to competently judge my new predicament. We spent a great evening together, but all through it I sensed I was already a goner, a done deal. He kissed me at my front door a few minutes after midnight, and went back to college to discover bigger and better girl- centered adventures, I'm certain. And in those following wee minutes of 1972, I anxiously sat in 1208 W. Freeman's front picture window while my mother snored in the next room and awaited Chuck's promised 2:00 am arrival following the conclusion of his New Years' Eve Payge III gig in Benton, bright eyed and resolute, steering his Stepvan over to the side of the snowy street in front of my house, jumping out, slamming its door shut with a thud and sprinting up to my front door.

We built ideas and discussed and argued and we developed a meeting of the minds and grew a physical and emotional life as one. I loudly chased o? loose female rock-star suitors throughout the early years in the rock 'n roll biz and shook my finger in his face and drew lines in the sand. We lived in Milwaukee for a little bit and married, and drove all the way across the country to California in his new band's Dodge Van with our two pet birds singing and swinging on a clothesline he strung from window to window. We never came back to Carbondale for more than quick family visits and funerals, built a full life together and raised two kids we desperately loved, moved in and out of Los Angeles houses that we tore up and fixed and used as laboratories to learn about our creative preferences and limitations. We learned about how we wanted this life to go and found cool things to do together in the process and — I guess I can actually say with confidence — lived happily ever after.

Freedom. Truth. Cars. Good decisions and bad ones. As kids growing up together, each of us in Carbondale learned to sort out and examine these things, alone as well as together within the confines of constantly moving boxes in the forms of cars, trucks, boats — we rode and literally lived on rubber tires as life's scenery passed by through windows. I wonder if life is still that way for kids in my little hometown. I know it's very di?erent for their present-day Los Angeles counterparts, which makes me feel sad for them. They've been chau?eured around while being quizzed, counseled and lectured by parent types. They've missed something for sure. I wonder if their generation is bewildered by all of that handling they experienced as a sign of the times.

I'm grateful for tender moments lived within the Carbondale bubble — driving, riding, talking, driving, laughing, crying, riding. Teenaged Cathy Frailey served as a carrier of a key message to me in 1969, one briefly fashioned and led by an inherently free spirit. I had much to learn from her in that brief moment, and I'm grateful to have ridden those wild highway miles alongside her as well as in the company of all others who came after her. Those encounters shaped my core values. I wouldn't trade them for the entire pack of full-blown heady, pretentious times and people constantly appearing in front of me since that time — false gods cherished and protected by the world at large. I choose Little Egypt.

And I choose you guys.

WELCOME HOME G.I. JOE

By Bruce Fohr

Harassing me, and my friends, was my big brother Johnny's entertainment.   This was especially true after we moved to Carbondale, Illinois, in 1962—the beginning of his junior year in high school.   Our dad, a business professor at Michigan State University in East Lansing, where I was born, was recruited by President Delyte Morris in his efforts to upgrade SIU's growing schools and colleges by attracting faculty members from Big 10 universities.   Our dad told us that one of the "perks" he was pitched by SIU was the University's highly acclaimed University School (U-School) for faculty and staff children.   Kind of like having a private school on campus without the big tuition fees.   So, my brother became a "U-lee."   There were no slots for a sixth grader, so I attended Winkler Elementary—where I would meet my future Best Man, Tom Blase, and several other close, life-long friends including John Wham, Terry Etherton, Dick LeFevre, and Ann Portz—whose mother was my sixth grade teacher.

While I grew physically at a "normal pace," my brother was always big for his age—more than six feet tall in eighth grade; and six foot three when he was sixteen—the year we moved to Carbondale. He had been an athlete in Michigan—playing for his East Lansing High School football, basketball and baseball teams.   But when he came to Carbondale—which he thought was the end of the earth and hillbilly heaven—he developed a bit of a rebellious attitude and identity.   He wanted to be a sort of James Dean-type… a cool outsider, not a joiner.

He thought that it would much cooler to be a lady's man, a fantastic dancer at sock hops (he won several dance contests around town), and a tough guy—that nobody messed with. He had his share of scuffles at Teen Town—and began to get a reputation as a "bad ass" who was quick to "kick butt" if provoked. In Michigan, where he began high school, he made me think that high school was going to be one big, on-going fight. "If you ever walk in to a Boys bathroom and you're the only white guy, you've got to be ready," he would tell me. I cringed at the thought of high school as a fifth grader in Michigan.

Moving to Southern Illinois was an adventure for me. No one I grew up with in Michigan ever moved anywhere. Not even out of their neighborhoods. So I enjoyed everything about the new world of Carbondale—where I could walk six blocks to my school every day. And virtually all my new friends, that I seemingly met instantly—all lived within about the same distance from our home on Briarwood Drive. For my brother, Johnny, it was a tougher transition. While he made friends very quickly also, including one of the more popular, attractive girls in his class, he simply resented leaving what he called a "Big 10 City" for this little hayseed, back water town with only one McDonald's. "I went down there to get something to eat at the McDonald's and this hillbilly wearing overalls in front of me says to the counter person, 'Burger and fries.' Anything to drink, she asks? 'Burger and fries.' Anything for dessert? 'Burger and fries,' he says again and nothing more. What kind of hick place is this?" he asked, shaking his head. It started just with me in Michigan. My brother enjoyed hassling, irritating and bullying me just to make me miserable and to get away with it. I later thought that he just resented me for "replacing him" by my birth and becoming the new "cute little guy" that others seem to pay more attention to. It was never fighting—as many brothers do growing up. It was just him picking on me or simply beating me up—generally for nothing other than his entertainment. "Mom, Johnny just hit me for no reason," I would complain. "Johnny, why did you do that?" "He called me a name," he said, just making something up. "No, I didn't! Why would I do that?" I shot back. "Well, one of you is lying," said our mother. "Yes, and it's him... Johnny just hit me for no reason!" "OK, since I can't tell whose lying, you both just go to your rooms," demanded mom, trying to end the episode. Johnny had won again, smiling, as he walked away.

As my new Carbondale friends started to come over to our house to hangout or to get something to eat, we tried to stay clear of my brother and his friends—who he encouraged to join him in the little brother "harassment fun." We didn't always get away. "Watch this," Johnny would say, as he picked up John Wham by his feet and started to bounce his head off the floor. "That's pretty cool. Let me try that," said Johnny's U-School buddy, Dave McCoy. "Let's get out here," Wham shouted, "these guys are psycho."

Southern Illinois in the early 60's seemed carefree and fun-- for high schoolers and for grade schoolers.... looking forward to Junior High. While Johnny was successful at the social scene at U-School-- making some close and good friends (most of whom were achievement and academic-oriented) Johnny just didn't like school that much. Nothing really excited him. He didn't have a passion or a goal. He just wanted to graduate and take it easy for a while. He didn't want to have to get up early each morning to go to class. So, after graduating in 1964—before Vietnam was really even happening, Johnny took off the first quarter of college in the Fall of 1964. He was tired of hearing our dad stomping down the hall each morning, saying "Johnny get up, Johnny get up... damnit, Johnny get up." He wanted a brief reprieve. When he started attending SIU in the Winter of 1965, if he didn't like a class, got bored, or fell a bit behind in his assignments, he'd just withdraw from the class. He wasn't in a hurry to accomplish anything. Then things changed. A lot.

The Vietnam War started and the draft started. And a "student deferment" was the only way to stay out of the conflict—unless you had a medical condition that would disqualify you. Johnny didn't have one. His academic pattern and hiatus resulted in him being far behind the student deferment "8-ball" of what was needed to stay I-S. He took every course he could at a local junior college trying to catch up to the required hours needed. He didn't make it in time for the September 1966 draft—one of the largest monthly call-ups ever.

He first had to report to Fort Leonard Wood, Missouri, for basic training. It was an eye-opening experience, with many firsts for Johnny. Even though the Civil Rights Act of 1964 resulted in the integration of Carbondale's segregated schools in 1965-- our first year of high school-- there weren't really any black students at University High in 1964 —or at least none that Johnny came in contact with. His first experience of being in close quarters with African-Americans was at Ft. Leonard Wood. On my first trip to visit Johnny with my parents, he told us of how guys were put on KP (Kitchen Police) duty if they screwed something up. "They call it the 'Grease Trap.' That's how they refer to KP. 'I'm going throw you in the Grease Trap, man!' a drill sergeant would scream at a new recruit. "This black guy in my company from some real small town got in trouble the other day," Johnny explained. "They told him that they were going to 'throw him in the grease trap'."

He looked at me in horror and asked, "You ever seen 'm grease a man up before?"

Johnny did very well in Army boot camp. He tested well. He was one of the sharpest guys in his company. "Maybe I'll get a good assignment and not have to leave the states," he hoped. Because he was "a college boy" and he tested so well, the Army thought that the medical field would be a good assignment for Johnny. He was ordered to Ft. Sam Houston in San Antonio, Texas, as his next training base. "Maybe I'll get assigned to a hospital there and learn a lot about the medical field—and stay away from the action," he told us on the phone. In Texas, Johnny did very well again- with his tests, his knowledge, and overall performance as a military man. A hospital assignment? It didn't seem out of the question or unreasonable. No such luck. His orders: Vietnam. Field Medic. He's going to Nam… in April, 1967.

All of his and our worse fears were being realized. He was going to Vietnam… not only to try to survive; but to have to deal with the worst part of the conflict… patching up and trying to save the lives of young men, like him, who would be shot, blown-up, or otherwise injured in all sorts of horrible ways. He was 20 years old. I had just turned 16 the month before. Our parents, especially our dad, with whom my brother had more than a few run-ins with growing up… including the unwanted move to Southern Illinois…were in shock and disbelief. There were strong emotions of dread.

Our dad, an academic, grew up very poor in the inner city of Milwaukee, saw education as the only way for one to advance him or herself. With virtually no other family member graduating even from high school, our dad worked his way through Marquette, with no assistance from anyone, joined the Army, served in World War II, returned and completed his Master's and Doctorate at Michigan State. The year before we moved to Carbondale, he was the acting Dean of the College of Business at MSU. He didn't like administration. He wanted to do research and teach students. That was the appeal of SIU to him. He was able to do both. His oldest son, his namesake, did not see the relevance, importance or even appeal of anything regarding school. There were many clashes between my father and brother. Now, ironically, because Johnny did so well on the medical and other aptitude tests, he earned his way to being a field medic in Vietnam.

Our dad was raised Catholic. Our mom was not. Yet she had to agree to the children being raised Catholic. So Johnny and I went to Catholic school in East Lansing—where you are required to go to church every day. Our dad never attended church, except Christmas and Easter. He later said that while he wanted his children to be Catholic, with having to go to Catholic grade school, junior high, high school, and college, he'd had enough church to last him a lifetime or two. When Johnny was sent to Vietnam, dad got religion again. He made pacts with God. Many promises. Just bring his son home, he prayed. It was excruciating. Virtually every day. Especially the way the national television network news covered the war. Each night there would be a casualty count… how many VC (Viet Cong) died that day. How many US troops died. Where the big battles were being fought. "Oh my God, Johnny said that he was in that area a week ago," Dad would say in a panic, referring to a recent letter.

Letters to Vietnam

Having Johnny go to Vietnam was not all bad for me. I had just turned 16 and got my driver's license. I got his room, his motorcycle, his stereo system, some of his cooler clothes—that I was starting to fit in to--and no more of his terrorizing and harassment. It was kind of nice. But thinking of him in Vietnam where guys were dying—virtually every day—really got to me. Johnny was my only brother; my only sibling. Even though we'd never really gotten along, the idea of him not coming back was scary and unthinkable. But I thought about it all the time. I also thought about the time he defended me from a bully.

Still, at first, it was hard to write to my brother. He was my life-long tormentor. We had always pursued different paths. He was always pre-occupied about being cool, hanging out with the coolest kids, looking good, having a great looking girlfriend, wearing the newest-style clothes, knowing how to do the newest dance; and caring very little about school—except to keep his Student Deferment—for as long as he could. His friends in high school—either in East Lansing or Carbondale—were always among the "cool kids"—especially those who were a little on the "bad boy" side—the trouble-makers; the guys who occasionally got caught skipping school or stealing beer or cars from their parents. Some didn't care about their grades, because they knew that their family would take of them. Several of Johnny's friends were from privileged families or backgrounds—but while they knew how to party and play, they also knew how to take care of business—especially in school. At least enough to keep up their Student Deferments or had an "in" with the National Guard—which turned out to be a doubled-edge sword.

I always felt that it was my good fortune to have friends who, while they liked to have fun and party, also thought it was "cool" to be a good student and/or to be involved with school—the teams, the organizations, the school paper, etc. I never felt that I wanted to be different or better than my brother, it was just that we were different in many ways. Still, I idolized him. He was always so big and strong—especially compared to me and my friends—the guys he liked to harass and terrorize.   During his U-School days he developed a reputation for being a "bad ass" that no one messed with.   I always thought that the reason I never really got hassled by older guys in Carbondale was because most knew of them that I was John Fohr's little brother.   One time our freshman year, a U-School junior, Richard Davenport (who would have been a freshman when Johnny was a senior), decided to act tough and try to bully my friend, John Wham (mostly) and me when we were hanging out at the Carbondale Bowling Alley.   He threatened us and made us think that hanging out at the bowling alley was not going to be a good idea for some time.   He wanted us to think that he was the new U-School tough guy and we had just better watch out.   He really seemed to dislike Wham for some reason.   Unfortunately for him, Johnny, now attending SIU and living at home was still in town.   And Johnny really disliked the idea of "this punk" Davenport (as he remembered the guy) giving shit and acting tough to his little brother.   "Just call me if he ever shows up and starts to bother you," he told me.   That day came soon.   Like the next week.   I called Johnny.   My brother quickly drove the family red Grand Prix down to the bowling alley and pulled in right next to Davenport's GTO.   As Johnny jumped out of the car, terror filled the face of Davenport.   "If I ever hear of you messing with my brother or any of his friends, I'm going the kick the shit out of you so bad...." Johnny began.   "No problem, man... I didn't know he was your brother... it won't happen again... believe me," said the "punk" as he got in his car and sped off.

I really don't ever remember even seeing that guy again while I was in high school.   He probably just avoided me.   It was the first time Johnny ever defended me.   "No one, especially that punk, is going to hassle my brother," he told me, saying that he wanted me to tell him if the guy ever tried to rough us up again.   "I want an excuse to kick his ass."   It never happened.

I started to write Johnny letters-- soon after he left for 'Nam in April, 1967.   But I couldn't finish them.   I'd tear them up.   He doesn't want to hear about me or what I'm doing, I thought.   It would just make him depressed to tell him how good of a time I'm having.   I knew my parents (and other family members) were writing to him.   But would he really want to hear from his kid brother?

Our dad always had a difficult time communicating with his family. It seemed like he just couldn't express himself-- or act like he cared or loved anyone in the family—even our mom.   As unbelievable as it may seem, I literally never hear him say the word "love" when I was growing up and I never heard him say "please" or "thank you" for anything we wanted or asked for. In fact, he never really asked for anything: "Give me that salt," he might say at the dinner table. It was just the environment that we got used to. No body hugged or ever showed affection. Years later, when he was a grandfather to our children, I confronted him about this memory. He didn't deny it. "My father was from Germany," he explained about the grandfather I never met or knew (because he died during the Depression when my dad was 17 years old.) "He told me that a man never has to ask for anything in his house... he's the king of the castle." My dad and brother had the most strained relationship as we were growing up. My brother even resented his name. "I hate that he named me after himself," said Johnny, adding that he thought that it put extra pressure on him to be "like his dad"—with whom he had little in common. He thought that it made his academic short-comings and lack of interest feel more like "failure" because he wasn't "living up" to his name. Our dad, who had a doctorate in Communications, could not communicate with his family, and especially his oldest son. Not until Vietnam.

Dad started writing Johnny letters—long, type-written, single-spaced on SIU Business Research Bureau stationary—at least weekly—from the moment he had an address to send letters to. He tried to write about things he thought Johnny would be interested in; that he would think was funny; or about family developments and insights. The letters always reflected his strong affection for his son, his concern, and his desire to know anything about what was going on--and hopefully something positive-- about Johnny's situation, location, or safety. In one of his earliest letters to Johnny, dated April 28, 1967, dad wrote: "My dear son: Apparently you have been kept occupied since you wrote your last letter, or, I hope, you have been replying to other letters which friends of yours have written to you... I trust that you are in good shape, both mentally and physically. We are still hoping that you will be assigned to work which involve a lesser amount of hazard. According to recent news reports, most of the severe action has been taking place near the northern demilitarized zone (DMZ). I assume that you are still in the Saigon area?"

Dad's letter mostly described his trip to St. Louis with a group of SIU business students, whose association—SAM—Society for the Advancement of Management— he was the faculty advisor for. The "SAM boys", as dad called them, had toured a brewery and stopped by the St. Louis Playboy Club, afterward. Dad described a wild adventure and the "souvenirs-- the boys bought me a Bunny cigarette lighter, and a mug which contained some 'fireball' booze called a 'Herbie'. I am saving the items for you," he wrote. The theme of many of his letters were about things he was doing or buying in anticipation of Johnny's return—to give him a motivation to come home (and survive the ordeal.) He ended this letter: "Johnny... I hope that next year you will be on furlough at home and will be able to join my SAM boys on our annual St. Louis bacchanalia. Best wishes to my very dear Son, Dad."

Johnny saved every letter our father wrote to him in Vietnam. He saved every letter I wrote him as well. And I saved every letter he wrote me. It took nearly two months for me to write Johnny my first letter. On June 5, 1967—just a few days before the end of our sophomore year at CCHS—I finally did it. It really was a curious time to write a seven- page letter. It was literally on the night before semester finals. I was little unfocused on school my sophomore year—for a variety of reasons. Maybe I was trying to be more like my big brother. Maybe it was the shock of having him leave home for the first time and being alone—without someone to protect me or to be my buffer with the parents. Or maybe it was the 18-year-old college freshman coed from CCHS-- who had been up for Homecoming and Prom Queen our freshman year--that I was dating and constantly spending time with, and all her college friends. Here I was, just in my second year of high school, and I didn't want anything to do with high school... I wanted to be with all these older, cooler college kids. I was trying to be like my brother.

Something else had shaken me in December of 1966. It was the incredible loss of our classmate, John Crawshaw, at age 15. He had been diagnosed with leukemia in September and just three short months later he died. Crawshaw had been one of my first friends in Carbondale, when I was placed at Winkler Elementary instead of U-School. John and I sat next to each other in the back row of Mrs. Portz's Sixth Grade class. We talked in class all the time and got in a bit of trouble for it occasionally. He was my first friend in Carbondale who invited me for an over-night at his home. We became good buds and playmates. He later developed a bit of a reputation as a bully and tough guy, but in sixth grade he was very nice to me-- the new kid. In fact, one Saturday, when we were playing basketball at SIU's Women's Gym, he showed me a pamphlet that he "stole" from school. It had been used for the 5th Grade "Girls only" Health Class. It was about the human reproduction system and all the things that young girls need to know when they come into puberty. It even had pictures. I was shocked, but said to John, "some neighborhood kids in Michigan told me about this stuff when I was in the third grade, but I didn't believe them. 'My mom would never let my dad do that to her,' I remembered saying to them." Like I said, I'd never hear the word "love" spoken between my parents growing up. I only remember seeing them kiss once or twice—on New Year's Eve or their anniversary.

Now, Crawshaw was gone. The guy who had first taught me the "facts of life." Death was something I had never been faced with in Michigan. Nobody I'd ever known had anyone in their family die, except maybe a grandparent... like me-- who I'd never met. I never knew anyone who died.

In Carbondale, death was far more common among my new friends. In fact, one kid, who would have been a classmate at Winkler had died before I moved to town from a suicide. Another had been killed riding his bike in a car accident near Murdale Shopping Center. I never knew him either. John Wham didn't remember much of his dad, who died one night when he was three years old. Now a close friend, only 15, had died suddenly of something we'd never heard of before. So, the idea of my brother dying in Vietnam was real. And, I thought a real possibility. So I began writing him. "I just got finished reading your last letter," I started my first letter to him. "And I suddenly realized that my excuse for not writing because I was too busy is kind of poor. I am real sorry for waiting so long to finally get down and write you... I really have been busy lately, however, I decided that no matter how busy I get, it would never be as busy as you are over there and you still find time to write." I continued writing, "I hopefully will try and write regularly from now on. I know you are overjoyed with the prospect of hearing from your runt brother; but just so you remember you have one I might as well tell you the little I know about as the soul brothers would say, 'Whas goin on.'" I proceeded to write how I was "keeping the Fohr tradition of beer drinking intact." And how our gang had discovered the Cliffs at Devil's Kitchen Lake. "However, after six or seven weekends at the Cliffs, the local fuss got wise and patrolled the place. Therefore, the Cliffs are no longer 'the place.'... Today, I just got back from swimming out at Midland Hills. Of course, we had a few beers along to add a little pleasure. I feel kind of bad telling you all this stuff that's going on, because I know you sure would like to be here doing it yourself." I wrote Johnny about his dog—who he probably missed the most. I knew he'd enjoy hearing a story of how our family dog, Hansy, a 14-year old black dachshund, had bit our dad as he scolded the old dog for having a "bathroom" accident in the house. I also told him of how his good friend, John Lewis, was in North Carolina going through National Guard Basic Training. Lewis, whose father was a prominent doctor in the area, had the right "connections" to get Lewis in the National Guard, instead of having to register for the draft. Years later, Lewis told me the "deal" wasn't so good—as the National Guard was called up repeatedly

due to campus protest riots and even race riots after Dr. Martin Luther
King was assassinated. "He only had to do two years," Lewis said about
my brother. "I've got to do this crap for six years!"
I also thought my brother would like hearing about my "athletic"
pursuits.   In Michigan, Johnny was an outstanding athlete and one of
the stars of his class.   While I was a good athlete, I was far from being
one of the stars of our exceptional class.   Still, as a freshman in high
school, I was on the freshman football, freshman basketball, and varsity
track team—as part of the Freshman Relay team.   I actually was one of
only eight members of our freshman class to earn a varsity letter… and it
was a black Champs letter, since our varsity track team won the first-ever
South Seven Conference Championship for CCHS.   Our team picture
was even put in the trophy case at school, with the freshmen relay team
holding the trophy.

So, I continued my letter by writing, "Last Saturday, Given and me
and Lutz wanted to play some 'ball' so we went lookin' around for
someone else to play. We couldn't find anybody good so we went over
to the 'Slob's' house (that's Freeburg's new nickname—The Slob) He
was playing whiffle ball with McCoy. We decided the 'Slob' was too
hurtin' to play with us so we asked McCoy. He gladly excepted and left
the 'Slob' standing. We went to Given's house where he has a goal.
We decided to play 2 on 2 up to 40 points and then alternate players.
For some odd reason, the team who had McCoy always won."   I
thought that Johnny would like to hear that I was keeping in touch with
his best friends from high school—Lewis and McCoy.

I also thought that he'd like to hear about school fights or my
classmates starting to act tough… like he'd always made me feel was
part of high school. "About four weeks ago, it was almost Sophomore
'kick ass on freshmen' day," I wrote. "It seems that the stupid freshmen
have a ridiculous past time of throwing each other in trash barrels by
grabbing individuals and placing them in the barrel. We thought this was
perfectly permissible, providing they stuck to their own class for victims.
However, one day they chose to pick on a sophomore guinea pig and
guess who they chose—you're probably right—Wham! Without the
help of fellow sophs to come to his aid, he was successfully dispensed in
a trash barrel. This seemed to most of us to be humorous. Although
one or two took it as an insult to the Sophomore Class… It did seem
degrading to have lowly freshmen throw one of our 'great 69ers' in a
trash barrel. So, a group of about 20 of us decided that all freshmen
would get their ass kicked after school. (However), the cool seniors or at
least some of them thought that they should defend the little frosh.
Nevertheless, we all jumped in our cars and went out to the cemetery to

have it out.   The rumble was getting ready to start when the 'Man' showed up. Somehow, someone finked... Sorry about that—all that reading for nothing!   Well, that reminds me, its two days to haircut time for the upcoming freshmen. I finally made it! By the time you get this I will be an official upperclassmen and I will probably have cut a number of freshmen scalps! Come to think of it, I'll probably be in jail for hazing." My June 5th letter was signed:

Good luck, your little brother, Bruce
P.S. I hope I haven't bored you with some of these things
P.P.S. The Grand Prix is alright, except young mother (as expected) bashed it into the garage once—but it was repaired OK.   Your cycle's OK, too—but the Dad hardly ever lets me drive it.

As it turned out, I never got in any serious trouble "initiating" freshman—by giving them creative haircuts.   In my next letter, less than two weeks later, on June 15th, I wrote, "I am now a 'cool' upperclassman. And, of course, I have initiated my right as a cool junior by becoming the 'master barber' of freshmen heads.   The night the graders graduated, me and Wham and a few other guys got a hold of some frosh who were asking us to cut their hair.   Of course, we obliged." I explained how we had to go to a local laundromat and did get caught by a policeman—who took names.   But no one got in trouble because the kids parents didn't want to press charges.   I explained how I "became the first barber of the Class of '69 and now I lead all barbers with a total of 18 shaved heads.   The most popular style is called 'The bartender"— it was designed by the Oaf."   I even drew a picture of what it looked like on a "punk Frosh."   Ironically, there was one incoming freshman who was supposed to be a tough guy who claimed that no one was going to cut his hair.   And that he'd kick the ass of anyone who tried.   His name was Johnny Paul Phillips.   One day we saw him walking down Highway 13—just across from the McDonalds.   I said, "We're picking him up and cutting his hair.   He's not that tough."   As we pulled over he gave us no grief and actually asked us to drive him to his home, because his dad thought that it would be cool.   It was amazing.   On his parent's carport, we pulled up a chair, sat down Phillips and gave him a Bartender (where we cut all the hair on top and leave it on the side... so the kid looks like an old man bartender.)   Phillips dad took a home movie, thinking this was so funny.   What didn't turn out so funny was that Johnny Paul Phillips became a serial murderer.   He was convicted of raping and killing three women between 1975 and 1981.   He was sentenced to death in 1986 and died on Death Row in 1993.   So while he may not have been such a tough guy in 1967, he was certainly disturbed.

The return address on the envelope of my June 15th letter included our home address in Carbondale. Just below it, I added: (Basketball Capital of the World). Although it happened before he shipped out to 'Nam, Johnny was away at Army training on the greatest day in Carbondale Basketball History in March, 1967. On the same day, SIU's Saluki Basketball team won the NIT Tournament in New York City and the Carbondale Community High School Terrier basketball team played in the semi-finals and final of the Illinois State Basketball Championship. It was too much for the Terriers to pull off winning the championship-- with just three hours between the two games—and the first one going into overtime. After beating the State's No. 1, No. 2, and No 3 teams—in that order—to reach the final-- it was widely recognized that the CCHS basketball team was the best in the state. Still, it was amazing that little Carbondale, Illinois, had two such high-profile successful basketball teams at the same time. So, sharing stories about local sports was something I incorporated in my letters to Johnny. In late Fall of 1967, I gave him detailed descriptions of two of the most significant sporting events that had occurred that fall. The first was recounting SIU's magnificent football upset of highly rated national power, Tulsa—resulting in the goalposts being torn down by rioting students for the first time since 1933. Then, I told him something that I promised would "blow his mind!" After detailing how I had "caught a 20-yard pass" in the homecoming game against West Frankfort, I set up the story of how our Carbondale Terrier varsity football team came from behind in storybook fashion to beat Mt Vernon in the last game of the year and thereby win the South Seven Championship—the first time ever in football. I provided Johnny a play-by-play report of the game and the heroics of individual players like Mike Cochran, Jim McAdamis, Pete Brown and back-up quarterback, Billy Resnick, filling in for star quarterback, Bob Pankey-- who'd been ejected from the game for fighting. I also went on and on in the letter, describing all manner of activities and developments involving sports, beer-drinking, using fake IDs to get beer, a trip to St. Louis, and our fancy new Oldsmobile Tornado that our dad bought as another "motivation" for Johnny to make it home.

Our dad even let me drive the new car to St. Louis—"Don't worry," I wrote Johnny, "the kid soloed perfectly in the Tornado—not a scratch! And that's an accomplishment in St. Louis. Those drivers are worse than Murphy drivers." I ended the letter, "Well, that's about all the cool things that have happened since you left. I'm sure glad to hear you're out of the miserable field. I hope you start seeing a better time in that no-good, worthless country. I hope your Christmas isn't too bad.

I've had a real hard time trying find something to send you. I know you wouldn't want anything really nice because it would probably get swiped or rot."

Coming Home… But Not Really

When I referred to "since you left" it was not from when he first shipped out. He got to come home in the middle of his tour. In early September of 1967, our dad's mother, who had lived with us for nearly 10 years, died of a heart attack at age 65—just a few weeks before her 66th birthday. Because she had lived with us so long, she was considered part of the immediate family. Deaths in the immediate family were the only way someone in the war zone could come home on a brief furlough. Our dad did everything he could to ensure that Johnny would be able to get that furlough. It worked. So, literally in the middle of his 12-month Vietnam tour, my brother was able to fly back home to attend the funeral of his grandmother. He flew directly to Milwaukee, where dad was raised, and all his other family members were buried. I originally was not going to go to Milwaukee. There had already been a funeral for grandma in Carbondale. It wasn't certain that Johnny would be able to get home when they left, and my parents didn't want me to miss school. I couldn't believe it. I was going to be able to stay home—alone—for the entire weekend. Wow, what a party I had planned! It was going to be epic. Then on Friday, in second period Chemistry, I was called out of class. "Bruce, your brother is coming home from Vietnam… just for the weekend. You're parents want you to come to Milwaukee," I was told by a school secretary.

Great! But how was I supposed to get there? Did they want me to drive? They already took the family car. I wasn't sure if my old '60 Chevy beater would be able to make it that far. "They want you to take the train. It leaves in about an hour."

It was a bit of an ordeal and somewhat scary for a 16-year-old traveling alone for the first time and having to make a terminal switch in Chicago. Some old bum saw me alone in the main terminal and started to panhandle me. I acted like I was meeting someone and rushed away. My parents picked me up in Milwaukee and drove me to my aunt's home, where they told me the good news and the bad news. The good: In an hour or so we'd be picking up Johnny at the airport. The bad news: Johnny's dog, Hansy, died during the night—literally just hours before Johnny would have been able to see him—at least one last time. "Don't say anything to Johnny about the dog," my dad said. "He will really take it hard."

When I first saw Johnny step out of the terminal, I thought "Wow, he looks like an old man." He looked so different. He was much thinner than I'd ever seen him. He showed hardly any emotion. He looked serious and professional. He had medals on his uniform—that he was required to wear while traveling. He had just turned 21 over the summer. Boy, I thought. The things he's seen. He's a grown man— with a lot of life (and death) experiences that I could only imagine. And some, I never wanted to think about. Still, there he was. Thank God he was back OK. We went right to the funeral home for the Catholic "viewing" and prayer ceremony. The next day was the funeral. As we pulled back into the driveway of my aunt's home, it finally hit Johnny. "Hey, where's Hansy?" he asked, knowing that he went everywhere the family went. Hansy was never left at home or taken to a kennel. "Johnny, I'm sorry," dad said, beginning to cry, "We tried our best. He just couldn't hold on. He died last night." Johnny immediately took his Army cap off and threw it on the floor of the car. "This world sucks," he shouted, clearly shaken and showing strong emotions of hurt and despair—for the first time. Things he had seen in Vietnam did not seem to bother him. Learning that our grandmother had died did not seem to affect him. Losing his dog devastated him. Something else no one saw coming was that he was going to able to return to Carbondale with us and await his orders to return. There was no set return date. This was truly amazing. How did this happen? Apparently, I learned many years later, that he was required to take a specific military "hop" (as they were called) to California, and then return to Vietnam by commercial aircraft. It was very strange, but no one was complaining. We all thought every day he's here, he's not in Vietnam and he's not in danger. What did he do for almost four weeks? He drank every day. A lot. In fact, one night, after he and his friend, Dave McCoy, and our dad had been drinking all day, he got in our new 1967 Oldsmobile Tornado and drove it directly into a parked car one block from our home. He apparently just blacked out. The small Dodge car he hit was totaled. The damage to the Tornado was about $2,000. Fortunately, neither he nor McCoy were seriously hurt and my dad just told the neighbor that he'd take care of their totaled car. The police were not called. There were no tickets issued.

When I had a few moments alone with Johnny, as any 16-year-old boy might want to know from his "experienced" older brother, I asked, "What's it like over there?" He said, "I'll tell you one thing. I vowed that no one I worked on or treated, would die. So far, I've kept my promise." "Have you shot any VC?" I asked. "I've seen thousands of dead VC over there," he explained. "But I've only seen one alive." "What did you do?" I asked. "I ducked down and put my M-16 over my head and shot every bullet I had in his direction," said Johnny. "Did you get him?" I asked.

"I don't know. I never looked. And then we were moving again," he said. "Wow" was the only thing his kid brother could say.

A Life Changing Question

I also asked Johnny a question that would affect me the rest of my life. "How are things really going over there? Is it going to be over before I might have to go—like after college?" I asked. "Here's what I can tell you," he said. "That war has been going on for 20 years. And will likely be going on for 20 more. I can also tell you this: we are not winning over there." It was at that moment that I realized that I would have to take into account dealing with Vietnam myself. And that I would likely be in the military—in some form—one way or another. I remember thinking, our grandparents had World War I. Our parents, World War II. This is the war our generation has to deal with. It's just the cards we were dealt.

The War Heats Up and So Does Vietnam

Getting Johnny out of Vietnam and coming home—for whatever time it was—would have seemed nothing but good. At least in my family's mind. Not so much in Johnny's. "It was the hardest thing I ever had to do," he told me later. "When I went there for the first time, I didn't know what I was getting myself into," he said. "When I had to go back, I knew exactly how bad it was and what I was returning to. When I had to change planes in Anchorage, Alaska, I looked at those beautiful mountains and said to myself, 'I could get lost up there pretty easy and no one would find me.' The idea passed, but I did think about it." It was not only hard to go back to Vietnam. Things there got much harder and really started to heat up at the end of 1967.

In my last letter to Johnny before Christmas, 1967, I ended by writing, "Well we know one thing for sure: you won't be having a White Christmas." He didn't. He also almost didn't make Christmas. In one of his last missions with his platoon before Christmas, he was working on one of the guys who had been hit. He was bent over the guy when another member of the platoon pulled the tripwire on a Claymore Mine—that had been placed on the perimeter of their camp. Unfortunately, the VC—who had gotten wise to these anti-personnel weapons—had turned the mine around—so it would shoot it's ordinance (similar to shotgun bee-bees) in the opposite direction—at the US troops. Johnny and the guy he was working on were right next to mine. Fortunately, they were very close and the metal balls that shot out when the tripwire is pulled, go out at a 45 degree angle. Since Johnny and the injured troop were so close, most of the blast went over them. A few pellets got Johnny in his side. He knew he was hit and worried that he might have a punctured lung. He took some deep breaths and realized that he was OK—just a few bee-bees stuck in his ribs. He kept working on the guy and they made it back to the base. It was the second close call he had after returning from his Carbondale hiatus.

A few weeks before, on Dec. 6, 1967, Johnny was involved in a search and destroy mission when he and his company came under intense fire from a large enemy force. Guys were being hit and crying out for the medic (or in some cases, their moms). The platoon leader told Johnny to lay low and not go help the wounded. "I can't afford to lose you too," he told him. As it turned out, Chaplain Angelo (Charlie) Liteky was also with the company that day. Johnny later told me, "This Catholic priest I served with in Nam was the bravest guy I ever saw there." Chaplain Liteky was there primarily to administer last rites to the Catholic troops who were dying in the field. He carried no weapon. But on this day, as he heard the cries of the wounded men, Chaplain Liteky ended up personally carrying over 20 men to the landing zone for evacuation. He sustained hits in his neck and foot, but was the hero of the day. He was later awarded the Medal of Honor for his incredible bravery and inspiration.

Johnny and his buddy, Father Charlie, were able to celebrate Christmas—such as it was in the jungle war zone. His other medic friends took a picture of him and Charlie next to a miniature Christmas tree, and with other buddies enjoying "Christmas dinner"—that looked like fancy C-rations or something—with Santa Claus and other festive decorations in the bleak-looking camp. At least they did get Christmas Day off from the fighting and general misery. More of that was to come in a month.

On January 28, 1968, I wrote Johnny a letter, that began, "With the semester over, things are just gonna start going downhill all the way until you get back (58 days, if I calculate correctly.)" Thinking again that Johnny would want to hear that I was trying to "keep up his tradition" of partying and having a good time whenever possible, I wrote about our almost daily "partying and drinking" over the Christmas break. "I had a very cool set-up," I wrote. "Denny Pankey was home from Leonard Wood and me and Bob went and drank with him and played cards over at John Budslick's house. He's got a house of his own—right in the middle of town, next to the Alaby."

In trying to keep him up on the local sports, I talked about the Carbondale Holiday Tournament results and some of the highlights. Then I wrote, "On the third night of the tournament, Pankey set me up with this girl—I didn't have a date or anything, but we all went to Italian Village and her old boyfriend saw us there. He was a little high and asked me to step outside. Evidently he still liked her and she had dumped him. Well, I couldn't reason with the young man. I tried to explain that there was nothing to fight about because I really didn't have a date with her and I didn't know if I ever would... Then he got out of hand—he tore a button off my shirt. I proceeded to pound him—he never laid a hand on me. I told him that if I wanted to date the girl I would. I did and I still am. She's very nice and very tough. I realize the stupidest thing in the world to fight about is a girl, but as you can see I was cornered into it, and besides that he tore a button off my shirt—quite uncalled for." While trying to explain why I shouldn't have gotten into a fight (my only one in high school), I was really trying to make my brother proud that his little brother could hold his own in a scuffle—just like him. The truth was (and I didn't realize it at the time) that when Bob Bain took a swipe at me, he missed but hit Bob Pankey, who was there to back me up, in case other guys got involved. So when I swung back and made contact, so did Pankey—who also swung back as a natural reaction to being hit. Bain went flying back and was immediately out of it. A two-second fight. As it turned out, the girl Pankey had set me up with was Wendy Meyer, who I ended up dating for the next four years—the balance of high school and nearly three years of college.

I went on in my letter to talk about playing basketball with friends, including Bob Pankey's older brother, Denny, who somehow had become "permanently" stationed at Ft. Leonard Wood—where he had also gone to basic training after being drafted. I wrote, "By the way, Denny, as you know, has been at Leonard Wood for about 15 months and he says there's a high possibility he may be going to 'Nam in March. He's on the March call, however, if he does—he'll be a typist, so there's really not much sweat. But as you, above all know, any place in 'Nam isn't going to be too comfortable." I ended the letter, "We just can't wait for your return—"Good Times a Comin'"! This town better start getting ready because it is going to know when you get back! Your Brother, Bruce"

What neither of us knew was coming for Johnny was the Tet Offensive. Two days after I wrote my letter, it started. It was one of the largest military campaigns of the Vietnam War. It was a series of surprise attacks against military and civilian command and control centers throughout South Vietnam. Over two weeks, nearly 3,500 allied troops were killed and more than 12,000 wounded. It was far worse for the VC and North Vietnamese Army—nearly 39,000 were killed. Of the allied deaths about one-third were US troops. The date on the Vietnam Wall in Washington, DC, with the most deaths is January

31, 1968.

Johnny later told us that Tet was like the Japanese Kamikaze attacks—they were going all out—regardless of how many died—to see if they could defeat and over-run the US military installations. Johnny told me that his base near Saigon was over run and many guys he knew died there. Fortunately for him, he was in Saigon, working in a hospital—at the exact time of the attacks. Not that it was safe in Saigon. It was not. But it was relatively safer than his Army Post at Long Binh that had been one of the targets.

For almost two months, from the middle of January to early March, 1968, Johnny sent no letters. It was excruciating for our parents, especially our dad. He wrote letter after letter, in each one asking for some type of status update or just some word that things were OK. Nothing came. Not for weeks. Later, we learned why. The Tet Offensive continued, actually for most of 1968. But the Phase I campaign, which was the most hot and heavy (and dangerous) went through February. Johnny was scheduled to finish his tour in late March.

Finally, a letter came from Johnny in March. He apologized for not writing sooner, but he really didn't have a lot of opportunity. Plus, things were so bad, he didn't want to worry the family. Not hearing from him those many weeks… right at the end of his tour… almost did our dad in. It was painful and worrisome. And it got all of us to pray. A lot. His letter answered our prayers. He told us that that he was rotating out of the field (the dangerous patrols out in the jungle). He would be primarily back at the Base Camp… now secured, with the major threat defeated. In just a few more weeks, he was coming home… for good.

During March of 1968, I contracted mononucleosis. I had lumps on my neck and felt tired all the time. I couldn't go to school. I primarily laid around the house. Took naps. Watched day time TV shows. Ate soup. And toward the end, as I was feeling a little better, but still not able to go to school, I spent a full day creating a large house-size sign with a roll of mural paper that read: in big block letters down the side of the house: "WELCOME HOME" (in red) and across the entire front of the house: "GI JOE" (in red) "NOW the BUD (in the shape of a red frosty mug) IS GONNA FLOW" (in black). It almost killed me and took the most time for me to tape and tack the giant sign to our house. I wanted Johnny to know how much joy and how glad we all were that he made it back. We could all breathe again. Now we could really party!

Everything changed between Johnny and me after Vietnam. I
wasn't the punk little kid he loved to harass and torment. We now were
actually close in height and weight... especially with all the weight he
had lost and I had gained-- just growing up. Our nearly five years of
difference in age didn't seem like that much anymore, with me now 17
and he still 21. After 'Nam, Johnny was assigned to Fort Gordon,
Georgia, for his last six months in the service. It was a piece of cake
for him. Still, he couldn't wait to get out of the Army and restart his
life. He had survived Vietnam and during one of the worst times anyone
could have served there. He never spoke again of the vow he made "to
not let anyone die, who he worked on." He achieved it for the first six
months. But not the last six. I knew it and never asked him about it.

Johnny never harassed me again. Our relationship became close,
special and fun. We always had a good time together. Laughing about
the old days and especially our dad, who was one of our primary topics
of "entertainment." All the things that he'd said to us, or had happened
to him, like the dog biting him, had us rolling on the floor when we were
together, reminiscing. "I'll tell you one thing about dad," Johnny said
to me one night as we were having a few beers, "he doesn't know how to
talk or relate to us, but he sure writes incredible letters. Every one of
them was amazing."

It was during one of my trips to St. Louis to visit my friend from
sixth grade, Tom Blase, when his older brother, Sparky, told me that he
was planning on attending the Air Force Academy. "Isn't that like West
Point, but for the Air Force," I asked with surprise? "Yes," he said, as
Tom added that he too was considering going there. They explained
their reasons, which all seemed to make a lot of sense, especially in light
of Vietnam, the draft, and the fact that my brother was there. I

mentioned this discussion to my dad. He took it from there. Yes, he could write amazing letters. And he knew how to prepare a resume highlighting all my activities, achievements, and academic success. He didn't want another son in the "rice patties" to worry about. Johnny had returned to Carbondale in the fall of 1968 when I learned that I had been nominated by Congressman Kenneth Gray to attend the Air Force Academy. There was an article in the **Southern Illinoisan** about it. Johnny wasn't happy about. When the Air Force Academy football recruiter came to our home to speak to me about "trying out" for football at the Academy (due to the recommendation of our football coach, Vern Pollack, not my talent), Johnny told him that he was against my going to the Academy. He didn't want to see me in the military in any way, shape or form. "Why is that?" the Air Force officer asked Johnny? "I know what it's like in the military," said Johnny. "I don't want to see my brother harassed and hassled like that." Yes, everything had changed between my big brother, Johnny and me.

Postscript: *I did go to the Air Force Academy and attended for two and a half years, before resigning in the middle of my Junior Year, then going on active duty for two years in the Air Force, serving as the Editor of the Holloman Air Force Base newspaper, beginning a life-long career in the media. My brother John, eventually got back into the medical field by becoming a Dental Technician. He died in 1982 in Arizona in a single vehicle accident, after he passed out driving his car home late at night. We had been together earlier that evening, celebrating my wife, Janet's birthday. I still have all of his Polaroid photos of Vietnam and his Homecoming, and the letters he received from me and our dad.*

THE CHILD IS FATHER OF THE MAN

By Charles Larry

Three main things helped me survive my childhood in Southern Illinois: reading, art, and nature. This short piece will attempt to weave the three together, although the emphasis will be on nature.

I was a voracious reader. I would walk about a mile each way to the public library to borrow books or, sometimes several times a week, to UDs (University Drugs) to purchase paperbacks, bought with money earned mowing five lawns in the summers. Years later I would walk to 710. Growing up I had all kinds of nature books. I had a great many of the *How and Why Wonder Books* series and also the *All About* book series. These were books on wide-ranging subjects of science and nature. Later I had the *Time/Life Nature* series. I was mostly interested in the prehistoric earth, geology, and plants and animals.

After my father was killed in a tragic accident when I was six, my mother realized she needed a college education to get a good job, so the summer before my fifth-grade year we moved from Cairo, IL to Carbondale. Moving from the swampy land of three rivers (Mississippi, Ohio and Cache) to the eastern edge of the Ozarks was quite a change for me and opened up a new world. Just about a two minute walk from my house was a small woods with a creek running through it. As now, I was an early riser then and would go out into that woods long before anyone in my family, or even the neighborhood, was up. The little woods had a variety of things to interest a young boy. There were trees to climb, especially an old mulberry, which grew on a hill covered with violets.

There were places where the Japanese honeysuckle grew so thick I could make "caves" that would shelter me from rain. There were grapevines to swing on. And there was the creek which harbored crayfish, snakes, frogs and many different insects. I spent countless hours in that woods, sometimes with other kids but mostly by myself. I sometimes took my *Boy Scout Handbook* with me, studying the chapters on stalking and tracking animals or other aspects of woodscraft. Then, in sixth grade, new things happened.

Our sixth grade teacher at Lakeland Elementary School was Gaylin Fligor, in his first year teaching. His teaching methods were not just rote learning out of books but experiential. In the warm spring months he would take our class out on nature hikes in the woods and fields near the school. We would identify butterflies and other insects, flowers, and any other things we saw that would have been of interest. For everyone in class he made copies of a tree key, a hierarchical method of identifying characteristics of a species of tree and by elimination gradually narrowing the choices down to one—the tree you were looking at. I took this key into my woods and worked at identifying every tree I found. I also started to expand my range of exploration and made my way several miles to Brush Hill, then wild and uncultivated. This was a much larger woods than the one near my home. On two separate occasions I was treed by packs of wild dogs. Only when they finally got bored and moved on could I climb down and return home. These experiences made real the events in my favorite book at the time, *Fire-Hunter* by Jim Kjelgaard.

Fire-Hunter is the story of Hawk and Willow who are abandoned by their tribe of prehistoric peoples. Hawk invents a throwing stick and later a bow and arrow. He becomes so successful at hunting and surviving, eventually he and Willow are accepted back into the tribe. I think *Fire-Hunter* was read by every boy my sixth grade class. It was our bible. Our neighborhood boys formed a tribe: the Lantana Tribe (Lantana was the name of our subdivision) and across the creek was the Tatum Heights Tribe. We all had spears (willow shafts cut in the woods) and we played at being prehistoric hunters. I made a crude throwing stick that I don't think would have hurt any woolly mammoths or saber tooth tigers but I learned the principle. I also made fire by making a bow with a stick and string of rawhide. Using another stick as a spindle, entwined in the rawhide, positioning it between two pieces of flat board where small cavities were hollowed out with a pocket knife to hold the spindle in place, I made a sawing motion with the bow to rotate the spindle rapidly, eventually creating smoke and then setting fire to some dry grass placed around the rotating spindle on the bottom board.

I also loved to look at books on painters. The artists I looked at most as a child were: John Constable, J.M.W. Turner and Jacob van Ruisdael, all landscape painters. I was also fascinated by Chinese landscape painting and still am today. I've been drawing all my life, mostly from animation in the earlier phases of my life. I wanted to work for Walt Disney. In 1959, Disney's movie *Sleeping Beauty* came out. I was astounded by the beauty of the imagery in this movie—especially the backgrounds. In high school, I thought very seriously (and romantically) of becoming a painter. I would sketch and paint some of the beautiful sights in Southern Illinois, like Giant City State Park, Little Grand Canyon, Garden of the Gods, or Bell Smith Springs, etc. Southern Illinois is so incredibly beautiful and I wanted to capture that in paint. Exploring these sites, to be walking among the huge rock formations, was turning back time for me. I was in heaven, but something was missing.

Mrs. Treece was my French teacher in high school. But it wasn't French that has had a lasting influence on me, it was from something she said one day in class. She said that she kept a copy of Henry David Thoreau's *Walden* on her bedside table and read a passage from it every night before going to sleep, and this gave her an abiding sense of peace. That peaked my curiosity, so on my next visit to 710, I bought a copy and read it. Slowly. Very slowly. It's that kind of book. Sometimes a single sentence is enough to carry with you for the day. "In wildness is the preservation of the world." This should be the world's mantra, when we're losing species of plant and animal life at an alarming rate. I don't think any book has had a more profound influence on me than *Walden*. I read in it frequently and re-read it entirely every few years. It has deepened my experiences in nature and led to other influences, such as the photography of Ansel Adams, Galen Rowell, and Art Wolfe.

Photography has always been of interest to me. I would browse and drool through the photography magazines in the library at CCHS. I knew I couldn't be serious about pursuing photography at that time, though, for three reasons: 1) I couldn't afford it; 2) to really get photos that showed what a photographer wanted to show meant working in a darkroom with various chemicals and I couldn't see that happening then with me; and 3) I couldn't afford it. Digital changed all that. Currently my passion is photography. I take photos mainly for The Nature Conservancy, which has a big project in Southern Illinois in the Cache River Wetlands. There is

Design Above....by Charles Larry

nothing I enjoy more than being out in nature, taking photographs. William Wordsworth was right when he said, "the child is father of the man." Not a day goes by when I'm not aware of something I experienced, or read, or was taught in Southern Illinois that has shaped and nurtured me in some way. I'm very grateful for that. day goes by when I'm not aware of something I experienced, or read, or was taught in Southern Illinois that has shaped and nurtured me in some way. I'm very grateful for that.

THE LAST GRADUATE FROM UNIVERSITY SCHOOL (I THINK)

By John Samford

"Yesterday, upon the stair,
I met a man who wasn't there!
He wasn't there again today,
Oh how I wish he'd go away!
"**Antigonish,**" an 1899 poem by American educator and poet William
Hughes Mearns

I never attended Carbondale Community High School. It is part of a large pantheon of such institutions: Harvard, the University of Southern North Dakota at Hoople, Trump University and many more. Never there.

But I came close! As a (then) life-long inmate of Southern Illinois University's University High School (actually beginning with pre-nursery across the street from Pulliam Hall), I was a part of the class of 1969 -- the first **not** to graduate from U School.

If memory serves, we were informed of U school was to be closed at the end of the summer of 1968 in an assembly in Furr Auditorium toward the end of 1967. It wasn't news to my parents, as my father was on the SIU faculty in the school of education, located in the Wham Education Building (named for a classmate's Grandfather) down a long glass corridor from U school, past the art wing. There was to be one more year (my Junior) and then oblivion.

Some folks "jumped ship" early, not waiting for the last trumpet. Classes got smaller. Teachers picked up extra responsibilities. Coupled with the usual teenage angst, I'd say I had a pretty rough year. (Did I mention my parents decided to move one town, sixteen miles, south to Cobden so I had virtually no social life?) It was a time to wander the echoing halls and come to terms with the inevitable change life brings.

What alternative for my senior year? CCHS! My friends registered. I registered. We picked out classes, wondering how we "refugees" would be treated. The mighty Lynx were rivals of the Terriers, not that I was athletic enough for that to be a consideration! CCHS was actually closer to my house than U School and my brother Lloyd had blazed the trail there, achieving some notoriety in basketball.

Two bright spots stand out. The first is the experimental math program which had come to U School a few years earlier moved "downtown" to the Benning Building at Washington and Main—a less gloomy place to go to pursue mathematical knowledge and eventually to get my first real job. The second is an opportunity to take a college freshman level English class at SIU in **old Main**, a building which subsequently succumbed to arson the following year and from which I helped carry things during the fire, once I'd finished my Sunday Southern Illinoisan paper route which culminated at the end of S. University Ave--site of the conflagration.

Taking a 3rd quarter college level class as a high school student felt a bit intimidating until the first class began. Everyone else in class was a college freshman taking a required class, I, on the other hand, was a go-getting High School student with a promise if I got an A in the class, I'd be given three quarters' college credit. This was credit both at the High School and college levels: I had to get an A. I wrote essays the instructor read aloud in class ("If you all could write like this…"), I raised my hand to every question. I was a real pain. But it worked: I got an A and could say I'd taken a class where no one would subsequently ever do so again. (No, I'm *not* responsible for the still-unsolved arson!)

A plan was forming in my mind…Suddenly I saw how it might be possible to cram my senior year into my Junior year and the following summer. The next step was to enlist my father's help in applying for an American History correspondence class, a requirement I needed to graduate and didn't have time to take. It turns out my birth in Laramie Wyoming at the Health Service of the University of Wyoming (go Cowboys!) where my father was on the faculty, was useful. Because Wyoming is such a sparsely settled state, it wasn't uncommon for high schoolers to take correspondence classes through the U of Y. Dad had been on the doctorate committee of the professor who "taught" the correspondence course.

Oh and I did research! I discovered in the basement of SIU's Morris Library a great variety of "secondary" (i.e. high school) textbooks. Including the one I was using for American History. Including its workbook. With an answer key. I checked all my answers and was turning in perfect work. Until the day the answer key went missing. I looked all over nearby shelves, under bookcases, etc. I asked a librarian for help. It turns out the key had never been formally checked into the library's system and couldn't be tracked. I was devastated: I could've walked out with it the first day and simply told the book checker at the door it was mine.

Book checking must have been a dream job for anyone wanting to be paid for reading. They sat near the exit at the end of an ornate multi-story hall and when someone left, they had to show their books to assure they were properly checked out. Today, of course, there'd be a chip in a book which would set off sirens and lights if it weren't deactivated at checkout. And who checks out books anyway? They're all on the internet.

For example, I just found a link to a booklet published at SIU in 1959, "Objectives of Southern Illinois University" which has photos from that time illustrating the University's mission statement which happened to have been lettered on Southern Illinois marble in the great entrance hall of Morris Library. Stretching ceiling to floor, often I only read the last part to avoid craning my neck: "TO BECOME A CENTER OF ORDER AND LIGHT..."

Being familiar with that lofty goal, I chuckled seeing some SIU students wearing tee shirts emblazoned "Chaos and Darkness."

I was part of the class of 1969. The class of 1968 was U School's last graduating class. I attended the June ceremony and in fact played the requisite "Pomp and Circumstance." A teacher subsequently told me she'd never seen me sit as straight as on the piano bench for the inevitable speeches. I played them out and into history. But there was still a summer school session beginning the next day and with the classes I took in it, I met the requirements for graduation from University High School by August 1968. I'll never forget the poignant ceremony when I sauntered into the school office and Principal Knewitz handed me my diploma. I don't know for certain, but I may have been the very last U School graduate.

And so, I did not have to carry through with my CCHS registration. In subsequent years, I've returned to Carbondale from my home in Ann Arbor where I went to college and am still trying to figure out what to do with my life. Some of those trips have been to U School reunions (smaller and smaller) and a couple were CCHS where I knew some of the folks who finished high school there. Memories have become sufficiently blurry that I recall 1969 CCHS Senior Class President Glen Freeburg reminiscing about me sitting on some hang-out bench at CCHS.

Nope. Wasn't me. I'm the little man who wasn't there!

FROM SOUTHERN ILLINOIS TO SOUTHERN MISSISSIPPI: A FIFTY-YEAR JOURNEY

By Cheryl McBride Mueller

The first almost twenty-three years of my life were spent in the same house in Carbondale with Dad Randal, Mom Marie, and sister Donna. My maternal grandparents, Tom and Ethel King, lived with us off and on during my childhood. We were a blue-collar family with not a lot of money. I never ever thought of us as poor or in need. In retrospect that was because our lives were rich in things other than money. My sister and I never wanted for anything. I even enjoyed wearing her hand-me-down clothes. One of my most vivid dinner table memories was of my Dad's being sure there was sliced white bread to eat with each evening meal. I learned at some point that was because his very large family of origin often did not have enough to eat, even bread.

Our home was in the west end of Carbondale in an area called Oak Grove Heights with a mailing address of RFD #2. When the 911 system went into effect and there needed to be more precise addresses, it became 1104 West Jefferson.

My best friends growing up were my across the street neighbor, Leilani Weiss, who died much too young, and Patty Raines who lived down the road. Our other playmates were the Woolard clan when they moved in across from Leilani and the rest of the Raines kids.

I grew up in the church that my mother grew up in, Grace (United) Methodist Church on the corner of Marion and Hester Streets. I went to Sunday school and church every Sunday followed by lunch at Grandma and Grandpa King's house just down the street. Every summer there was Bible School down in the church basement where I remember making lambs from a bar of Ivory soap wrapped carefully in a white wash cloth (why would I remember that?) My dad, sister, and I were baptized together there and I was married there. During high school, I taught a Sunday school class of five year old boys – Randy Black (now a music professor and my Facebook friend), the Golliher boy (deceased), Chris Smith in his little wheelchair (my forever friend – now on Facebook) who served as acolytes at my wedding. Talk about precious memories and how they linger.....

Weather permitting, we walked to and from Springmore Elementary. When we did walk, we often stopped at Leilani's Dad's auto shop for a Popsicle. I remember rest time in Kindergarten on our individual rugs we brought from home – geez that must have been uncomfortable... Moved on to first grade with Mrs. Tripp and for some reason, I cannot for the life of me remember my second grade teacher's name. I do vividly remember Ms. Bevis, my third grade teacher, who was maybe retired military and had a reputation for being a hard teacher. Fear was my first reaction on day one of third grade – love and respect were my reactions on the last day of third grade. I learned SO much that year!

The next memory that jumps out is having a real German man come teach us German in the fifth grade. I could listen to him talk for hours. Somewhere in there, we also learned French. German and French are languages I never used again.

I'm thinking our class was the first to consolidate with other Carbondale schools for sixth grade at Lincoln Junior High School. We thought we were really hot stuff going to the junior high a year early. The seventh and eighth graders soon let us know that we were not!

During those three years, I had lunch almost every day with my grandmother. She lived a few blocks away on Hester Street and I would walk there to a homemade lunch! What special memories. She and grandpa lived with Anna Mae Montgomery in a large house that had several bedrooms rented out to male SIU students. Lunch was often shared with these guys who became a part of our family during their stay there.

Wilburn Boyd lived two doors down from my grandparents and he was my first puppy love. His name is engraved on the Vietnam Wall in Washington, DC – killed in 1967-68. I can remember my first visit to that wall and having to make several rubbings of his name because I was crying so hard the tears soaked up each of those little pieces of paper they provide for the rubbings.

I had such a great time with a real diverse bunch of kids. I loved moving from class to class and especially enjoyed being a cheerleader. When we couldn't go out for "recess", they would play records in the gym and we would dance. The boys sat on one side of the gym and the girls on the other, waiting for the boys to come over and ask us to dance! If memory serves me correctly, everyone danced – must have been an adult there being sure of that.... A new boy, Richie, moved to town and I went gaga over him. He was the epitome of "the bad boy" – black leather jacket, slicked back black hair – my oh my. We were boyfriend-girlfriend for quite a while – in a junior high kind of time frame!

Once again, weather permitting we walked to and from school. All the way across town! If we had any spending money, we would stop at the Rexall Drug store just down from the Ben Franklin and get a flavored fountain coke. My flavor of choice then (and now!) was chocolate.

Then along came high school. Carbondale Community High School. Kids from University School came over. African American kids from Attucks came over. We were a mixed bag and a loving bag. Looking back and remembering those days, I can truly say there were absolutely no racial problems or concerns. It seems we saw no color lines, only other humans that we learned with, played with, and truly loved. Maybe we were unique. I don't know, but now, having lived in the south and seen so much of their history, I thank God for my multi-colored CCHS class of 1964! I recently shared with a friend who is a native Mississippian that our homecoming queen in 1963 was African American (beautiful, wonderful Hazel Scott) and my friend was amazed. We weren't......

I was disappointed that I wasn't a cheerleader my Freshman or Sophomore years, but was fortunate enough to be one my Junior and Senior years. I was class treasurer all four years of high school, so I knew everyone in my class as I collected that $1.00/year class dues! (I don't remember what we did with those dues....) I have no doubt there were ups and downs in high school especially since I really liked boys and tried to have a boyfriend at all times, but my memories of 1960-1964 are great! Speaking of boys, my friends and I often cruised around Murphysboro and occasionally DuQuoin on Saturday and Sunday afternoons to see who else was out and about that we could talk with and maybe get asked out on a date. Date nights often ended at Crab Orchard Lake, "making out" in the back seat. I can say that now, I'm 73 for goodness sake! I wasn't all about fun and games though. Not to brag, but I was an excellent student. Graduated as a Top Ten Senior and was chosen by that group to present our graduation speech. I have no idea what I said in that speech, but it was certainly an honor that I cherish to this day.

My ACT scores gave me a full ride to SIU, so I started college the summer after I graduated from high school. Since room and board were not a part of my scholarship, I lived at home. I never ever thought I was missing out on anything by living at home. I worked 20 hours a week in the Home Ec Dean's office while taking classes. By this time, my fantastic dad was a Captain on the SIU Police force so I had lunch with him every day at his office. Mom would pack our lunches in his black metal lunch pail. How I loved that man and those times. This was an example of our not having much money I guess, but that thought never crossed my mind. It was what it was and I enjoyed it!

I couldn't afford the Greek Life, but I was an active leader in the Home Economics honor society at SIU where I made wonderful friends. Of course, there was still the guy thing and dating and etc. etc. I did have a good time that might not have always been approved of by the parental units. I did manage to stay out of trouble though.

Summer of 1965 before my sophomore year at SIU, some girlfriends and I went to the infamous Jacob Day Homecoming celebration near the big city of Jacob, Illinois (it is on the map). I met this handsome, tanned young man who was in the area picking tomatoes that summer to save up for college expenses. He had six beers on his person – two in each hand and one each in his shirt pockets. Love at first sight! Four years later we were married. Twenty-eight years later we were divorced. But that's a whole other saga!

College blew by in what is now pretty much a blur. What I do know is that I was preparing myself to save the world – probably through working with children. Although my major was in Home Economics, my area of concentration was Child & Family Studies with dual minors in Psychology and Sociology. My first job upon graduating in June 1968 was with the Illinois Department of Mental Health. I was an outreach worker going into homes to work with individuals in hopes that they could remain at home and not have to be institutionalized because of their mental illnesses. Totally not prepared for that job, but muddled through and as far as I know, did no permanent harm to any of my clients.

At this time in my life, I left Carbondale to never return except for visits. Bill, the tan tomato picker, and I got married in April 1969 and moved to the Detroit, MI area where he was an Industrial Technologist with Ford Motor Company. I got a job as a welfare worker (that's what it was called back then) in the inner city of Detroit. Talk about a change of pace from Southern Illinois! The first time my parents came to visit and I took them to see my office, my dad said "Don't you dare come back to work in this area!" Of course, I did. I got more life education there than a thousand years in a classroom with textbooks. I also became an expert in the use of profanity – something really different for me.

Hubby and I both worked and went to night school to get our Master's degrees at Eastern Michigan University in Ypsilanti. We bought our first home there and had our first son (he still can't spell his city of birth ☺) I worked for a time as a liaison between the Department of Welfare and Ypsilanti State Hospital – another lifetime education. I didn't have to use as much profanity though.

Illness in my husband's family brought us back to Illinois where we eventually bought a little eight-acre farm near Olney, IL, the birthplace of our second son. A total 180 degrees from my previous life, I learned to operate a tractor with a belly-mounted mower, gather eggs from the hens, buy cows at auction to raise out for meat and other odd and sundry country-livin' stuff. This was as close as we ever lived to Carbondale....

Our next move was to Covington, TN just north of Memphis and, of course, this was where our third son was born (he, too, can spell his birth city). After eight years as a stay at home mom, I returned to part-time work as a nursery school teacher at the local First Baptist Church – another life altering change!

My final move was to Hattiesburg, MS in 1984. No new kids were added....Sons grew up and left the nest. Husband moved on and became my ex (but still my friend). After teaching adjunct and continuing education courses, I started full-time in 1989 at the University of Southern Mississippi teaching Child & Family courses and directing the campus Child Development Center. Kind of full circle from a Child & Family Studies student at SIU to teaching those courses at USM! I left there in 2006 and became a part of the Early Childhood Institute through MS State University. At that time, we focused primarily on helping early childhood programs get re-established on the MS Gulf Coast following Hurricane Katrina.

In the fall of 2011, I tried to die with pneumonia caused by Legionella bacteria. That led me to semi-retire AND to be grateful for every new day. I had long before re-established my Methodist roots and now have an opportunity to be involved with many, many church activities.

In the intervening years, I became a mother-in-law to two wonderful gals and grandmother to five boys (we just seem to have a thing about boys). None live in Hattiesburg today, so I travel a lot!

As I look back over this composition, it amazes me to think that one can sure cram a lot into 73 years! With my parents gone (Dad in 1984 and Mom in 2004) and my widowed sister living in Louisiana, I have no family left in the Carbondale area anymore. I have made it back for class reunions, but Carbondale is now a memory of another life. Strong foundations were laid there. Precious memories were made there. Losses of loved ones were endured there. I look back with tears and smiles.

MY MEMORIES OF CARBONDALE

By W.J. "Jeff" Lee

The Neighborhood

The doors were propped open on the new ranch house located on the Giant City Blacktop near Old Illinois Route 13. Several people were going in and out carrying lamps, furniture and other items. I was running around in the house noticing that the rugs placed on the wooden floors would slide if you jumped on them the right way. Friends of the family who were helping were asking "how do you like your new home, Jeff?" I liked the new place; however, when it approached bedtime and learning that I was not sleeping in my old bedroom anymore, I became less comfortable with the idea of moving. It was December 1960 and I was about three months shy of the age of three years. My father, William "Doug" Lee, my mom, Betty Lee, and I moved from Pittsburg, Illinois located northeast of Marion. The birth of my brother Michael would come a few years later. Both sides of my family have a long history in Southern Illinois.

The neighborhood was very different back then. The Giant City Blacktop ended at Old Route 13, now frequently referred to as Walnut Street. The East Campus of Carbondale Community High School was yet to be built; that area was always planted with corn, milo, or the like. For mailing purposes our address was not Giant City Road back then. If I recall, it was first "Route 3" and later "Route 5." Traffic on the blacktop was not nearly as heavy as it is today. The area had sort of a rural, bucolic flavor. The neighborhood was populated by very nice families, families with whom we became very close over the years. To the immediate north lived the Henderson family. Their youngest daughter was named Kay who was about 7 years older than I who frequently played with me and even taught me how to ride a bike. To the south lived the Holmes family. J.D. Holmes was the fellow who built our home along with his and the one two doors to the south of our home. This latter house was originally the home of the Kirk family. Later, the Fox family moved into the Holmes house next door to us. The Gibsons lived down at the corner of Giant City Road and Old Route 13. Between the Gibson property and Henderson property was a house owned by a Mrs. Piquard. Later, the O'Neal family would move into that house. The Cannons lived on the gravel road that went along the side of our house, later to be occupied by the Piquard family (a different Piquard family than the one who earlier had lived in a different nearby house). All these homes were occupied by wonderful people. I remember hearing stories told by the older folks sitting around outside on summer nights as the bugs in the trees were starting to chirp at dusk. At the time this area was outside the city limits of Carbondale. The University Mall was not even a thought at that time.

Behind our house, on the other side of the fence, there was a wooded area that was very thick with underbrush. Unfortunately, it was inhabited by such animals as field rats and snakes. They would occasionally travel onto our land uninvited. One time the Cannons had a copperhead snake in a windowsill. As we got a little older, my brother and I, as well as other kids, would build forts back in the wooded area. Not too long after we moved to this home, a trailer court was established further to the east of the wooded area. My parents contemplated moving to another location in Carbondale a few times, wanting a larger home, but always decided to stay put. We did enlarge the house in 1969.

When very young, I would frequently look out the front picture window and watch cars go by. A frequent site would be coal trucks coming through as well as those amphibious vehicles referred to as "ducks." The reason for the frequent appearance of the duck vehicles was the presence of many beautiful lakes in the area; e.g., Crab Orchard, Little Grassy, Devil's Kitchen, Kincaid, Cedar Creek and other lakes. At one time (before my time) Crab Orchard Lake was the largest manmade lake in the country. Now it's not even as big as Rend Lake, located up north by Benton, Illinois. Because of the presence of all these lakes, many things carry the moniker "Lakeland" or some other name hinting at the presence of nearby lakes. My first school and the church we attended both had the name "Lakeland."

The area is also blessed with resplendent scenery. Apparently, when glaciers came through North America, they flattened much of Illinois and nearby states, but luckily Southern Illinois was spared of this phenomenon. Among the natural jewels of Southern Illinois are Giant City State Park, an area replete with bluffs, large rock formations, manmade trails, and evidence of early human existence in the area. Also, there is the Shawnee National Forest and the Garden of the Gods.

My mom would take us on frequent excursions to nearby Giant City State Park on summer afternoons. I remember an area that was fenced in that was home to deer. In the 1960s deer were almost extinct in the area so it was interesting to view these beautiful animals that were residents of this sequestered area. It may seem unreal to younger folks that deer were almost non-existent in Southern Illinois back then given their ubiquitous existence these days. Also, coyotes were extremely rare in Southern Illinois five decades ago. And who would have even thought that armadillos would take up residence in the area in more modern times?!

Our backyard was fairly large. My brother and I had a sandbox (actually, just sand on the ground) under a wild cherry tree. Many a battle was fought there with army men and tanks. Someday an archeological dig may uncover plastic soldiers and the old spoons with which we used to dig. There was considerable clover growing in our yard and honeybees were everywhere. Also, one could catch numerous monarch or swallowtail butterflies in the area. When I was very young, because there weren't very many kids my immediate age in the neighborhood, I would frequently occupy myself by getting my dad's shovel and digging huge holes in the backyard, pretending I was doing something productive like creating a swimming pool. Luckily, most of these holes were back at the end of the lot!

As we got older many nights our dad would hit grounders and fly balls to my brother and me. Or he would pitch batting practice to us. During the day when my dad was at work (and when my brother was still too young to play baseball), I would take five or six baseballs outside with a bat and would throw the balls up in the air and hit them—and then go out and retrieve them. Sometimes a hit would go long much to my joy but was then followed by disappointment as the ball was irretrievably lost in the aforementioned underbrush behind the fence.

Another interesting activity we got to do a couple of times is hunt for arrow heads on a farm located south of town near Giant City Road. The fields on this farm were apparently home to ancient peoples centuries ago. Once the fields were plowed, one could find 10 or 20 arrowheads and rocks cut to tan hides with within an hour or two.

Grocery shopping was done at Pick's Grocery Store on East Main, or the A&P downtown between University and Illinois Avenues. Later it would be done at the Sav-Mart store that came in, and even later Penny's when it had a grocery store. My dad would stop by Gray's Market near the intersection of Wall and East Main on Sunday mornings to get a newspaper before they were delivered to our area (and sometimes Pick's). And I would usually get candy at Gray's or Pick's, one of my favorites being Necco wafers. I also remember buying clothes at a store called "Goldie's" downtown.

Schooling

The first school I attended was Lakeland School. During a recent visit to Carbondale I noticed that the signature chimney had been removed from the building. At one time there was a very tall chimney attached to the building. If I recall, Winkler and Thomas Schools were built in the same manner. To this day I can remember the green tile floors in the school (except for the gym, which had sort of a light-tan color of tile), the squeaking noise made by the swings when in use, the banter of children playing, the bad food in the cafeteria that somehow seems to be requisite for most schools. There were lots of good kids that attended that school, some with whom I keep in touch from time to time. My teachers were Miss Watkins, kindergarten; Mrs. Drake, first grade; Mrs. Cherry, second grade; Mrs. Ashley, third grade; Mrs. Greer, fourth grade; and Mrs. Hall, fifth grade. My home was too close to school to ride the bus, but also too far away to walk by myself in the lower grades. We had a carpool arrangement with three other families who lived on Old 13. After fifth grade the school district implemented a busing program to promote diversity. As such, I attended Lewis School during sixth grade. My sixth-grade year was also the first year in which we "changed classes" throughout the day. In other words, one teacher taught math, another spelling/language arts, etc. During grade school my mom would many times have treats waiting for us as we walked into our house from school (she was an amazing cook and made wonderful birthday cakes and deserts too).

During sixth grade we would hear "scary" stories about Lincoln School. An assistant principal, we were told, was very strict (later I would realize he was a pretty nice guy; he just wanted to enforce good behavior given that many seventh and eighth graders can probably be difficult). Lincoln's building was very old, dark, and dreary looking (they now have a newer building). However, I really enjoyed those years. It was an opportunity to meet people from all over town and it was also a time of gaining more independence in the process of growing up.

The Lincoln years were followed by high school: freshman year was at the East Campus of Carbondale Community High School near my home and I attended the main campus on North Springer Street for the other three years. Many friendships were forged at this time as additional kids came in from DeSoto, Giant City, Glendale, and Unity Point schools. Because I worked at the store so much, I was not involved in too many extracurricular activities, other than playing on the junior varsity baseball team during my freshman year.

The Appliance and TV Store

I remember my dad saying that the week I was born was a busy one. Not only did I arrive, but my dad purchased half of Durall Appliance Store and, unfortunately, my paternal grandfather passed away—eight days before I was born. The year was 1958. Irv Hillyer also invested in the store. Irv was a professor of plant and soil science at SIUC. He was a very good friend of the family and seemed like an uncle to my brother and me. My earliest memories of the store are when it was located at 413 South Illinois Avenue, right across the street from the Varsity Theatre (now a parking lot for the train station). I still remember the telephone number, 618-457-8090. I can also remember the smells of different rooms, the sounds that doors made when they were closed, the tile on the floor on the appliance side of the showroom, and the carpeting on the TV and stereo side. Those memories are very dear to me. I idolized my dad, who was the managing partner, and also my mom who, at that time, was a stay-at-home mom (later she would return to bookkeeping—and she was an extraordinary bookkeeper—if someone had a question about bookkeeping she was an excellent resource). Originally, the Hines Restaurant was located to the south of the store with Western Auto on the other side. There was also a shoe repair business nearby. Later, the store would become Lee & Hillyer Appliance Center and would take over the space that was occupied by Hines Restaurant. We also had a warehouse that was located behind the shoe repair shop and other stores. At one time we also had a furniture store up the street. This was our location until about 1974 when we moved to 1308 West Main Street. But getting back to Illinois Avenue, next to the Varsity Theatre, was the Varsity Grill. At lunch time you would nearly always see the friendly regulars, Sam from the locksmith store, Larry from Larry's Veach/Gulf, Dave from the watch repair shop, Tony Luckenbach, Larry Doyle, along Vicky and Jean behind the counter.

Our store was fortunate to have so many employees who were "the salt of the earth." They quickly became friends of the family as well as employees and we valued them dearly. I was offered the opportunity to work at the store from the age of 13. Because I physically grew rather early, I was already able to help lift appliances and TVs. Much of my first duties were to vacuum and dust, and the like. One thing my family still laughs about to this day is that after the first day on the job when driving home with my dad I was telling him that I should get a raise because I was worth much more to the company!

When handling appliances there will occasionally be a mishap. One time when installing an air conditioner in the fifth floor of the high rise for the elderly at Marion and Walnut, we accidentally dropped an air conditioner out of a window. Luckily, the first floor extended out farther than the rest of the building, so the errant air conditioner landed on the roof of the first floor. I remember climbing on the extended roof with an elderly lady looking out her window helping me locate various pieces of the former air conditioner. This event caused excitement with the residents of the building!

During summers I would frequent the nearby Dairy Queen up to three times per day. Thanks to hard manual labor and a high metabolism (at the time) weight gain was not an issue. If I recall, at one time a large chocolate shake would cost 55 cents and a large hot-fudge sundae would cost 65 cents.

At the age of 17, during my senior year in high school, my dad placed me on the sales floor. I felt like I matured considerably during that year. Surprisingly, I did rather well in sales.
My dad and mom were as honest as they come. We were more like "consultants" on the sales floor rather than salespeople. My dad wanted every customer to be extremely happy. To this day, I still occasionally hear people say, when faced with a difficult decision, they would ask themselves, "what would Doug Lee do?"

Riots

During the late 1960s there was considerable unrest because of the Vietnam War. As such, many students and young people held large riots that caused considerable damage to the business district of South Illinois Avenue. Our store's windows were damaged at least a few times along with appliances and TVs that were near the front of the showroom that were struck by the thrown rocks. During one riot my dad went down to the store despite my mom's worried advice not to. Luckily, he was not hurt.
I also remember the Illinois National Guard camping on the campus of the East High School during one of the riotous times (I think additional Guard soldiers also camped at another site in Carbondale as well). Also, when I was in the sixth grade or so, I remember we were returning to school in a bus from the SIUC campus, having been on a field trip. We drove by an area, roughly around S. Illinois Avenue and Grand Avenue that was lined up with various law-enforcement personnel, donning

helmets, standing shoulder-to-shoulder, armed with Billy Clubs. The stores' windows were still boarded up and the authorities were expecting additional activity. Carbondale made national news during the years of protests.

Recreation

Our family had basketball season tickets for years at the SIU Arena (now called Banterra Center). I remember when SIU won the NIT championship in 1967, a time when it was roughly on par with the NCAA tournament for college basketball. Walt Frazier was on the team as well as Dick Garrett. Both would go on to have professional careers in basketball with Frazier being named one of the top 50 NBA players of all time. Later would come the era when Mike Glenn, Joe C. Merriweather, Corky Abrams and others played on some excellent teams (Glenn and Merriweather also had NBA careers as well).

SIU had great baseball teams back then as well, particularly when Richard "Itchy" Jones was at the helm. Also, a track star for SIU, Ivory Crockett, would eventually break the world's record in the 100-yard dash in 1974 (an event that, I believe, has since been replaced by the 100-*meter* dash).

Carbondale Community High School had excellent football and basketball teams in the late 1960s and early 1970s (as they have in many other eras as well).

Occasional trips to watch the St. Louis Cardinals was also the norm for us.

My family also enjoyed fishing and did so quite a bit, mostly at the pond of a family who were friends with my family, but also at various lakes.

My brother and I played baseball in Little League, Pony League, and I went on to the Colt League.

Carbondale Junior Sports

My dad was involved in many community organizations such as Rotary (of which he was president at one time), United Way, teaching adult Bible study at our church, etc. In the early 1970s he became active with Carbondale Junior Sports. He eventually became president of the organization. If memory serves, when he took over the helm there was about a $7,000 deficit that had been there for at least a while (that would be equivalent to more than $30,000 in 2019 dollars). He eliminated the deficit in a very short time. First, he devised a plan with Burger King with which the kids would go door-to-door and sell tickets that gave the buyer credit toward purchases at the restaurant and Burger King would give part of the proceeds to Junior Sports. Additionally, he encouraged some very fine people to donate money so that lights could be installed for night games, grass was planted on at least one of the infields, etc. There were many good people who volunteered their time and talent to the organization, all of whom worked to ameliorate the program in different ways. They made a great team! After games sometimes there were kids who didn't have a ride home. My dad would take them to their homes or make sure they had rides, even if they lived fairly close to the park. Despite these accomplishments, my dad was a very modest man who didn't seek praise. My mother is the same.

May 29, 1976

This unfortunate day is burned into my memory. It was a Saturday; we were at the store working that day. For most of the day it was a very normal, uneventful day. Everyone seemed to be healthy with many more years of life in store for them. I was 18 at that time and high school graduation would be the following weekend. As many kids did back then, I was going out that night. I remember saying bye to my dad as he was outside talking with a neighbor. They were laughing about some story and it was a beautiful spring evening. I headed over to Eckert's parking lot, which was a frequent hangout for high school kids. I was driving around West Main and Emerald Lane and saw flashing lights behind my car; I was being pulled over by a Carbondale policeman. He informed me that I needed to get to Carbondale Memorial Hospital because my dad had had a heart attack but was likely going to be okay and for me to drive safely.

While driving to the hospital (probably not in a safe manner) I was already envisioning my dad sitting up in the bed with my worried mom telling him that he needs to take it easy and not work so hard. However, that vision was very far from reality. I walked into a waiting room to see my mom heavily in prayer urging me to pray, which I did. Some time later all we heard was: "Sorry Mrs. Lee, we did all we could do." We were handed his wallet and a few other items to take with us. We had the task of telling my younger brother who was only 12 at the time. In the following days we were making decisions about a burial location, funeral arrangements, etc. My mom, consumed with grief, bravely reopened the store a few days later. I was doing a good job being in charge of the sales floor that summer; however, I was going to college and being able to assist customers on the showroom floor is only a part of running a business.

We made a difficult decision to sell the business and the deal was consummated in the fall of 1976. My dad's cousin along with another fellow bought the store. Because of agreements made during the deal the store would now be called Lee Appliance Center, rather than Lee and Hillyer, even though no one with the last name of Lee now owned the business (a common practice is to keep a former name or some derivative of a former name when businesses are purchased). The fact that my mom, brother and I worked there part time seemed to cause people to believe, erroneously, that we owned and operated the store. Later the store moved to where the old Sav-Mart store was located at Route 13 and Reed Station Road and was rebranded as MidAmerica Appliance and TV (or some similar name—I was no longer working there at that time). Later the store would be bought by Tipton's, a large appliance/TV chain based in St. Louis. Even later it would become a Circuit City store. Even though I visit Carbondale frequently, I don't know what is located there now.

Doug Lee Park

Not long after my dad passed away, Carbondale Junior Sports honored my father by naming the baseball fields and surrounding amenities "Doug Lee Park." Originally, the park was located down the hill from Lewis School on Grand Street (where the new junior high school is now located). Later, the ballparks at the Carbondale Superblock would carry that name. The Lee family is grateful and honored that my dad's memory and service to Junior Sports was recognized in such a nice way.

College Years

Having practically grown up on Illinois Avenue because of my dad's business I was, in some ways, well aware of how students lived, that the campus was large with probably about 24,000 students back then, the school nationally known, etc.; however, I was a bit overwhelmed when I registered there for the first time. I would go to one place to be told I needed to go elsewhere first. When I arrived at "elsewhere" I was told that I got incorrect information and to go back to the original place. It was sort of a circuitous process it seemed. I was also sort of an outsider in a school in my own hometown as I was a local and still lived with my mom and brother. It took me a semester or so to become accustomed to this environment. I graduated with a bachelor of science degree in finance and in short order obtained a master's degree in business administration—the latter at the age of 23. Subsequent to obtaining an MBA I was invited to join the faculty as a lecturer/instructor, teaching undergraduate investments courses and corporate finance courses. This was an extreme honor to me as SIUC's finance faculty at that time was ranked very high relative to those of other schools. Several of the faculty members were getting published in the most prestigious of finance journals. To be clear, I was not involved in this department honor of being nationally ranked. I was just teaching undergraduate courses and that was it. Nevertheless, it was exciting to be around the professors who made this distinction possible.

Carbondale and the World today:

A job offer from Emerson Electric Co in St. Louis was the catalyst for my leaving Carbondale in late 1982. The time was bittersweet: I loved the area but there weren't many opportunities for one to put an MBA to full use in a small town. My wife and three daughters and I have lived in the St. Louis area ever since (I continue to work in the field of investment/financial research and do some teaching at local universities), but I visit Carbondale about once a month. The area around Giant City Road and Walnut Street has changed considerably over the years. Giant City Road now goes all the way through to Route 13 and has for two or three decades. There are businesses along North Giant City Road where farmers' fields were once planted. The East Campus of Carbondale, which formerly housed just freshmen, is now the home to the entire four-year high school—and is no longer referred to as "East." Some of the houses around our family home are now rental properties or have been torn down. Traffic on the once sleepy Giant City Rd can cause delays when school is letting out at the high school campus.

Televisions and appliances are sold mostly at large chain stores.

Necco wafers are no longer produced, I believe.

With inflation over the past decades, large shakes cost well more than 55 cents and large sundaes more than 65 cents.

Once when I was at a gas station near Eckert's parking lot, I asked a young fellow if kids still congregated in the parking lot. His answer was in the negative and he had a look on his face as if to say: "Why would anyone do that?"

My brother and his family, ironically, live in the house in Pittsburg, Illinois in which we lived before he was born.

As the Greek philosopher Heraclitus said, "change is the only constant in life."

FROM LAKE HEIGHTS TO SOUTHERN ILLINOIS UNIVERSITY

By Lynette Damhoff

The neighborhood I grew up in was known as Lake Heights. My family moved there in 1963, when I was eight. It is located behind the mall on the east side of town. There are no lakes in the neighborhood and never have been. Lake Heights was a poor neighborhood inhabited by a mix of families and students. You turned into the neighborhood off the highway and had a choice of driving down three dead end streets. My family lived on the shortest street. There were six houses and one trailer.

Our family home was small. Downstairs there were four small rooms and one bath. Upstairs was a good size room that extended the width of the house. There were four children in our family; one boy and three girls. When we first lived there, we rented the upstairs room to students. My sisters and I slept on a hide-a-bed in the living room. Since we didn't have a second bathroom, the students used the family bathroom. They had to walk through the living room to get to it. There sure was no privacy. As my sisters and I got a little older, my parents gave up renting and let me and my sisters move into the upstairs room. I, being the oldest and the neat freak of the trio, got one half of the room to myself. It was great! I set up my own little reading corner with a little library. I spent many, many hours in that corner. My sister thinks I don't remember much of our childhood because I was always in a book. My sisters used their room to hide fly swatters from our Mom. That is what we got spanked with. We also occasionally hid a cat up there. We always seemed to get caught. It was rather warm up in that room and we had no air conditioning. The floors were tile. They were the coolest thing in the room. On really hot nights, I would lay directly on the tile. When one spot got hot, I just rolled over to a cool spot. I prefer air conditioning now.

There were no personal computers, game boys or any other electronic devices when I was a kid. I remember when my brother got a radio. We listened to KXOK out of St. Louis. We did not get a TV until I started high school. Kids really did play outside and use their imaginations. You either played with your siblings or other neighborhood kids. We played Hide and Seek, Ghost, House, and School. We played Tetherball, hunted for Crawdads, and caught lightening bugs. If there was an abandoned house in the area, we spent hours exploring it. Not everyone can include that in their list of childhood activities, but it was one of my favorites. I had quite a collection of wine bottles from these homes.

Our best neighbor was Ruth Biggs. She was like a grandmother to me and my siblings. She had two grandchildren near our ages and they were our faithful playmates for many years. Our driveway was made of old coal cinders. They were rough and sharp to fall on. Ruth had a cement sidewalk. She let us ride our tricycles on her sidewalk. She also let us watch her TV sometimes. I watched the moon landing at her house.

Some of our other neighbors I don't have such fond memories of. One evening I was at neighbor's house eating supper. The mother had just come home from the hospital after having had surgery. I am not sure how it came to be, that I was even there that night, but, she made us all supper and called us in the eat. She had forgotten to put a plate of bread on the table. Her husband demanded she get up and get the bread. Even as a kid I was appalled. By the way, he was a police officer, and his nickname was "Trigger". Really?

There was another family that had five children. They were a rough group of kids. I witnessed one of the older boys pick his sister up by her pony tail and swing her around in the air. That same sister pushed my brother down onto the peat gravel street in front of our house. She shoved his head down into the peat gravel as hard as she could. Now I wasn't one to fight, but I couldn't let her do that. I jumped on top of her and knocked her off of my brother. I then ran home as fast as I could because I thought she was going to kill me.

However, maybe the most memorable experience was witnessing what appeared to be a kidnapping. One summer evening there were a bunch of kids outside playing. A large white station wagon pulled onto our street. A woman got out and called the new neighbor kid over to her car. He didn't act like he wanted to, but he got in and they drove off in a hurry. Later we learned his Dad had taken him first and his mother had come to retrieve him.

The first school I attended was Lakeland Grade School. It was the school for the southeast end of town. The fall I was in third grade John Kennedy was shot and killed. Our teacher announced this to the class. There were a lot of tears, even from the teacher. The thing I remember about 4th grade was the sudden death of the teacher's husband. I think he had a heart attack. This was the teacher that gave me bad handwriting grades because I used the wrong hand. I was left- handed. I recently learned that my grandmother tried to convince my parents to make me use my right hand. My 5th grade teacher was my favorite. She was nice and read to us in the afternoon. The book I remember liking was "A Door in the Wall." It was a Newberry winner. In 6th grade I had my first male teacher. He was ok, but played favorites. I never liked it when a teacher did this, even if I was a favorite. The incident that I remember from 6th grade involved a girl I didn't really like. She was snooty. One quarter the teacher handed out report cards. This girl normally got straight A's. On this report card she had a B. She started sobbing and said she couldn't go home with this grade. Her Dad would beat her. She had seen her brother beaten every time report cards came out. I think the whole class felt sorry for her. The teacher changed her grade to an A. I liked both of them better after that day.

Behind Lakeland School was a large grassy playground. One side was bordered by a corn field. At the edge of the corn field a group of us would set up a little camp. We played "Tornado". It was a version of House, but we would pretend that we were being blown away by a tornado and would hide behind the corn stalks. There were swings and monkey bars. Girls were required to wear dresses, so for modesty we wore shorts under our dresses. Twice a year there was a music program; Christmas and Spring. We practiced a lot to get ready for these. In 5th grade our class learned Mary Poppins songs. We learned to the say the word. Supercalifragilisticexpialidocious. We were super cool!

If only I could have stayed at Lakeland and not had to go to Lincoln Junior High. I don't have one good memory of that place. I lived in fear the whole two years I attended school there. I can't understand how a town with so many educated people let that school get so bad. In 7th grade I had Mr. Horst for homeroom. I may have just been a kid, but I thought he was a mentally unstable bully. White slips were given out as a form of punishment. If you got so many of them, other more severe punishment waited. Mr. Horst seemed to relish giving these out. He gave one to a kid once for having a weapon in class. It was a safety pin. Another one of his quirks was to require the students to keep all of their papers in a three-ring binder.

Every so often he would walk around the room and pick your notebook up and shake it. If any papers fell out, you got a White slip. His biggest pet peeve was anyone walking into his class with mud on their shoes. One day I made this mistake. He screamed at me to go out and clean my shoes off. On the surface that doesn't seem like such a bad request. What made it horrifying, was getting caught in the hall by Mr. Allen, the guidance counselor. His form of counseling was to patrol the halls looking for kids to beat with his big wooden paddle. I was absolutely terrified. I did manage to avoid Mr. Allen that day. I shared this story with some of my friends that didn't have Mr. Horst. A few weeks later one of my friends was teasing me about this and trying to push me into a mud puddle. She underestimated my fear. I turned to her and pushed her as hard as I could. She fell into the mud puddle and was covered head to toe in mud. She needed to go inside and clean up. When she asked a teacher for permission, the teacher asked her what happened. She stated she fell into the puddle. That was the best lie ever!

I managed to escape any beating by Mr. Allen, but my brother was not so lucky. My brother was legally blind and had to get up close to things to be able to see things. One day while standing in line for lunch, he stepped out of line to look at a picture on the wall. You guessed it. Mr. Allen took him away and beat him for this. My mother paid a visit to the school after this and told them none of her kids were ever to be touched again. We weren't.

By the time I started High School, Carbondale East had been built and was open for classes. Only Freshman attended here. I think my whole class breathed a collective sigh of relief to be away from the Junior High School. For me personally, my freshman year was uneventful. Not so for the world. Protests and riots against the Vietnam War were on the rise. Classes were cancelled at SIU that spring. They were also cancelled at CCHS East for a week so the National Guard troops had a place to stay. There were no mass school shootings, but a girl in my class was kidnapped and murdered coming home from school one day. The body was found after about a week and an arrest was made. It was a scary time. Her name was Lisa Levering.

Sophomores moved to the main school campus on the northwest side of town. Here students sat on the wall and bought mostly junk food from the store across the street. My favorites were plain Dorito Chips and Vanilla Zingers. I don't think either are made any more. Girls were allowed to wear slacks to school and boys grew their hair long.

It was during my sophomore year that I killed a baby chicken in Biology class. We were doing an egg incubation experiment. One week I opened my egg to find an almost ready to hatch baby. It wasn't developed enough and I watched it die. I was so distraught that the teacher did not make me continue with the experiment. It was also during my sophomore year that I met my first "love". I thought the world of this boy. Let's just say that this relationship did not have a good outcome for me. I was as heartbroken as a sixteen-year old can be. At the time I thought it was the worst thing that could happen to me. I was wrong.

My junior and senior years I studied and worked on getting good grades. I attended football and basketball games. Working on the homecoming floats was fun. I did a lot of babysitting and my Senior year I worked at Ideal Bakery. I did end up earning a scholarship to college. I also received an award from a local organization and was asked to attend a dinner in honor of the recipients. What I remember about the evening was struggling with how to eat the fried chicken without using my fingers.

During my senior year my family moved across town to Tower Road. Across the street was a nursing home. It housed a wing of severely mentally and physically challenged children. Most of them had been abandoned by their families. I began doing volunteer work there and often went twice a day to help feed the children. It was horrible and was run by nurse similar to Nurse Ratched, from "One Flew Over the Cuckoo's Nest." She was mean. I was horrified by some of the things I witnessed staff doing. I eventually voiced my opinion and got kicked out. One good thing that happened was the adoption of my favorite little girl by a local family. This experience sparked my interest in Social Work. I worked in the social work field for thirty years, most of that time in the medical field. I had several close friends growing up. Diana was my best friend in grade school. She lived just down the highway from me. There was a barn behind her house. The house she lived in was unique. She and her family lived in one half of the house and her grandparents lived on the other side. The two sides were connected by an entryway. There were six kids in her family and only two bedrooms. Her parents had to be creative to fit them all in. I spent many hours playing with Diana and her siblings. Diana was quiet and a very good girl. I remember only one time we got into trouble. She lived near where CCHS-East was being built. One day we were walking home from school and we decided to cut across the construction site to her house. It was muddy. Very muddy. By the time we got to her house we were covered in mud and had both ruined our shoes. Our parents were not happy. New shoes were not in the budget. I attended Lakeland Baptist Church with her and for two summers we went to church camp together. Church camp is one of my favorite childhood memories. This surprises me since it was quite primitive. There was no indoor plumbing and we had to use an outhouse. We carried buckets of water to the cabin so we could wash up. We sang, went swimming, and did crafts. Diana's favorite hymn was "What A Friend We Have In Jesus". I always think of her when I hear this song.

In Junior High I made friends with Janet. She lived across town in Parrish Acres in a very nice home. It was nicely decorated and her mother was an immaculate housekeeper. Janet had three younger sisters. Her parents owned PKs on the strip. I read that her mother recently died. We did not hang out at PK's, but occasionally would go in there to talk to her parents. A funny memory I have of Janet was the time she crocheted herself a beautiful lavender mini
dress. She wore it to school. As the day went on the dress stretched out and became a midi length dress.

Sue Ellen was a good friend in Junior High and High School. We spent countless hours just hanging out and riding our bicycles all over town. Her parents were strict, but this didn't seem to slow Sue Ellen down very much. She was beautiful and popular. One night we snuck to a party at Harry Edelman's house. His parents were out of town. Sue Ellen was meeting her boyfriend there and I was tagging along. They disappeared and, being the dork that I was, I sat and watched TV. I wasn't about to drink. Sneaking out was enough bad for one night. When the Mary Tyler Moore show came on, Harry and some of his friends came in to watch. It turned
out that Ed Asner was Harry's uncle. He played Lou Grant on the show. Sue Ellen and I left before the police showed up, but we still got caught. One of her mother's coworkers lived next door to Harry.

By the time I graduated from high school I was ready to move on. I didn't actually move too far since my scholarship was for SIU, but I did enter a whole new world. I liked college. I made new friends and met people from all over the United States and the world. I learned to think in new ways and see the world from other points of view. I often have said I learned as much
outside of the classroom as I did in it.

I was fortunate to work at the Information Desk at the Student Center. This was a wonderful way to meet and help lots of people. One of the best experiences involved a student who had just arrived from

Asia. He had gone to the bathroom at the Student Center and left his billfold lay by the sink. When he went back it was gone. He came to me in a panic. All his money was in the billfold. I took his information and told him I would see what I could do. A little later a man showed up at the Info Desk with the billfold. All the money was there. It was a happy day.

I recently visited that Student Center. The Information Desk has been replaced by a Starbucks. I had two thoughts about this. How can students afford Starbucks and who is going to cheer when a billfold is turned in with all the money intact? There is now a computer screen people can click on to get information.

I also worked in the Check Cashing Department. This was on the second floor of the Student Center. We cashed checks all day long. This was how students could get cash from their hometown banks. There were two or three employees working all day and evening. We cashed hundreds of checks a day. Now there is one window with a sign that says "Ring the Bell for a Assist." I am guessing debit and credit cards have replaced checks.

The SIU Bookstore is still there. It should probably be renamed. They had clothes and other SIU memorabilia, but not many books. The text book end of the store was empty. It was sad looking at the empty shelves. I always loved books and spent many hours at Morris Library. I have to admit, even I rarely go to the library now. I have a smart phone and it is kind of like having a library with me all the time. I am kind of ashamed of this. The large Student Center cafeteria had been replaced by fast food restaurants and the TV lounge was empty. In the 1970's it was packed at noon with students watching "All My Children."

Carbondale was a unique place to grow up. It was part old south and part a progressive university town. In 1963 the town was segregated by race and money. The southeast was inhabited by poor white people, the northeast by black Americans, the northwest by middle class whites and the southwest by rich people. At least that was the way it seemed to me. Not long after my family moved to Carbondale the schools were integrated. This didn't go over to well with some people. They wanted to stay in their neighborhood schools. I wasn't raised in a racist family and didn't understand why people were prejudiced. In junior high the PE teacher had some issues with this and I didn't like it. I made friends with a black student, Kathy. She was as big and strong as I was little and weak. We liked to pretend we were arguing so the teacher would get all worked up. She just couldn't believe we could be friends. I remember Kathy telling me that her family didn't listen to "honky" music. I was shocked. It made me realize prejudice can come from all sides. Some sides just had more power and some more hurt

The University was the hub of the town. There were concerts, bands, and plays. There was political unrest, riots, partying on the strip. Famous people often came to town. I saw George Bush Sr., Jimmy Carter, and Ted Kennedy. Gale Sayers was the Athletic Director for a few years. The first time I saw him, he had on a full-length fur coat and platform shoes. This was not the athletic look I was used to.

Many Carbondale residents either worked for the University or went to school there. There were almost as many students as there were permanent residents. When classes were in session, the population swelled and when classes were done, Carbondale almost became a ghost town.

The strip was famous and SIU was known as a party school. The strip saw a lot of action. Some of it was harmless fun, like streaking and some was not good. The train tracks were next to the strip. It seemed like every year a student was killed when they stumbled in front of a train. Illegal drugs were common. The odor of Pot was often present. I can't speak with much authority about the strip because I didn't spend much time there. I didn't enjoy being in crowds of intoxicated people listening to loud music. SIU was known for partying, but there were many students who did not participate in this lifestyle.

The countryside around Carbondale was beautiful and offered many outdoor activities. The lakes were plentiful. My family often went swimming at Carb Orchard Lake. I learned to swim there. My favorite lake activity was playing on the island at Campus Lake. My sisters and I would pretend we were castaways on a deserted island. I enjoyed the Cardboard races held on Campus Lake. We also spent time at Giant City. There were trails to hike, bluffs to conquer, and creeks to explore. My family camped there in a tent.

During my recent visit to Carbondale I drove around looking for familiar things. The biggest surprise to me was the growth of the east side of town. The town has flipped flopped where the center of business is, from the west side to the east side. When I was growing up, on the east side, we had Cousin Fred's, Picks Grocery Store and Vic Koenig Chevrolet. The town ended at Vic Koenig. Now it seems as if there are stores all the way to Marion. Murdale Shopping Center is still standing, but I don't think any of the stores are the same as when I lived there. The new bakery did sell the pinked iced sugar cookies that were sold at Ideal Bakery years ago.

I bought three of them and ate them all in a short period of time.

Many of the schools have closed down and have been replaced with new buildings or consolidated. I was not sad to see that Lincoln Junior High had been torn down. It was kind of sad to see the high school no longer being used as the high school. Carbondale East has been expanded and all students attend there now. There were many buildings I recognized but many were empty or being used for other things. I was disappointed at how unkempt the town appeared. Many homes were in disrepair and yards needed tending. I was glad to see that the campus had been well maintained and was as beautiful as I remembered it. I have visited many college campuses in my life time and SIU is still one of the prettiest.

I realized during this recent visit that I no longer feel like Carbondale is home. There were glimpses of "my" Carbondale, but it has changed as much as I have. You move away, change and age, but still, a part of you is that sixteen-year old girl trying to find her way.

FIRST FIVE

By Denny Pankey

During the Sumner between my 7th and 8th Grade Year, I played Baseball with a group of Friends, who would become future teammates and life-long friends. We made the Finals of the City League, coached by Bud Allen, along with His Son John, Chuck Grace, David Mercer, Kurt DeWeese and other SW Carbondale Boys. Our time together during that Summer went far beyond the Baseball Diamond and when School was about to begin, I convinced my Parents to let me transfer from University High School to Lincoln Junior High School to continue to participate in Athletics with my Friends.

They agreed, and I made the First Five for the Leopards 8th Grade Basketball Team. Football, even though I had some success in football, that came much later. Basketball was to be my sport, having been coached by one of the best, Bud Stotlar in 6th and 7th Grade at U-High.

Along with Jim Shafter, Chuck Grace, Lynn Howterton (C.C,H,S, Terrier Hall of Famer,) and Jim Phillips, we had a great season, advancing from Regionals and Sectional Play, only to loose to Chester at the State Tournament, a team we had beaten twice in regular season.

One thing I remember, was C.C.H.S. Terrier Head Coach, attending most of our Home Games, sitting in the Stands taking notes. I always somehow thought how dedicated He must be to be out and away from his Family on either a Tuesday or Thursday night at a Junior High School Basketball Game.

I played Freshman Football for Coach Cherry, but as I said, this was to be a stepping-stone to greater achievements on the Basketball Court. Remembering back to those days, I recalled Coach asking me one day what size shoe I wore but thought nothing about it.

On the first day of Basketball Tryouts, outside the Varsity Locker Room, was a long row of bins with equipment including a reversible practice jersey, tube socks, shorts and Basketball Shoes all numbered for identification purposes. At the end of the row were 4 Bins with names above them. Our Lincoln Junior High First Five, excluding Shafter, whose Father accepted a position in Oklahoma over the Summer and Jim had moved away. That was truly a proud moment, that Coach had pre-selected us to be a part of the program, which would include First Team Freshman and 2nd Team Junior Varsity.

I was feeling pretty proud of myself and played very hard as to live up to the confidence that Coach had placed with me. On about the third day of practice, I was warming up and Coach Cherry walked onto the court as I was shooting free throws. He said, "Would you like to play a short game of one-on-one?" I said sure and just knew that my defense would shut Him down. When He started dribbling, He went right, then left, then right again, passing the ball between my wide-spread legs, retrieved the ball and made an easy lay-up. I was really embarrassed. He said, "That move surprised a lot of Players along the way, So work on your defense and you'll be a good one too."

Soon, we were introduced to our Freshman Coach, Sam Hardwick. A science teacher I had 3rd Hour. Seems, there was a shortage of qualified coaches and the staff had to dig deep for a volunteer to guide us to stardom. Our Season ended up about 500 for the year and a tribute to Coach Hardwick, for giving it His all, without much practical experience. Some of the players made fun of Coach, but I was brought up better than that and always gave Him the credit and respect He deserved.

Our Senior Year, the First Annual Carbondale Holiday Tournament began, with outstanding teams from around the State, including Jacksonville and Decatur St. Teressa. We advanced to the Semi-finals and had to play State-ranked Decatur. Coach Cherry, always inspired us to play top-notch Basketball and made terrific pre-game speeches. On this occasion, He simply walked into the locker room, waited for the noise to subside, pulled a telegram out of His pocket and began to read. "Team, it has been a long time since we have been together, but I read where you were playing a great Basketball Team in the Semi-finals tonight. I'm sure, you'll remember all the great things I taught you as Freshman, as I had the very good fortune to have been selected as your Coach, so go out and play for Coach Cherry and I'll be rooting for you,"

Signed Sam Hardwick.

We went on to beat Decatur in the Game and advanced to the Finals against Jacksonville. Decatur had beat us down and we could only give Jacksonville a good half and finished in 2nd Place. Our Season ended, losing to Marion in Regionals, who advanced to the State Tournament.

Life lessons were learned by yours truly. Respect for Coaches, who give up time away from their own Family's, who work hard to mentor young men and teach skills away from the playing fields that last a lot longer than their playing days.

I am sure many of you reading this remember the names and have stories of your own about Coaches, Vern Pollack, Frank Bleyer, Gordon Butler, Walt Moore, and John "Coach" Cherry. I was privileged, to have played for them.

GROWING UP IN CARBONDALE ON WALNUT STREET

BY NANCY VOGLER BAIN

It really wasn't until I was much older that I realized what an idyllic childhood I had growing up on Walnut Street. Carbondale was such a safe place in the 50's and 60's and kids were free to walk and ride their bikes anywhere. And from where I lived, I could walk practically anyplace around town. And Walnut Street in the 50's and early 60's (until 1968) was a quiet, tree-lined, brick street – not the thoroughfare it is today.

Helen and John Gilbert and their children Pam, Gail, and Phill lived next door to me on Walnut. Phil was closest to me in age and graduated CCHS 1967. I never understood how his address could be 513 W. Walnut and mine was 601 W. Walnut when we lived right next door to each other! Whenever the Gilberts had parties, I could watch the gathering in their kitchen from my bedroom window. I would run and hide under Phil's big sister Gail's bed when my sister Ann was after me! Between our two houses in the back, was a half court basketball court. Lots of hours were spent on that court by all the neighborhood kids, including me! In the fall we would rake leaves into a long pile in the middle of our two drive-ways and roast marshmallows. I'll never forget how it smelled and felt on those cool, crisp nights with the fire to warm us and the smell of roasted (I.e.burned!) marshmallows!

Dr. Dan Foley and his wife Jean lived next door to the Gilberts. Their house is the oldest in Carbondale. It was nice having Dr. Dan so close – he would make house calls! A little further up from them was the

Dr. Leo Brown family– his daughter Dorothy was 2 years older than me. The Monroes (Mike Monroe, et.) lived down the street on the corner of Walnut and Springer. Kathy McGowan lived on the corner of Walnut and Poplar. Dr. Marty Powell and his family lived in the big white house two doors down from me – this was the house the Jabr's moved into later. James Johnson (aka Jim Johnson) lived on a little street just off of Walnut Street near Oakland Ave. I remember as a very little girl going to his house for play dates. Later on, I would go to John Samford's house on Poplar – he had a big buckeye tree in his yard. Other frequent playmates included Mary Lewis and Gigi Reese. And I loved to spend the night with Mary Swindell, in their apartment above her Dad's car dealership! They even had a swing set on the roof!

Across from the Gilbert house is where Dr. John and Liz Lewis lived with their family of 6 children. Mary Lewis was my age. The family left Walnut Street when Mary was still a little girl and the Phi Kappa Tau fraternity moved in. In the spring, they would entertain the neighborhood by singing on the steps of the house while they were practicing for the Greek sing, a singing competition for the Greek fraternities at SIU. People from the neighborhood would either stand or bring a chair to sit on the lawn so that they could hear the singing. The fraternity also decorated the house for Halloween and had treats for all the neighborhood kids.

The Edwin Vogler family lived on the corner of Maple and Main Street but they were really just a few houses away from 601 W. Walnut. The Vogler kids from both Vogler houses and the Gilberts were really all just like one big family. The Gilberts and my family even shared a dog named Peggy. She liked to come to our house and sleep in front of the heat register but at night, she would always go home to the Gilberts.

In the 50's and early 60's, we had milk delivered from the New Era Dairy to our side door, under the drive-through carport area. It was my job, on many cold mornings, to retrieve the milk from the carport. The empty glass bottles went back to the dairy to be re-used. Later home deliveries included Charlie's chips and Schwann ice cream. Interesting how we were all recylcing and didn't know it!

I went to pre-nursery somewhere on the SIU campus as a 3 year old– this just happen to coincide with the year my brother was born! Then I went to U-school . U-school was where the Education students from SIU practiced teaching. In Kindergarten , I had a wonderful teacher named Dr. Mott. In our classroom, we had a fountain with a real live turtle in it . We also had a bee hive, encased in clear plastic with the exit and entrance to the hive outside the window. (No bees in the classroom!) We could watch the bees and pick out the Queen. We learned our letters, basic hygiene, took naps, and had snacks of crackers with sugared butter on them. We took wonderful field trips over to the Shryock Auditorium on SIU campus where we saw some musical productions. (Bill Shryock was in my class). Dr. Mott had us grab onto a knot on a long rope and that's what we held on to as we walked behind her. Once we made little stuffed monkies out of monkey socks. I remember John Wham sewed his monkey to his pants! We had a wonderful music teacher, Dr. Thomas. He would pass out the tambourines, autoharps, bells, and xylophones and we would make beautiful music! We loved it when he sang "Mama's going to make a little shortening bread"! We also had a really great art class and occasionally some of our art work was selected to hang in the student center at SIU.

The boys outnumbered the girls at U-school in my kindergarten and for many years after. Some of the kids in my class included Bill Brown, Glen Freeburg, Harry Schulz, Bill Shryock, Harold Koplowitz, Kalman Eldelman, Ron Muich, Bob Pankey, John Crawshaw, John Wham, John Sanford, Anne Gates,Mary Swindell, and Mary Lewis just to name a few. If I got anyone wrong, I'm sorry! Remember, this is MY memory and it is 60+ years old!

There were two swimming pools at the school and we swam twice a week. Until 3rd grade, the boys and girls changed into their swim suits in the same locker room – and we all wore the same waist high, red bathing suit! I was so excited the week we were going to learn how to breathe when we swam because I thought we were going to learn how to breathe underwater!

We got almost all our immunizations at U-school, usually timed to be given on a swim day. We would all line up in the hallway by the art building – most of us were terrified but too embarrassed to cry! I remember the nurses used reusable, glass syringes.

Even as a lst grader, I could walk to school on my own. Sometimes I would walk with John Crawshaw and later I remembering walking with my cousin Jimmy Vogler. On the way home from school, I would stop at Entsmingers and buy candy cigarettes, lick-a-maid, and bubble gum. I loved to chew gum and blow bubbles as a kid and I still do! Some days John's Mom and my Mom would pick us up and we would go to UD's(University Drugs) for lunch. John's Dad, Gene Paul, worked behind the lunch counter and made the best French fries, served in a little plastic basket with a greasy piece of wax paper!

There was no cafeteria at U-school but they did offer hot sandwiches downstairs next to the rec room. They had the absolute best hot dogs with a maidrite mixture on top. Or we could walk over to Woody Hall on the campus and go through the line with all the big girls. Woody Hall was a dorm for female students at Southern Illinois University (SIU). I once dropped my tray and was so embarrassed – my friends pretended not to know me! Lunches were 50 cents at both places. Everyday I had a 50 cent piece to take to school with me.

I remember most of my teachers at U-school until the 5th grade when we had more than one. Tina Goodwin was the 1st grade teacher and she was mean! If you did anything wrong, she would grab you by the shoulders and shake you! Very intimidating to a 6 year old! Mrs.Bricker was the 2nd grade teacher, Dr. Treece was 3rd, and Mrs. Meehan was 4th. I remember going to St. Louis on a field trip with Dr. Treece – I believe we went to see King Tut! Somewhere during the next few years I had Mr. Harvey Teel, who lived right behind my house on Elm Street. They were really excellent teachers and I am blessed to have received an amazing early education!

As a middle schooler, a group of us kids were always walking or riding our bikes to the SIU campus. There we would do stupid stuff like go to the library, walk up to the top of the stairs and then drop something over the side of the banister just to watch it fall, sometimes we would just spit!. Or we would climb up the circular fire escapes and slide down. I remember one day the U-school kids encountered some rowdy Lincoln Jr. High kids doing the same thing! Occasionally we would find that the door at the top of the fire escape wasn't locked and we could go through into a classroom. We thought we were really getting away with something to be in a building closed over the weekend! I went to U-school through 8th grade and when my parents heard that U-school was going to close, they sent me to CCHS.

And I loved CCHS!! Always before I had been in a class of about 18 and now I was in a class of 300! I met so many wonderful people there and I'm still friends with many of them. I met my husband, Bob Bain, on the second day of school, during lunch on High Street. Our first date was on the train to the football game in Centralia.

I walked to school most days because it was an easy walk from my house. Gathering outside the front of the school when it was warm enough was a tradition before school. And later it seemed we all went in the back door by the gym and gathered in the big glass hallway. I remember changing classes on cold rainy days when we had to run between buildings! I didn't mind cafeteria food and ate there most days. Occasionally I would go to the store on high street and get a barbeque sandwich – they had the *best* barbeque! When we got old enough to drive, it was a treat to go to McDonalds, out by the bowling alley. For $1, I could get a coke, French fries, and a hamburger, and get change back!!

McDonalds seemed to be THE place to hang out. I remember when I was a junior, riding in Louise Tolle's car, a 1951 black limo which at one time had belonged to a funeral home, with Sherry Winn and others. We bought cokes at McDonalds and would put sloe gin in them. (I have no idea where we got the sloe gin!) Then we would cruise around C'dale looking for something to do! We never drank much, just enough to make us silly, and fortunately never got caught!

Back in the Walnut Street neighborhood, It seemed like we always had things to do during the summer. Kids played ball, rode bikes, walked to the Varsity movie theater, went to the Dairy Queen, went swimming or played in the garden hose outside, or spent time at the library. I don't ever remember being bored as a kid – our playground on Walnut Street extended up to Poplar, down to Springer and all the way down to Maple and Main. The Easterleys on Maple street had a two seater ferris wheel which was a lot of fun! We made clover chains and stretched them out across the street and waited for the cars to run over them. My cousin Jim had tubs of turtles on his porch that we could watch and play with. . The Gilberts had a ping pong table. I could always play Canasta with my Grandmother or unwind a golf ball around a pencil. As I said, there was always something to do!

Summer evenings were quiet and calm with only cricket noises to hear. There weren't any air conditioners coming on and off to interrupt the quiet, no one had air conditioning when I was a kid! At night to help cool the house, we had a huge attic fan.

We practically slept in our window sills trying to catch the cool air being pulled in! I remember many late afternoons riding my bike to Senkosky's store for something to grill out. After dinner we would stay outside as long as possible, catching lightning bugs, playing kick the can or hide-and-seek. When we heard the mosquito sprayer coming, we would chase it down the street, running in the fog behind it.

We could easily walk downtown to Atwoods drug store. This was a favorite of my sister and I when we were teenagers! We would also walk to Stroups, (later known as Bleyers), and to the record store. We could go in a little glass booth and listen to 45's to decide if we wanted to buy them. As a teenager, I walked to Kay's and The Alice Fly store to spend my hard earned money on clothes! We were completely safe – there was no crime and certainly no childhood abductions when I was growing up! Fortunately, not that I appreciated it then, there were plenty of parental eyes watching and if anyone saw anyone's children doing something wrong, the parents would hear about it!

During the summer before my sophomore year, I worked at Spudnuts, a place where they made the donuts out of potato flakes. When they were warm and newly iced, they were to die for! Right across from Spudnuts was the Moo and Cackle fast food restaurant.. I was sorry to see them go out of business because they had the best chicken sandwich. This was also the summer I took the only summer class I ever took – typing! My sister Ann had left for college and I was sad and lonely and tried to fill all my hours!

Major changes came to Walnut Street in the summer of 1968 when the street was widened. The bricks were pulled up and trees cut down.

Dr. Leo Brown salvaged many of the bricks for a patio around his pool. Helen Gilbert cried when the big tree in her front yard was cut down. Of course it was in the city right of way so it really belonged to the city but it felt like hers! It was a beautiful, big tree with a huge trunk and everyone hated to see it go. For months while the widening was in process, we had to park our cars either at the end of Maple Street or on Elm Street behind our house. It was the quietest summer ever at night because there were no vehicles on Walnut Street. Whenever it rained, it was a muddy mess! This was the summer I worked at the DairyQueen, starting out under the watchful eye of Jack Kloever, a really wonderful man. Working at Dairy Queen (DQ) was really fun, we hand-made Dilly Bars and Peanut butter Buster bars and we experimented making different kinds of sundaes. The "turtle" sundae with hot fudge, caramel, and pecans, was my favorite!. After I was trained at the main DQ by the Varsity theater, I went to work at the Dairy Queen on Main Street, across from Picks Grocery. I usually worked 6-8 hours/week and I loved it!

And of course I worked for my Dad at Vogler Motor Company. In high school, I got all the grunt jobs, i.e. the ones no one else wanted to do!! Mostly I hung signs in the showroom windows. Around Thanksgiving, I would dress warmly and help with inventory in the parts department. Every part had to be counted - on the shelves in the parts department and in the attic and basement. It took three days and it was cold, dirty work. In the early 70's, my Dad took a computer class at SIU and wrote a program to inventory all the parts. With the push of a button, every Sunday night, he could get a complete, accurate parts inventory!

The basement at Vogler Motor Company had once been designated a fallout shelter and there were still signs that indicated this. This was left over from the "cold war" days! I remember drills in elementary school, when we were instructed to sit on the floor under the heavy wooden tables, but these were more fun than scary! Such a worrisome time for our parents but I don't remember being scared at all. I'm glad I had a real childhood where I was oblivious to the scary things going on in the world! I'm not sure kids today have that option.

I remember attending the First Christian Church with my Mom and family. For several years, I would go to Sunday School first and then church. So many wonderful families went to this little church. The Pankey family (Denny, Bob, and Tommy), the Maurizios (Mike, Bob, and Steve), Gigi Reese, Amy Huffman, Dia Parr, Mary Lewis, and John Samford. Mary, Gigi , and I were all Baptized with each other. Almost every Sunday after church, my family would eat at my grandparent's house on Springer Street. My grandmother would fry chicken before church and leave it simmering in an electric skillet while we were at church. If we didn't eat here, we might go to Bevis's – in the same block as UD's. They had a wonderful, delicious Sunday buffet!!

Carbondale in the 50's and 60's was just a quiet little town with a bustling university. So many of my friends came to Carbondale because their parents taught at SIU. It was a town full of diversity – different races, different religions, different opinions. I feel very fortunate to have grown up in a place like this – I am sure that my whole being was influenced by it. And I am thankful for the wonderful memories!

"OH BOYS, BOYS, OVER HERE…"
ON BEING THE NEW KID

By David White

It was a few days before the first day of school in 1965. It wasn't going to be just the first day of school, it will be the first day of high school! High school! Where over the course of a summer students evolve from grade school big shots to faux adults with an overriding and constant pressure to be cool. We went from being BMOC's at our junior high schools to be the low person on the high school totem pole. Hormones are raging. Positions of status were beginning to be staked out. For some it is a second chance to reintroduce themselves or even try on a new identity. For the new kid from out of town it is terrifying and the most pressure a 13 or 14 year old has ever faced. Thrown into a new environment the most basic and most frightening question that needs an immediate answer is "Where do I fit in?" That's when I learned that excitement and anxiety are two sides of the same coin.

It was on this day that I was still getting settled into a new home in a new city. We lived in a small rental house on Oakland across from the fire house. After a light breakfast I was calmly watching one of the 4 TV channels we could get. My mom was walking through the combination dining room/little brother's bedroom and looked out the front window. She suddenly picked up her pace and went out on the front porch.

Suddenly I heard my mom shout "Oh boys, boys, over here!" I had no idea what she was doing. Then much to my chagrin she then said what became the most horrifying sentence I had ever heard come out of her mouth "I'd like you boys to meet my son." The horror, the shame, the embarrassment, the overwhelming desire to run out the back door and never look back over took me. Realizing that I was trapped, I took what seemed like an innumerable number of deep breaths and sighs then I headed out to the porch to confront my fate.

There across the street were four boys that looked to be about my age. They seemed to confer amongst themselves and then one boy took the lead and they came across the street to meet me at the behest of my mom. As they approached, I felt my throat tighten and my palms sweat. I swear I could feel stress zits popping out! To this day I don't know if I ever looked any of them in the eye. Can you imagine what it feels like to have your mom solicit friends for you at age 13?? Add a heaping amount of new kid in school-itis and you have yourself a real male teenage catastrophe.

The boys introduced themselves with the lead person, Bruce Fohr, going first. I sheepishly introduced myself. The others followed. I have no idea what else was said. All I could do was manage a stupid smile while imagining what was going to be said among them once they escape the crazy woman on the porch. Once they departed, I seriously considered hitchhiking back to Decatur rather than going to school and facing these guys again. Those boys with Bruce were Dick Lefevre, John Wham and I think Terry Etherton. Of all the guys to witness this!! Four boys who were later to become some of the kids I hung around with the most in high school. But, my oh my what a beginning!

A little backstory: We moved to Carbondale just prior to the start of our Freshman year because of a couple of factors: 1) my dad's alcoholism had gotten out of control and he had lost a series of jobs. We were essentially destitute and had lost our house in Decatur, immediately casting my older brother, a senior at SIU working part time at Sohns, into the role of being the primary breadwinner for a family of three and 2) my mom told me the main reason we had to move out of town and not stay in Decatur was because I was running with a bad crew and she was afraid as to where that would lead.

During my 8th grade year in Decatur, I skipped school over 40 times, I engaged in underage drinking beginning at age 12. Snuck out at night for no good reason. The final straw for her occurred the summer after my 8th grade year and prior to when my mom made the decision to move to Carbondale. My buddies and I broke into the grade school that we had previously attended and did significant vandalism with the worst damage being me using a knife to damage a portrait of the principal. We were arrested and although not formally charged we did have to make restitution. My mom must have been prescient for three years later some of the guys I hung around with were involved in a botched burglary resulting in someone being killed.

So not only was I dealing with separation anxiety from my home town and friends, but also the guilt that my actions and my actions alone must have caused the break up and relocation of my family. After all, wasn't everything about me when I was 13! So, to be amid that and then to have my mom embarrass the wholly shit out of me doing what she did only exacerbated my stress and put me in a very dark place. Not exactly a Leave It To Beaver way to start high school. For years after I certainly was not charitable toward her actions however well intended.

During high school we tended to give each other very mean-spirited nicknames. Most of those nicknames dealt with some part of a person's appearance. Some were based upon actions of the individual that were ripe for ridicule. During our high school years, LBJ declared "War on Poverty" this prompted the creation of my nickname, White Poverty. This nickname impelled Mike Vanhorn in front of everyone to present me with a shoeshine box that he made in shop labelled "White Poverty". The joke was, that I can now make some money giving shoeshines.

The other nickname/insult was being called a non-athlete in a class that was probably the best group of athletes in the history of the school. I had undergone a serious operation during my 7th grade year that put me in the hospital for 3 weeks and out of school for 6 weeks total. Because of the surgery and despite clearance from my doctor, my mom would not let me go out for football. And as we know from history, I was on the outside looking in on an incredible undefeated season that I could only participate in vicariously. I certainly don't think I had the skills to make any great impact on the field, but the sense of belonging, bonding and camaraderie were things that I desperately wanted.

This prompted unhealthy behavior on my part to try and fit in. My shouting of insults at Terry Etherton and others during a JV football game while seated comfortably in the stands with the varsity cheerleaders certainly did not help and resulted in me becoming a well-deserved outcast for a while cowering in our house while guys came to confront me. I would have wanted to kick my ass too! I humbly and belatedly ask for forgiveness from those I maligned.

It has always been my feeling that sometimes the friends one makes in high school are based on tenuous and expedient reasons while once away from high school one has more independence in choosing friends with similar values etc. The collection of guys known as the Gang was the closest I felt to being accepted in high school but understandably, as a new kid I was not quite a full-fledged member because I had no common history with those guys.

However, with all of Facebook's faults, I must laud one of the benefits from social media. I have become reacquainted with many high school classmates through Facebook and found many who seem to share my same values and interests. And conversely some friends I was close to don't. I have visited with some former classmates in person and we have gotten to know each other as adults. The effect is that I am truly looking forward to our 50th reunion! I don't know that I had this same feeling at previous reunions.

I do not want this to sound as a continuation of the 1965 pity party that I threw for myself or a self-serving screed of poor me but rather an acknowledgement of what happened and that my story as the new kid is not unique and what it can mean. Every new kid has a backstory and a need for stability and a feeling of belonging.

When I read Bob Pankey's call for essays regarding Carbondale and CCHS I first imagined penning a light hearted and humorous anecdote regarding my mom embarrassing me. The fact that she called boys over to "meet her son" was cringeworthy and would meet with some laughs.

However, my first draft changed dramatically because of a very recent email from one of the boys that was there, Bruce Fohr. I hadn't had any communication with Bruce probably for over 30 years. He saw that the title of my essay was "Oh Boys, Boys Over Here". He remembered his role in this little vignette and rather than laugh at it again, he told me that at the time he felt for me and my embarrassment and related to "being a new kid". He admired what my mom was trying to do. His gracious effort in reaching out made me rethink the whole tenor of this essay. Rather than going for the cheap laugh by criticizing my mom for putting me in such an untenable position for a teenager, I went in another direction. So, sincerest gratitude to Bruce for graciously reaching out and demonstrating a caring compassion towards me that I did not realize that I still needed at age 67.

Thanks to my big brother for assuming a role that he had not asked nor planned for.

Most of all, a belated and regrettably too late thanks to my mom for what she did for me and not castigating her for what she did to me.

On you Terriers!!

THE WONDER YEARS, 1962-65

by John Wham

<u>*July 2019, New Mexico*</u>
At this time of year, Old John often has baseball on his mind. He is a lifelong fan and competes in an MLB fantasy league online. Since it is All-Star break, no points are accruing to his fantasy players, so he has time to let his baseball mind wander. His aging imagination wanders back into a summer fifty-seven years ago, just before he entered junior high. For him and his friends, Old John thinks, that summer might have marked the season opener of their Wonder Years.

<u>The Sandlots, 1962</u>
Johnny's home on Emerald Lane made him neighbors with boys who would challenge other neighborhoods to baseball games. The Emerald Lane kids had their own sandlot. Mike Van Horn commanded another, the lot across from the little green store. Tom and Sparky Blase's backyard was the home field for their players to show off baseball prowess, with teammates like the mighty Bobby and Wally Crane Brothers and the wicked Higgins Boys, Pinky and Piko.

Sandlot play bled into the official Bantam League games at Oakland Field. This year was proving special for Johnny's team, the Lynx, with their undefeated record heading into the final games. But now they must face the Royals, with their leftie wild child Steve Vavra. He, along with Ron Perry, Wayne Kraft, and Mike Cochran, were the hardest throwers in the league. The Lynx were outmatched this particular day. With two out in the final inning, the Lynx loaded the bases with a walk, an error, and an infield single. Then Terrence comes to the plate. He seems all of a sudden to realize what is at stake. His bat begins to shake. To Johnny, his teammate seems on the verge of tears. Out to the batter's box trots coach Al Van Horn, signaling to the umpire for a time out. In words known only to the two of them, the coach calms the batter. Terrence then, with a serene look and a level swing, lofts the ball into right field for a two-run single and a walk-off win. The Lynx would post a final 16-0 record for the championship, along the way beating an All-star team from neighboring Murphysboro.

"Where have you gone, Joe DiMaggio?" Old John shuffles into his retirement man cave to listen to the latest thumb drive collection of golden oldies that his neighbor, a long-ago L.A. radio deejay, has left in his mailbox. "...our nation turns its lonely eyes to you, woo, woo, woo...." For that matter, he wonders, where have they all gone, those boys of summer of that championship season? Bobby E, Bobby W, Jay W, Buzzy B, Larry W, Mike V, Steve I, Ernie G? Terrence, and John himself, went into the Army on the buddy system right after high school and both ended up in Tucson. But where are the others now? Old John recalls that a few of them took part in other exploits with him, way back when.

Gang Life in Carbondale

Living in a university town, especially one known for its partying ways, must have rubbed off on Johnny and friends. From someone's older brother, the Gang found out about a bigger and badder place to spend time: the SIU campus, home to Old Main with its many fire escapes dating back to the 1870s. Wally Crane, aka "Spiderman", would climb the vines adhering to the outside walls until he reached the second floor windows. He would always find one unlocked, slide in, then walk downstairs and let the Gang into the building. They could then slide down the fire escapes, which were slippery chutes that would deposit them abruptly onto the ground at the end of each ride.

Sitting down now to his breakfast of raisin bran and 2%, Old John notices a dog hair on his floor. That's from Heisenberg, his trusty German shepherd, but the dog hair isn't what he's thinking about. Is he losing his touch? he wonders. His lifelong habit of daily mopping has recently dwindled to twice a week. Yet something about how the light shaft is coming in through his window and highlighting the dog hair reminds him of the Gang's discovery of the belfry.

"Hey, you guys," some boy challenged the rest. "My brother said nobody has been in the belfry for more than 20 years."
"Let's go up there!"
"It's three stories. You first."
The door creaked as each entered warily in the absolute dark, an indescribable stench blinding their noses. At the top of the steps, though, a shaft of light! Coming in through the belfry's long, dirty window, the haze revealed what looked like three inches of dust under a thick mosaic of bat and pigeon dung. "Look out! A bat!" someone shouted in the near-dark. Every boy picked up whatever he could find. For John it was a 2x4.

He had no choice but to kill the bat, he thinks now, drawing on his recent habit of explaining his boyish pranks through the morality of an old man. And besides, he adds to himself, it was suffocating hot in there, in the triple digits. And there was humidity.

The boys found that escaping from the tower was riskier than entering. They learned the hard way one afternoon. SIU was already holding classes, but the Gang was enjoying its last days of summer. Dickie Duba, leading the way down the dark staircase, missed a step and tumbled, knocking open a door and landing in the hallway just as a college class was letting out. The Gang picked him up, everyone running outside and hopping onto their bikes to escape the college boys, who looked remarkably like grown men as they briefly chased after on foot.

Old John recalls now that the Gang's break-ins to Old Main lasted into a second summer. But what exactly had ended the visits up to the belfry? Old John supposes that, for some of the boys, visiting with bats was not as interesting as having makeout sessions with girl classmates in the Main Hall first-floor teachers lounge.

The visits completely ended after the roundup by the campus police. Several boys were pinched, the police demanding to know their names. One of the Gang sent the police on a wild goose chase by giving the name of a boy who wasn't even there. When the police arrived at his home, Mr. Oakes had not been amused. Adults being adults, that was the end of that.

School Daze

When Young John showed up at Lincoln Junior High, just after Labor Day 1963, he learned that the system would assign him to either thin, balding, short-fused baseball coach Larry Drake, or to crew-cutted, hairy-armed, red-faced, zero body-fatted Charles Horst as homeroom teacher. Other than how they looked, he wasn't sure there was much difference.

Even though his fifth and sixth grade teachers at U-School and then at Winkler had also been males, John noticed at Lincoln that the testosterone of the teachers had kicked up a notch. Whereas Johnny had been bodily carried—desk and all—into the hallway by sixth grade teacher George Mendenhall for whizzing a Peewee football near the teacher's ear, now seventh grade teacher Charles Horst was adding a new dimension: the personal put-down.

Tuesday, 8:00 a.m: Horst scans the classroom looking for the least engaged student of the morning to call upon. "uh-John Wham!" he announces, thus gaining the young man's attention and, with it, the eyes upon him of every classmate. Young John scans his own formidable memory. He silently formulates an answer, proof that he has listened to some of Horst's lessons and memorized an answer from another day. "Prepositional phrase, adverbial in nature?" John offers, smiling smugly. Unfortunately, Horst has not yet even asked a question. He is merely establishing the setup for what will become the forever tone of their classroom interactions. Horst says again "uh-Wham?" then pauses dramatically before he forms a zero by joining the tip of his thumb to his forefinger...("uh-John Wham," he repeats again)... then puts the flourish on the physical gesture by extending his lower arm out from the elbow in a straight emphatic line. "uh-John Wham....skip it." Horst's vivid blue eyes (some might say Nazi-like, John thinks) then alight on a star pupil: "uh-Bruce Fohr. Can you help us out? Ah, yes. Nicely done."

Old John comforts himself by remembering Horst's many oddities. But also something else. Although the Skip-it Boy was not a member of Boys Honor Society, the faculty sponsor Horst evidently arranged in spring of 1964 that he be invited on the society's train trip to St. Louis, where they would attend a Cardinals game. John recalls (is it possible?)

that he is invited along again the next year, when he is not even in Horst's homeroom. He closes his eyes and sees Horst, lining up the boys on the train platform, making sure that all have dressed as he instructed: short-sleeve white shirt with a clip-on necktie. Horst will live on for Old John as the November 22, 1963, purveyor of the news that the world had suddenly changed as he announces: "Your President has been assassinated!" John hears now the meek voice of a classmate, pleading in a tone filled with puzzlement and fear. Could Mr. Horst explain what he just announced, because she does not understand. Horst repeats the news, a note of compassion slipping into his voice.

<u>Love Them, Do!</u>

Spring of 1964 found Lincoln Junior High students, along with the rest of America, trying to move forward from the dark days of November '63. There was foreign intervention: the British Invasion. Four classmates decided to enter the talent show with their rendition of the Beatles. At the auditions (a required preliminary round in front of the student council and the music teacher), the four appeared with fabricated, cardboard instruments. They made the cut, then lost one of their members to that time-honored condition known as "chickening out." So they picked up another member, a second girl. John had begun to notice that girls were more dependable in such matters. For the big day, Bruce, Anne, Sue, and John (aka Paul, John, Ringo, and George) borrowed real electric guitars and a drum kit. Although they shouted their lyrics into a live microphone, it is not certain that the Fabricated Four were actually heard, such was the frenzy of the crowd as the four sang along to Beatles 45s of "Love Me Do," "Twist and Shout," and "I Wanna Hold Your Hand."

Old John realizes that not until that day had he experienced crowd adulation. The fact that none of their star turn was captured on video or in photographs makes it possible for him to savor the day on his own terms. Maybe that day, he now thinks, is what gave him the impulse to become a Deadhead, and to collect more than 1500 LPs, cd's, and cassettes, all of which surround him in alphabetized bins in his man cave. John reaches for his treasure trove of rock concert ticket stubs. The Cardinals beer stein is crammed with hundreds of them.

To his embarrassment (although no one but Heisenberg is there to notice), Old John detects an old man lump-in-the-throat developing. And while an LP plays on, the memories flow. ...collecting an entire 1963 Topps baseball card set...Saturday matinees at the Varsity for 35 cents...hitting the pinball machines up and down Illinois Avenue...heading to U.D.'s, to play pinball, but also to visit with John Crawshaw, while their friend makes them malts, compliments of "the

Craw" and his father, who owns the place....Dicky Duba, bigger than all the rest of them, telling two friends to hop onto the handlebars and onto the back fender and effortlessly riding them home on his bicycle...the same Dicky Duba, indignant when he comes in one day and announces that his family is moving to Vietnam for a year, and no one looks up, so intent are they on their pinball....master sneaks in the summer...-- Heisenberg now interrupts Old John with a rubber ball. He wants to play. Old John picks up the ball, throwing into the distance of his yard, as far as his arm will take it, long enough for Old John to have one more memory from the Wonder Years before Heisenberg returns.

Family Matters

Petite, blond, 37-year-old Billie—nicknamed by the Gang as "Doris Day"—lays the sealed, stamped envelope with the school's return address on the supper table as she sits down to eat with her children, John and Debbie. Her son suspects he is the subject of the mailing. School principal Carl Jones recently stopped him in the hallway to say, "Young man, your grandfather must be turning over in his grave." John knows that Mr. Jones means George D. Wham, the first dean of SIU's school of education. John takes a bite of tuna casserole and wonders if he's getting a C in Citizenship again. He decides against the lime jello with fruit cocktail his mother now passes around, realizing there is no point in stalling.

Billie finishes her own last bite, then opens the letter. John can see there is a report card stapled on the back. She is sitting directly across from him. He follows his mother's eyes through each word as she reads what is in front of her. He sees the blue eyes change. Billie passes the letter across to John. His eyes go straight for the verdict. He is stunned by the closing sentence, just above the homeroom teacher's signature: "Basically, John is a good boy."

TOMMY PANKEY AND THE CARBONDALE SHARKS SWIM TEAM

By Dr. Bill Vogler

In the mid 1950's, Dr. Edward Shea, newly hired Dept. Chair of Physical Education at SIU, organized a Summer regional competitive age group swim program under the auspices of the Amateur Athletic Union (AAU). Centralia, Marion, Herrin, Carmi, Cairo, Alton, Edwardsville, Granite City and Carbondale communities to name some, fielded teams which culminated in a championship each August at the Marion city pool.

The early years saw a domination by the ever-powerful Centralia team with Carbondale always a distant second place. Dr. Bud Stotlar, PE teacher from the SIU University Lab School (U-School), was the first Carbondale swim team coach and was a persuasive recruiter to the team. As U-School alum Dave DeWeese years later put it, "When Bud Stotlar asked you to swim for the Carbondale team, you just said, "yes sir" and showed up for practice!" Dr. Stotlar eventually accumulated all the pieces needed and Carbondale took the championship crown from Centralia for the first time in 1960.

Prominent swimmers on the early team included Dr. Stotlar's kids, Dave and Connie, Amy Huffman, Billy Pugh, Ron Murphy, Camilla Patterson, Mike Stoelzle, Denny Heisler, the Jacobini brothers (Charles and Bob), Bill Simione, the Pankey brothers (Denny, Bob, and Tom), five Vogler kids (Cookie, Cynthia, Bill, Jim, and Barb), the DeWeeses (Dave, Kurt, & Debbie), the Franklins (Ross, Barbara, & Mark), Brad

Benzinger, Barb and Bill Borkon, Jan Franklin, Judy Raab, Sharon Danby, Emma Jean Talley, Betty and Barb Hong, John and Barb Shea, Marietta Muich, Jo Daugherty, Roberta Lewis, Harry Edleman, Bruce and Jim Johnson, Bonnie Crawshaw, PG Schoen, and David McCoy to name some.

There was a lot of good talent on the team and some even went on to swim collegiately (John Shea, Bill Borkon, and Bill and Jim Vogler) but perhaps the most talented swimmer on the team was Tommy Pankey and he displayed some of his talent in 1961 at a national caliber invitational swim meet held in Evansville, Indiana. The meet included then current world record holder and future Olympic gold medalist, Chet Jastremski, swimming for nationally prominent Indiana University and brought to the meet by the legendary coach Doc Councilman along with others from his NCAA national caliber team. Also attending were the premier age group teams from around the Midwest including the mighty Indianapolis (IN) Riviera Team, Indianapolis (IN) Athletic Club, Louisville (KY) Plantation Club, and the Chicago (IL) Portage Park Club.

In 1961, Dr. Stotlar turned over the coaching reigns to recent SIU graduate and swim team captain, Bob Steele, who would later become one of the most successful collegiate swimming coaches in NCAA history. Bob was a go-getter and took the already talented team to new heights with rigorous training and innovative coaching techniques. He gave a name to the team, the "Carbondale Sharks" and developed a team uniform (color coded team sweatshirt and team patch with a shark logo). The team rolled over all other teams in dual meet competition, relay meets, and at the annual Southern Illinois Championship meet in Marion that Summer but had one more swim meet to attend, the Evansville Invitational. In August of 1961, some 40-50 Carbondale Sharks and parents descended upon the 50M Hartke Pool in Evansville IN with great hopes for successful competition amongst the national caliber age group teams. Many of the Carbondale swimmers stayed in local campgrounds and motels, had common cookouts, and enjoyed the camaraderie amongst teammate families with common breakfasts and spaghetti dinners. It was a "big time" event and we had great expectations for our team! After all, we were the great Sharks from Carbondale, IL!!!

Competition started early on Saturday morning with the prelims of the butterfly, backstroke, breast stroke, freestyle and relay events. The finals, consisting of the top 8 swimmers from the "heat" competition earlier in the day would begin in the evening around 6 p.m. As the day wore on, the anticipation turned into disappointment as, one by one, the strong Shark swimmers succumbed to the stronger, more dominant kids from the "city" teams. It was an intimidating scene with Carbondale Sharks dressed in a dark blue cotton sweatshirt with a single shark patch competing against the larger and more powerful teams dressed in full fleece warm ups adorned with multiple patches. Back then, swimmers received a patch for each large invitational meet attended which were sewn on to the warmups. Our swimmers had no meet patches and looked rather outclassed by the "superior" opponents.

The disappointment turned into great joy for Carbondale, however, as one swimmer from the team was qualified for the finals, Tommy Pankey in the eight-year old and under 50 M butterfly. He would take on the best swimmers from the great cities of Chicago IL, Louisville KY, and Indianapolis, IN! No one else from C-Dale made it! It was up to Tommy Pankey to uphold the honor of the team, city and region. We were all so proud of Tommy and he would salvage our reputation.

Instead of pulling up stakes and heading for home, all the families of swimmers who didn't "qualify" from Carbondale stayed around to watch Tommy. He had a beautiful butterfly stroke with a nice rhythmic tempo to his dolphin kick. He was a strong and athletic eight-year old kid who looked every bit in place that evening as he approached the rather tall starting block for his event. The meet had been delayed by a thunder-storm so his swim was held after the sun had gone down and the rather dingy pool flood lights gave the pool an eerie and uncomfortable look.

Finally, all the eight-year olds in the "fly" event with Tommy took to the starting blocks. In the then quiet moment, with the storm gone, the winds died down to zero, and the rather large crowd quiet, the starter in almost a hushed tone said, "take your marks". The starting gun went off and the swimmers motored furiously down the 50 M pool. Tommy finished somewhere in the middle back part of the pack! Great news! Carbondale was vindicated! We had scored points in a national caliber swim meet! But wait! The judge walked over to Tommy's lane. He was disqualified! Somehow, his feet separated a bit so it appeared that he had a slight flutter in his dolphin kick which was deemed illegal. We were all crestfallen! Our chance to show the swimming world, we too can compete with the "big boys" was dashed! We were stunned and so disappointed!

I don't exactly remember the reaction by Tommy, the Pankey family, and Bob Steele the coach, but most of all we were disappointed that Tommy didn't get to prove his immense talent by scoring points against the "big boys". We weren't disappointed in Tommy but disappointed that he didn't get the chance to "realize" his "stuff". It must have made an impression on the Shark coach Bob Steele. Fifty-five years later when Bob was honored in Carbondale (2016) as an outstanding SIU career alum, he mentioned this story in his remarks at the alumni ceremony. Bob had later trained many champion swimmers including collegiate world record holders, All-Americans and Olympians, but in his first swim coaching job, coach of the Carbondale Sharks, this was his first big disappointment and he always remembered it.

Tommy, the Pankey brothers, many of the Carbondale swimmers, and Bob Steele would go onto successful athletic and otherwise professional careers but there would always remain that little "sting" of the thought of what might have been on that fateful night in Evansville, IN, back in 1961 when "real" Carbondale talent was denied a place in the spotlight!

Postscript: *It is with great appreciation that Bill Vogler has written this story of our brother, Tommy Pankey, and his moment of fame with the Carbondale Sharks. Tommy's life was unfortunately cut short due to a cancerous brain tumor.. He lived a full life, had three wonderful children and was a great athlete at CCHS. He will be remembered always by his brothers and family.*

THE WILD LIFE OF YOUTH AND ANIMALS

By Susan Ohlde-Isbell

We were free and the animals were too. Joanie, Lynne, and I lived in the same neighborhood, we knew each other since we were four years old and had many adventures together. There was the time in about 5th grade that we were sliding down an incline and at some point noticed that a huge snake was hanging a foot above us as we slid. We got Lynne's dad and he brought down a fencing sword to deal with the situation. There was the time that Joanie boasted she couldn't get poison ivy and rubbed it on herself. I always got it and it was frequently oozing down my leg. Unfortunately, Joanie ended up in the hospital.

I remember when Lynne's mother found a huge cockroach in a jar and asked if it was a pet before she threw it out; that house was an animal-friendly house! We lived in town, with Lynne and Lucy, the goose, and several chickens also hung there. There was also an iguana that lived in the tree at the house, apparently causing quite a stir when Lynn's mother was having a party and the iguana came down to visit.

My dog, Jinx, and Lynne's dog, Ted, lived without fences and went on daily treks together. One time Jinx was seen running through the neighborhood with a pan of food that he had stolen from someone's back yard. Another time Jinx took a steak off of someone's grill. We thought he was smart, although the neighbors may not have felt the same way.

Lynne and I had horses at one point and there was a problem with the stable, so the horses lived in Lynne's back yard for a bit. Amazing! Lynne and I spent many days riding on SIU land and doing some dangerous things, including swimming bareback and jumping handmade rigid jumps.

In Southern Illinois, where else could one spend the day caving? I remember Joanie got stuck while looking for rattlesnakes with Steve and David. Joanie, who appeared to be living safely, ended up in the hospital with mono. Who knew that poison ivy and kissing could be so dangerous.

A TRIBUTE TO THE DICK LEFEVRE

By Bill Vanmetre

I heard about Dick Sunday evening, as a matter of fact I called Larry and Joyce Eastwood to get his telephone number to give him a call, when Joyce told me they had just heard from Roger Medlen that he had passed..........talk about floored-how strange. We lost another icon of our class, quite frankly it never does get any easier does it. Hope you and yours are all doing well, stay in touch.

icon -Wikapedia defines it as: a name, face, picture or even a person readily recognized as having some well-known significance, or embodying certain qualities. They should have included a picture of Dick LeFevre beside their description. As I was driving through Carbondale yesterday I decided to go down Oakland Avenue then turn west on West Walkup street, a flood of memories filled my mind of the very

first time I can remember being invited to a birthday party, Dick Lefevre's 5th, wow was it something, everyone there got a present just for coming, these folks knew how to live! From those days of playing with tin soldiers and tanks and stuff, to tossing the old leather ball, to just last Fall in 2009, sitting at a table reminiscing of times gone by, it is so hard to think that he will no longer be making new memories.

Dick LeFevre had an eidetic memory to recant every little detail like it had just happened an hour ago. He had a meth-like personality, if you met him once you were hooked, and he would change your life forever, that was Dick. The guy who looked like the Frito Bandito, had a mind like Einstein, and was truly our very own John Belushi. Someone who was charismatic enough to draw a crowd wherever he went, sharing his life's journey and experiences with everyone he met, all the while, keeping you on the edge of your chair listening to his stories. Can you remember the "nick-name" he gave you? Mine was The Meter, amongst others that don't belong in this tribute. I can still hear his strong voice and warm greeting yet, "T H E M E T E R", reverberate in my ears today, no matter where you were or how long ago it was since you had last seen him, he made you feel like at that moment you were the only thing in the world that mattered to him.

What a quality! I have read the stories that Bob Pankey has sent to us all concerning Dick, each one is so heart felt and such a wonderful tribute, deserved for sure. I was just taking a shower and happened to remember our Freshman or Sophomore year football, where it was revealed in the shower room that LeFevre had drawn a heart with an arrow thru it, and the name MOM under that on his ass, with Coppertone Suntan lotion!

My deepest regrets to his family, all his family, father, mother, sisters, and yes to us, the people who knew him well enough to call him family. His passing is so hard here on earth for us, but let's know in our heart that he has been called home to finish his task. Thank you for the blessing of knowing him as long as we did, he will never be gone from our hearts.

Dr. Richard LeFevre – 1951 – 2010

John Richard (Dick) LeFevre Jr., 58, passed away Sunday, April 25, 2010, in Gainesville, Fla. Dick was a beloved son, friend and brother who embraced life and carried a compassion for humankind with an uncanny ability to make people laugh. Dick was born May 25, 1951, in Nashville, Tenn. His family moved to Carbondale as Dick reached pre-school age. He was a starting member of the Terrier football team's 1968-69 perfect 10-0 season and accepted an athletic scholarship to Michigan State University, where he played football until he was injured. He returned to Carbondale and completed his undergraduate degree at Southern Illinois University Carbondale in physiology. He entered Kansas City School of Osteopathic Medicine, where he received his medical degree then served as a doctor and lieutenant in the U.S. Air Force. Dick's medical career took him to Topeka, Kan., and central parts of Michigan before coming to Gainesville and assisting in the care of his parents. By his early teens, Dick was an accomplished coin, stamp and comic book collector, athlete, chess player, chemist and talented sketch artist. At 13, he was offered an art scholarship while attending American Community School in Saigon, Vietnam, but turned it down to ultimately become a doctor. Dick was a history buff with precise recall of dates, times, places, events, activities and people as well as military actions. And he had an encyclopedic knowledge of medicine and medical facts. His love of humor, enjoyment of earlier comic actors and his own personal delivery of comedic acts will be sorely missed. Dick is survived by his mother and father, Hazel LaVerne (Redus) and John Richard (Dick) LeFevre Sr. of Gainesville, Fla. (formerly of Carbondale); his sisters, Dr. Suzanne Elaine LeFevre ofNew Orleans and Linda LeFevre Stephens of Gainesville, Fla., and Southern Illinois; a nephew, Christopher James Stephens and his wife, Holly Ann (Witcher) Stephens, of Durham, N.C.; his greatniece, Abigail Claire Stephens of Durham, N.C.; and many, many endearing friends. Williams-Thomas Funeral Home, 404 N. Main Street, in Gainesville, Fla., is in charge of arrangements. In lieu of flowers, donations may be made to Carbondale Community High School Athletic Association in memory of Dick LeFevre

MAKE YOUR OWN KIND OF MUSIC

By Cindy Hagler Hardnett

Reflecting on my childhood in Carbondale Illinois, the sweetest memories I have are those of riding my golden Palomino, Pal. We rode the cinder trails behind Saluki Stables through pastures where the sweet-smelling honeysuckle vines arched high above my head, sun streaming through the green leaves and creating mystical shadows as we trotted along the trail. We side-stepped rocks in the creek below as we waded through the rippling water to our own pasture and the small barn that my dad built which was home to a few of the neighborhood horses. This was my peace and comfort, as a 12- year old girl navigating my way through a complicated and delicate adolescence. I got lost in the smell of horse sweat and hay and felt safe and secure here. After I fed Pal, brushed him down, picked his hooves and kissed him goodnight on his velvety nose I would hop on my green Schwinn five-speed and ride a few blocks home to find the smell of BBQ pork steaks on the grill wafting down the street. Best smell in the neighborhood, and my mom would have buttery corn on the cob, baked beans, and home-grown tomatoes ready. To top it off we would have homemade ice cream and either my favorite coconut cream pie or German chocolate cake for dessert. I had a lovely and loving family, gentle and humble souls who grew up in Carbondale and attended the same schools I attended. They were salt of the earth, solid people who raised our family in church and taught me good values— honesty, hard-work, compassion, and independence. I didn't have any idea that one day these values would be my warrior's shield, helping me survive difficult times ahead.

I spent first grade through sixth grade at the newly constructed and sparkling Parrish School. I was a bright-eyed, energetic straight-A kid, with a heart for all things good. I was a Brownie and Girl Scout, played clarinet and piano, sang in chorus, and marched as a baton twirler in the Apple Festival and SIU Homecoming parades with other friends from school. I spent weekends with the SIU Ecology Club and Touch of Nature testing soil samples and learning how to count the rings on a tree trunk to determine its age. I learned to rappel on the huge rocks in Giant City Park and relived pioneer days making candles by hand. I would write E-C-O-L-O-G-Y on my notebooks in big, loopy, neon letters, and was interested in saving the environment and keeping planet Earth clean. I was all about being outside in the sunshine every minute I could, whether I was walking my dog Frankie in the woods, riding horses on the wooded trails, swimming and waterskiing at Crab Orchard Lake, or just riding my bike to catch the breeze in my hair. I was in love with the outdoors and how free and alive the fresh outdoor air made me feel. Life was so good. I was a happy little girl, long blonde ponytail blowing in the wind and a smile on my face.

I can vividly recall the indelible impact that each of my grade schoolteachers left on me. Grandmotherly Mrs. Crackel allowed us to complete our first-grade math book at our own pace. A handful of kids finished the book long before the year was over, and we were given the privilege of watching film strips in the Kindergarten room across the hall. In second grade, Mrs. Corich visited our home when my baby brother was born. She brought him a gift to celebrate his arrival and it made me feel so special! Third grade teacher, Mrs. Nelson, spoke sternly and carried a ruler to swat kids, but softened my heart when she complimented my colorful artwork decorating my notebooks and asked where I bought my lime green fishnet stockings so she could buy her granddaughter some. Mrs. Brandon transported me to another world as she read the novel, *Island of the Dolphins,* to our fourth-grade class after recess every day. I was captivated by the Aleutian Islands. Her story time opened the whole world up to me and helped me travel there in my mind. In fifth grade, Mrs. Ramp allowed us to write creative stories, and I discovered the joy of expressing myself in writing. Sixth grade teacher, Mr. Fligor, was an encourager who constantly pulled my shoulders back reminding me to stand tall, head high, and not to slouch. I can't remember an unhappy time at Parrish School. It was everything school should be—safe, a beautiful environment, nice and friendly children and teachers, fun and challenging classes. I dearly loved school, and my grades showed it.

I learned about the world around me mainly through observation from the backseat of my dad's 1968 blue Impala. A couple times a week we had a family outing to the Dairy Queen where my brothers and I could buy a ten-cent treat—that was our limit. I always ordered a lemon-lime Mr. Misty. We sat in the backseat of the Impala and ate our treats with the car windows rolled down, looking across the street at Holden Hospital's big front lawn full of college kids. It was the "hippie" era in Carbondale, and college girls were dressed in bell bottom jeans or peasant dresses while the boys wore tie dyed shirts, headbands, and shoulder length hair. What fun it was to watch! "Flower power" and "Make Love not War" were common themes. I asked my mom what that meant, and she just told me be sure to never do it, whatever it was. I was mesmerized by the radical changes going on in the world even though I didn't fully understand them. I felt the pull of fierce independence and a tiny thread of rebellion stirring inside me. I could feel the need to dance to my own music, just like the song Mama Cass sang so sweetly.

"Nobody can tell you
There's only one song worth singing
They may try and sell you
Cause it hangs them up
To see someone like you.
But you've gotta make your own kind of music,
Sing your own special song
Make your own kind of music
Even if nobody else sings along."

I entered Lincoln Junior High School with a strong sense of adventure and independence, yet very shy and lacking in self-confidence. To say my transition from elementary school to junior high was a bit rocky is a vast understatement. I remember hearing my older brother and neighbor kids refer to it as a "dungeon" and "stinkin' Lincoln" and in my case, it lived up its infamous reputation. All the students from various grade schools throughout Carbondale were bussed to Lincoln, the city's only middle school, for seventh and eighth grades. I quickly discovered that friendships that had been formed in elementary school were seemingly abandoned in junior high. Girls like me who still wore knee socks with unshaven legs and a clean scrubbed face without a speck of makeup were not popular. What worked at Parrish School did not work at Lincoln Junior High. I recall showing up the first day of seventh grade in the basketball courts at Lincoln where kids would wait for the bell to ring before entering the building.

I felt so incredibly out of place. Little 12-year-old girls like me had their faces made up beautifully, so mature and sophisticated. I remember wishing the ground would just open and swallow me to escape the feeling of being the ugly duckling in a sea of beautiful swans. For the first time ever, I experienced what it felt like to be invisible and not belong.

As days passed, my friends from grade school were finding new groups of friends to be a part of, and I was stuck in place. I always scrambled at lunch time to find someone, anyone, to sit with to avoid being alone. I had a few friends to hang out with from time to time, but no real tight-knit group. Eventually, some other "loose end" sort of kids gravitated my way. I found them to be funny and engaging. I enjoyed their hilarious antics and laughing together 'til we cried. Nothing like a good belly laugh to make me feel all better. I had no idea about the unwritten rules against making friends with kids from the "wrong side of the tracks." I grew up being taught to "love my neighbor as myself," so I very naturally accepted people who were different than me. One of my favorite childhood songs I grew up singing at University Baptist Church on the corner of Oakland Avenue and Mill Street, helped form the foundation of my beliefs and values.

" Jesus loves the little children,
All the little children in the world,
Red and yellow, black and white,
They are precious in His sight,
Jesus loves the children of the world."

I was taught, by example, to treat those less fortunate than myself with an extra measure of kindness and helpfulness. Every year my mom and dad adopted a needy family to buy Christmas presents for. This was one of their Sunday school ministries at University Baptist Church. It was so much fun buying clothes and toys for these anonymous children whose only information we had were their first names, ages and sizes. I always imagined the looks of joy the children must have on Christmas morning when they found beautifully wrapped presents beneath their tree. My grandma Brooks was part of a friendship club at church, and she hosted dinners for international students from around the world. She was always excited to share her home and her delicious meals with them. Love and generosity were the norm in my family.

It was no wonder that I was caught off guard by the sudden shut-down I faced from friends and the school administration due to befriending kids from the other side of town. One day at a pep rally an old friend handed me a note that spelled it out clearly—I had a choice to make, and if I didn't give up my new friends I would be rejected by the old friends. I knew her intentions were good, and she was only trying to help, but still it stung. Despite the brewing turmoil, my schoolwork was a big positive for me. I had the toughest teachers, Mr. Horst for Language Arts, and Mr. Collmeyer for CEMREL math. I loved learning about logic and truth tables and tautologies, which I didn't see again until I got to college.

My life crumbled one day in March of 1972, the spring of my seventh-grade year. I broke a rule, albeit with good intentions. This particular day I became concerned when I heard a boy who we hung out with was dropping out of school—a 13-year-old boy who had a troubled home life, and who my heart went out to. I thought it was a good thing to try to help someone; it never occurred to me I could get in trouble for it. He had not been at school all week long, and since I had no way to contact him, a friend and I decided to walk across the street at our lunch period to see if he was at the Quick Shop where he would sometimes hang out and buy candy. Funny thing, he wasn't even there, and we just went right back to school. We weren't away from campus for 10 minutes. A bit later I was summoned from Science class, the period following lunch, to go to the Principal's office. When asked about leaving the front lawn of the junior high, I readily admitted I was attempting to check up on a friend who was in a dire situation. This all seemed so reasonable to me, but there was no compassion and very little discussion. I was told that this boy was "mentally deranged" and better off not at school, and to stay away from him. To drive the point home, I was given what amounted to a life sentence—not only did I receive a horrific, physical beating, but was also given 2 ½ months of detentions morning, noon and after school, until the end of the school year--nearly 150 detentions! I had never been punished in school—ever-- not so much as being sent to the hallway. I felt like a helpless lamb being led to the slaughter, a fly killed with the sledgehammer. They were doing whatever it took to break my spirit and change me. Indeed, that day changed the trajectory of my entire life.

I lost the anchor that kept me grounded, like a dandelion being blown into the wind to scatter about. All 90 pounds of me was beat with a thick wooden paddle administered by the Assistant Principal. He was a big man all the way around, easily weighing at least 350 pounds. I was forced to bend over and place my hands on the front of the principal's desk. I was wearing a little orange and yellow striped tee-shirt mini-dress, and when I bent over my undies were exposed and it made me feel terribly embarrassed and ashamed. The school Principal watched while the Assistant Principal beat me until I had welts, blisters, and blood marks on my bottom. My skin turned an ugly black and blue, and I couldn't sit down for over a week. I had never been paddled before, not even by my own parents. I recall wanting to scream but was too dignified to do anything other than allow the involuntary tears to stream down my face. They never asked my parent's permission. My parents were not aware of the incident until I arrived home later that day. Their faces showed their utter shock. I remember vividly how my mother gently applied ice and babied me. I stayed home from school for a few days because my injuries were so severe.

There were no words to describe the shame, humiliation, rejection and outright worthlessness instilled in me that day. My parents were sympathetic, but they were not of the mind to stand up to school authorities. They were raised in the day and age when authority figures were trusted without question. After all, they had attended this same junior high school. I saw the hurt and disillusionment in their eyes. I heard them discussing moving away to another town, but jobs and finances did not permit that.

On that day, the cycle of having blind trust for the powers that be stopped cold for me. Not only did I question their motives, rules and values, I challenged everything that was status quo. I was respectful, but fearless, nonetheless. Had it not been for the escape and solace I found in the songs running through my mind, books that took me to faraway places, and the soft whinny and nuzzling of my beloved horse Pal, I'm not sure how I would have coped. My mantra was the song by Jonathon Edwards, that sang my thoughts:

"Sunshine, go away today,
Don't feel much like dancing,
Some man's gone and tried to run my life
He don't know what he's askin'

When he tells me I better get in line
I can't hear what he's sayin'
When I grow up, I'm gonna make it mine
These ain't dues I been payin'

Well, how much does it cost? I'll buy it
The time is all we've lost, I'll try it
And he can't even run his own life
I'll be damned if he'll run mine, sunshine...

Sunshine, come back another day
I promise you, I'll be singin'
This old world, she's gonna turn around
Brand new bells will be ringin...'"

I did what I could to avoid the remaining months of detentions I was facing. I simply couldn't fathom sitting inside in the detention room wasting precious time doing nothing. Rather than serve morning detentions between the time when the bus dropped me off and when school began, I walked the two miles from my house to school and waited at the railroad tracks until the bell rang to enter school property. After school I walked home so I could leave campus right away rather than serve detention while waiting on the bus. I usually stopped by the Dairy Queen to buy a marshmallow Coke or lime Mr. Misty. It was springtime, and I enjoyed walking home. One time, a couple of kids of a different ethnic origin tagged along, and the Carbondale Police alerted the junior high principal who called me down to warn me and called my parents. There was no crime, no mischief, nothing —just innocent 13-year-old kids walking home from school in broad daylight laughing and having fun. I had a hard time understanding why everyone made such a big deal about little things, but at least I never got in trouble or punished again.

Instead of serving months of lunchtime detentions, I was able to work out a deal with the Science teacher to create a slide show of insects in his classroom during the lunch period. Anything to keep from having to sit in a detention room. I was proud of my insect project and presented it to the class when I finished. It was impressive!

The school year ended, and my last final report card of seventh grade had straight A's in every single subject throughout the entire year—except citizenship. The principal had failed me in this category for the last quarter of school. What a scarlet letter--I just couldn't accept it. In my mind everything about the situation was a failure, from the extreme discipline and social isolation imposed, to the emotional damage inside me. I changed the F to a B with a blue ink pen before showing my parents; I couldn't stand to see them hurt again. At the end of the school year my language arts teacher, Mr. Horst, told my parents I was the best student he had in 7 years and wondered what had gone wrong. That made two of us, Mr. Horst.

Eighth grade came and went uneventfully, with most of my efforts focused on schoolwork, riding my bike and my horse in my free time. I remained on Student Council for the second year in a row. The highlight of the year was our trip to St. Louis to see the musical, *Up, Up with People*, at the Fox Theater. I totally loved the happy music and energy! It planted the seed in my mind that other places were very different than Carbondale, and just maybe life would be kinder to me somewhere else. I would tuck this away for the day I turned 18 and got my birthday present – a one-way ticket out of Carbondale and off to California, along with some cherry red luggage!

The transition to high school was surprisingly refreshing. I enjoyed my freshman year at Carbondale Community High School (CCHS) East, which was a nearly new building. It was a fresh new environment and much nicer experience than my prior two years at junior high. I loved English with Mrs. Cook and Latin with Mrs. Olviera. Sophomore year brought another change as we moved over to the central campus. Central seemed old and scary to me. There were a few older bully girls who picked on me for no reason, and often made my life miserable. Other than that, my time at central campus was dotted with some happy highlights that still stand out in my mind. I took a photography class with Mr. Boetcher at the vocational school. What an awesome and inspiring teacher he was, and what a fun class! I loved taking photos with my 35mm camera and developing them in the dark room at school, applying special techniques to create moods and tell a story with my photos. I also enjoyed the liveliness and energy of chorus and swing choir. My most memorable social event of high school was the prom dance of my last year. I didn't have a boyfriend at the high school, but lucky for me, the boy I had a mad crush on in Kindergarten and again in junior high invited me to go to prom as friends. He wore a white tuxedo that complimented my flowing long, green dress. He brought me a beautiful yellow corsage and took me to a lovely dinner. He was a gentleman, and I felt like Cinderella that night. He never knew how much his gesture and that prom meant to me. It was the only high school dance I had ever gone to, and it is the nicest high school memory I have.

Most high school kids had a car when they got their driver's license, but for some reason my parents thought girls didn't need cars, so I relied upon my trusty green Schwinn to get me where I needed to go. I didn't have a regular group of high school girlfriends to hang out with, so to keep myself busy I ventured out on my bicycle. I rode around Campus Lake and out to Giant City State Park to enjoy the beautiful scenery, always thinking about what my future might hold. I met a handsome college guy who eventually became my best friend, and one day would become my husband. I liked the college scene and looked forward to moving on. I studied at the college library, went swimming at Campus Lake, worked at SIU's athletic events and went to many an outdoor concert on the college campus. I can still hear the sweet sounds of Chuck Mangione playing his trumpet behind Woody Hall at dusk dark on a hot, humid summer night. Ahh yes, "Feels So Good!" The music flowed through the air in sync with the humming mating calls of cicadas, while darkness fell and wrapped around me like a cozy blanket. Bikes, blankets and young people covered the grassy hill between Woody Hall and Pulliam Hall on these starlit summer nights. The sheer energy and excitement of new experiences and places were calling my name.

I graduated from CCHS in 1976, a year ahead of schedule. I was excited to start college classes at SIU Carbondale that very summer. Several of my high school teachers had touched my life in meaningful ways, preparing me for college and beyond. My junior English teacher, Mrs. Howell, introduced me to the books of Joyce Carol Oates where I found companionship and comfort. Anytime there was an opportunity for creative self-expression, I was all over it. I created a crazy awesome presentation on Bob Dylan songs in Mrs. Cook's freshman English class, and another crazy awesome slide show on famous American jazz musicians in Mr. Davis' summer history class my junior year. Mrs. Olviera and Mr. Mindriski inspired me to excel in Latin class, and honestly, that is most likely what helped me placement test out of nearly all my general studies at SIU. I wrote an amazing research paper in Mr.

Emme's government class that peeled back the onion on standardized testing; it stretched me, and I felt accomplished. Our high school principal, Dr. Black, was helpful and encouraging. He always told tell me I could be anything I wanted to be. He was the nicest principal I ever had. Years later, after I had graduated from college, our paths crossed again as we became colleagues working for the same employer in Springfield. What a small world!

Carbondale had plenty of endearing "Mayberry RFD" type of places that I dearly loved: Dillinger's Feed Store where I bought my horse feed; Ernie's over by the Phillips 66 station on North Illinois Avenue and Oak Street where my dad bought me Strawberry Crush soda while he had a beer, letting me twirl around on the bar stool until I went so fast I flew off; Kirby's grocery store on Sycamore Street where we bought deli bologna sandwiches at lunch period; and of course, the Dairy Queen on Illinois Avenue and the little wall where we sat and sipped our Mr. Misty's and watched people. When college was in session the town had a special energy and was truly magical. I loved those times, and often wondered, "Why me? Why was growing up so hard for me in the town I loved so much?" My grandma Brooks would tell me, "God won't give you more than you can bear." Words to last a lifetime.

When I was a junior psychology major at SIU Edwardsville in 1978, I discovered an author who had a life-changing healing influence in my life. Leo Buscaglia was a USC special education professor and motivational speaker, aka "Dr. Love." He seemed to write directly to my heart, like he knew all my innermost thoughts and experiences, and how my teenage years had shaped me. I learned the simple concepts that were not taught, or maybe even known of when I was growing up: self-esteem, self-worth, and self-love. The teaching of "Dr. Love", along with my family and new college friends, helped me learn to love and accept myself and step out of the past and into a wonderful and healthy life with unlimited possibilities.

I graduated SIU Edwardsville magna cum laude in 1980, began my graduate degree, took the plunge to get married and start a family, began my career, moved up, worked more, moved up more, and so the cycle continued. I felt affirmed, stable and in control of my own destiny. Where there was once rejection, I found acceptance. Where there was judgement, I found unconditional love. Where there was hopelessness, I found hope.

I never returned to Carbondale to live, but I have returned for occasional visits. I am always amazed at all the bittersweet memories and emotions that wash over me like giant waves. A part of me longs for a "re-do" of that delicate time in my life, to right all things wrong and bring the best version of myself to those situations that I was so ill equipped to deal with once upon a time. But since I can't turn back time, for now I'll just sing along with Demi Lovato….

"This is a story, that I have never told,
I've got to get this off my chest to let it go
I need to take back the light inside you stole
You're a criminal and you steal like you're a pro.

All the pain and the truth
I wear like a battle wound
So ashamed, so confused
I was broken and bruised.

Now I'm a warrior
Now I've got thicker skin
I'm a warrior
I'm stronger than I've ever been...

There's a part of me I can't get back,
A little girl grew up too fast
All it took was once, I'll never be the same.

Now I'm taking back my life today
Nothing left that you can say…

Now I'm a warrior
I got thicker skin,
I'm a warrior
I'm stronger than I've ever been,

And my armor,
Is made of steel, you can't get in,
I'm a warrior,
And you can never hurt me, again."

WILL THE CIRCLE BE UNBROKEN?

By Scott Dreher

*"I'm the son-of-a-*BEEP *that named you Sue!"*

The first time I heard those lyrics, from Johnny Cash's 1969 album "At San Quentin," I was in fourth grade and I was 80% sure I knew what word had been BEEPED – my dad, a professor at the Crime Studies Center at SIU, occasionally used that four-syllable sequence. Our family had recently moved into the red house atop the big hill off Giant City blacktop about a mile north of Boskydell Road, and my parents had purchased a mahogany stereo console with record changer for the family room.

I sat and listened, spellbound, to "At San Quentin," alternating with 1968's "At Folsom Prison." Those wood-encased speakers broadcast a rich stew of vinyl crackles, guitar strums, rhymes and melodies through the living room and onto the balcony looking towards Giant City State Park, seven miles south.

After a few plays I'd learned the lyrics to all the songs on both albums, along with the between-songs banter from Cash and his prison audiences (learned them so well, in fact, that I was able to hop onstage in Athens, Greece a decade later and sing "Folsom Prison Blues" at the invitation of a band at a hotel bar). But what was blocked by the "BEEP"? I needed to be certain.

I scoured the back side of the album cover, desperately trying to find the printed words to "A Boy Named Sue" and prove my assumption about that "BEEP." I removed the inner sleeve, but it was simply a white envelope with a hole in the middle though which the red "Columbia" record label was visible. I read the fine print on that label, as well, but found no lyrics, although I did notice names listed in parentheses next to the titles – "B. Dylan" – "J. Cash" - "J. Sebastian" – and deduced that they were the songwriters.

In October 1971 Cash was scheduled to play SIU Arena "in the round." As it happened my mom knew the guy at SIU who produced those shows. But I wasn't aware of this. What I did know was that Ms. Emery, my sixth grade English teacher at Giant City School, was pacing the front of our classroom talking about reports each of us would present to the class, and she began tossing out suggestions. "Scott! Johnny Cash!" she said, eyes locked on mine and pointing at me. What a great idea! Only many years later did I wonder how she got the idea.

At dinner that evening I informed my parents that I would be doing a report about Johnny Cash and that I needed them to take me to Morris Library to find books about him.

"And I'll need to bring a record player to school and play songs from his albums…" I couldn't wait to start a classroom discussion about "A Boy Named Sue" and the BEEP…

"He's playing in concert soon. How would you like to go backstage and meet him?" said Mom. My first concert!

The night of the show we were escorted into the dressing room. There sat Johnny Cash, dressed in black, and his wife, June Carter Cash; both were smiling and happy to see us. Mom had brought a cassette tape recorder and a camera. Johnny reached out and shook my hand, strong and firm. June then took my hand with both of hers, firmly but gently. "Very nice to meet you," she said, smiling at me. I explained that I was doing a report for my class.

"Hello, I'm Johnny Cash," he said into the cassette recorder microphone. "I want to say hello to the Sixth Grade class at Giant City School." "Always work hard and do your homework so you get good grades," added June. We talked for several minutes more, took a polaroid picture of them both, shook hands again, and went back out to watch the show.

As I'd hoped, Cash played "A Boy Named Sue" for the packed SIU Arena crowd. As I hadn't hoped, he actually sang the word "BEEP" after the words *"… son of a …"* while he, June Carter, Carl Perkins, The Statler Brothers, and the Tennessee Three moved slowly past on the rotating stage.

Mom wouldn't let me use "A Boy Named Sue" in my report to my class, so I chose "Folsom Prison Blues" instead. I got an A. I still have the cassette and the photo in a box in our garage.

That next year my father took sabbatical from SIU and we spent 1972-1973 living in England. One of my best friends there was a huge fan of Slade, the Sweet, and T-Rex and I returned home to Carbondale with more musical literacy, including knowledge about "B. Dylan," and a handful of 45-rpm records that he gave me. I wore them out.

When I was fifteen I got a job at Baskin Robbins in the University Mall. My under-16 wage of $1.25 an hour seemed like a fortune. I spent all of my 15-minute rest breaks and 30-minute lunch periods combing through The Record Bar, midway down the Mall's main promenade between JCPenney and the central fountain, reading the backs of the albums. The staff there would play the records if you asked, and by now the inner album sleeves usually contained printed lyrics whose meanings I pondered while listening to the songs. My birthday gift that year was a red AM transistor radio and I fell asleep every night listening to pop songs on St. Louis radio station KXOK. Mom and Dad always had fresh 9-volt batteries available for me when I asked.

By 1976 I had my own record player and an FM stereo receiver which included a rare 8-track tape player with recorder. I was earning enough money to buy albums rather than 45s, and now I had a driver's license to go get them. "My" car was Dad's 1969 Pontiac Firebird which he'd bought from one of our teachers, and my friend Marv Tucker helped me replace the stock single-speaker AM radio with a more potent FM/8-Track stereo unit and twin speakers on the rear window deck.

In that car I discovered Murphysboro FM radio station WTAO – playing musicians I'd never heard on an AM station: The Band, Poco, Santana, Bob Dylan, Vassar Clements, the Ramones, Papa John Creach. Every Sunday WTAO aired live concerts on a show called "King Biscuit Flower Hour" and I was a regular listener. I often bought what I heard, and then recorded those records onto 8-track tapes, so I could play them in that car. "American Beauty." "One of These Nights." "Blood on the Tracks." "Hurricane." "Desire." "Born to Run." "Darkness on the Edge of Town." "Hotel California." "Dirt, Silver & Gold." "Late for the Sky." "Running on Empty." I spent hours driving the Firebird around town – Illinois Avenue, Highway 51, Main Street, Parrish Acres, Douglas Drive around campus, Chautauqua Road -- simply to hear music, while drumming on the dashboard and singing verses.

But this music wasn't something we shared with adults, teachers, parents. The lyrics weren't serious, grown-up stuff, and these songs couldn't be real-world targets of study. Or were they? Could they? By senior year at CCHS I had worked up the nerve to find out. Ms. Sue Howell, our English teacher, had assigned us to write an essay about Hamlet, and I was convinced I could compare an aspect of Shakespeare's great play to Jackson Browne's song "The Pretender."

"*It's time to clean up your style*," Ms. Howell had written alongside the "A" she gave me on that Hamlet/Pretender paper. I didn't know I had a style, but I knew then that songs and lyrics were legitimate endeavors. They could contain magic. Duly encouraged, I began feverishly seeking out the good ones, the deep ones, studying them in the hope that I would understand them and be influenced by them.

I graduated college and left Carbondale for San Diego, California in 1982. Got married, had children, grew up in fits and starts along the way. Through it all Alyce and I made a point to share music with our kids and expose them to different musical styles, artists, songs, and lyrics.

As it happens I bought my own 1969 Firebird and we would drive it to concerts at legendary music venues such as L.A.'s Hotel Café, McCabe's Guitar Shop in Santa Monica, and Ben Harper's Folk Music Center, near Pasadena. The rule was, each of us would choose any CD we desired, and we would play them *en route*. The rest of us would have to listen. I might choose Dave Alvin's "Ashgrove" or John Hiatt's "Perfectly Good Guitar" while they might choose Green Day's "American Idiot" or something by Blink-182 or Switchfoot – very different, yet in some ways not so much. We were often pleasantly surprised to find ourselves enjoying things we hadn't heard or didn't think we'd like, when we took a chance and actually listened.

And we would move along the freeways and city streets, drumming on the dash or the armrests, singing various lyrics and pondering their meanings.

My kids' first live concert was Orange County punk band Social Distortion, at House of Blues. It was an all-ages show. One of my clients managed the place and got me four free tickets.

"How do *you* know about Social D?" my 14-year-old daughter Cassandra asks me, rolling her eyes, when I arrive home from work one evening and announce to the family that we'll be attending the concert.

"Listen, kiddo," I say. "They're *our* band, not yours. They have kids your age."

Mike Ness, Social D's lead singer and guitarist, is well known for breaking rules, and his fans are wonderfully irreverent. We join the raucous, jam-packed, alcohol-infused audience near the back edge of the darkened main floor (there are no seats at House of Blues) and begin jumping and dancing as the band plays their rough punk rock.

Ness is also well known for covering Johnny Cash's music, both with Social D and at his solo gigs. I'm beyond excited to hear the inevitable Cash number, punked-out and live.

Midway through the show Ness pauses center stage. "We're gonna play an adult song, now," he informs us, smirking slightly. And, as always happens at Social Distortion concerts, some guy near the front of the group hoists both middle fingers high, and waves them at the stage. Ness sees the flip-off.

"Fuck me??" Ness says into the microphone, smiling now and shaking his head. "Fuck *you*!"

The F-word. Twice. No BEEPs.

The crowd erupts, cheering and raising their beers in a toast of approval. My 10-year-old son Robbie's eyes are wide as saucers, his mouth agape, as he stares up at his mom.

"He sounds like Daddy..." Robbie says. My kids have heard me use those syllables.

"Yes, he does," Alyce answers. At that moment, I'm the proudest of fathers.

The drummer leads as the band rips into "Ring of Fire."

CARBONDALE BEFORE DARK

by H.B. Koplowitz

A tree stump clinging to a tiny grassy island, marooned in a parking lot a quarter-mile southwest of where I once went to school -- Pulliam Hall, the building with the iconic clock tower on the campus of Southern Illinois University-Carbondale -- is the last vestige of where I grew up from 1952, when I was in diapers, to 1964, when I was in puberty. Like other homes in the area, during the 1960s, ours was eminent domained by the university for the higher public purpose of providing academicians with a place to park their cars. SIU eventually demolished the house, yard and street, leaving behind a solitary oak tree that had been in our front yard. It survived on the island until May 2009, when it was felled by a derecho storm.

In February 2008, when the university began destroying the last 13 houses on my old stomping ground, an SIU Daily Egyptian *reporter interviewed me about what the area had been like in the 1950s and '60s when I was living there and attending University School, a nursery-12th grade training school for teachers that began closing in 1968. I'm afraid I wasn't much help to the reporter, and after getting off the phone I felt like I'd let down the 'hood, which had been unexceptional to grownups, but a virtual never-never land for kids.*

As the author of Carbondale After Dark, *I'd told the story of the town's notorious strip. Now that the last of my childhood strip was disappearing, it seemed the least I could do was put together a few sentences to mark its passing. I also found myself reminiscing about growing up in the rest of Carbondale during the 1950s and '60s, when the town was undergoing a seismic shift in race relations. (I won't pretend to know what it was like to be black in southern Illinois. For that, I suggest* Traces in the Dust *by Melvin LeRoy Green Macklin, who was born in Carbondale in 1945 and later moved to Texas. His copious history of the town's black community has a prelude called "The Wonder Years," in which he describes his 1950s upbringing in the "Hoodlums" neighborhood on the far northeast side.) So with apologies to myself, I humbly submit a prequel to* CAD *called "Carbondale Before Dark."*

In 1959, when Carbondale had 15,000 residents and 12,000 SIU students, I was 8 years old and living in a residential neighborhood west of U-School so full of kids it might have been called a baby boomer incubator. Our address was 906 W. Grand Ave., the middle house of three on the north side of Grand, between Elizabeth and Forest streets. Our square, white, frame house was modest, with a leaky basement and an unfinished attic. My younger brother Sandy and I shared one bedroom, our parents, Audrey and Julius, the other. We all shared the bathroom. We also shared a single black-and-white console TV connected to an antenna on the roof. Periodically, a repairman would drop by with a suitcase full of vacuum tubes to fix it. And we shared a single, black, rented telephone, attached to the wall, that had no buttons or even a dial. To make a call, we'd pick up the handset and a human operator would say, "number please." Unless a neighbor was on the party line, and then we'd eavesdrop.

The furnace in the basement had been converted from coal to fuel oil, and during the winter a man in a tank truck would drive down a gravel alley alongside our house and stick a hose through the coal chute to fill our tanks. New Era Dairy milk trucks also used the alley, to deliver and pick up bottles, as did peddlers and trash collectors, sometimes in a wooden wagon pulled by a couple of mules.

Carbondale was covered with foliage, and the spindly oak was the youngest tree on our property. The trees attracted birds, especially robins, cardinals and blue jays, while milkweed vines drew monarch butterflies. The town was also edible. Kids would pilfer from apple trees and chew on mint leaves a neighbor grew. We dangled the stems of wild wheat grasses from our mouths like they were cigarettes, and in the fall, maple seeds fell to the ground in pods that whirled like helicopters. We'd pinch the pods to squirt the seeds at each other, then suck on the leafy part until it was just the right consistency to make a perfect kid's noise -- somewhere between an air horn and a fart.

The neighborhood store was Kelley's, a mom and pop grocery in a wooden pole building around the corner on Forest Street. Owned by the family that later managed the Giant City State Park Lodge, Kelley's was my first hangout, where my recreational drug of choice was glucose in the form of Popsicles, candy bars, soda pop and bubble-gum. After school, the concrete porch in front of Kelley's would be full of kids getting their sugar fixes.

Spring and summer afternoons we'd chase after the ice cream truck, and at night we'd bicycle behind the "mosquito truck," a jeep with a loud contraption on the back that spewed a dense, white, smelly, plume of smoke that was probably toxic DDT. In the fall, families would drive past dorms and frat/sorority houses to view yard decorations that combined Halloween and Homecoming themes to depict the dastardly things the football team was going to do to the opposition. The best part of winter was Christmastime, with more festive yard and store decorations, and a live manger scene on the lawn of Holden Hospital, next to the Dairy Queen, which had been turned into a Christmas tree lot.

The hub of downtown was actually called The Hub, a cafe owned by Nick Masters on the southwest corner of Illinois Avenue and Main Street, in the same building one of the town's founding fathers, Daniel Brush, once had a general store. Beneath The Hub was a lounge called the Rathskeller, aka Rathole, one of the few downtown taverns in the 1950s except for the Levee, a black strip across the train tracks on North Washington Street.

Before South Illinois Avenue became known as the strip, it was dotted with eateries including the Alibi, Varsity Grill, Lavender's and UD's, where in my adolescence I played a lot of pinball. We went to the movies at the Varsity Theater, where blacks were supposedly segregated in the balcony, although white kids would sneak up there to make out.

We also made out at the drive-in, which in those days meant drive-in movie theaters, like the Waring (later Campus) on old Route 13 halfway to Murphysboro, and the Egyptian, outside Energy, which claimed to have the biggest outdoor screen in the country.

The first fast food drive-in I remember in Carbondale was the A&W root beer stand on East Main Street, where instead of a drive-thru, carhops would deliver the frothy brew in frosty glass mugs on metal trays that attached to the car window. Next came a Frostop on the north side, a Dog n Suds on the west side, and a McDonald's where Lenus Turley Park is now, across Glenview Drive from the town's first strip mall, the Murdale Shopping Center, which opened in 1958.

U.S. 51 used to be a two-lane highway that traversed Normal (University) Avenue. At the main gate to SIU it would jog west on Grand for a block, then turn south on Thompson Street, where the Faner Building is now, and head out of town west of the old campus and what would become the Arena. Shortly before I was born in 1951, the highway was rerouted east to Illinois Avenue, clearing the way for the college to expand west. U-School became the first major addition to the campus in 1950, followed by Woody Hall, which was a women's dorm and cafeteria.

If the definition of a private school is you have to pay tuition to get in, then U-School was a private school. However, being attached to the university, it was anything but parochial, with student teachers and experimental teaching methods. Many of the students were the children of SIU faculty, so the student body was more transient and cosmopolitan, yet more insulated, than the townie schools.

In addition to small and big gyms and small and big auditoriums, U-School had small and big swimming pools. The brick entryways to the younger classrooms were adorned with six small corner castings or renderings of classic fairy tales, including "Hansel and Gretel" and "Three Billy Goats Gruff." The nursery school and kindergarten were in the same classroom, which had a one-way mirror so adults could spy on us from an observation room. There was a shallow, indoor fountain for small aquatic turtles and metamorphosing tadpoles, and a hive encased in window panes, where bees manufactured honey. The highlight of those years were the field trips -- in nursery school we took a train to Anna and back, and as kindergarteners we rode a bus to the St. Louis Zoo. Dr. Mott taught nursery and kindergarten, Mrs. Goodman first grade, Mrs. Bricker second, Mrs. Treece third, and Mrs. Meehan fourth grade.

In high school I spent a lot of time at a place called the typing room, where students learned to use more than their thumbs to tap letters on something called a typewriter. The typing room doubled as the newsroom for the Tower Times mimeographed student newspaper, which is why I hung out there with fellow nerds, although at the time we considered ourselves pseudo-hippies.

U-School was on the grounds of SIU, which made the entire campus our playground, including Old Main. Built in 1887, it was the oldest building on campus until June 8, 1969, when it was apparently torched by an arsonist, motive unknown. Altgeld Hall, built in 1896 to resemble a medieval castle, had a natural history museum with dioramas and a gift shop that sold packets of Confederate money. We also infiltrated the nooks and crannies of Shryock Auditorium, got lost in a grid of World War II barracks that had been turned into married student housing, and explored the labyrinthine steam tunnels beneath the campus.

West of the Quad, past the Baptist Foundation and SIU President Delyte Morris' home, was the new Morris Library, which had three floors of open stacks and a basement with microfilms of old newspapers. The Life Science Building, with its odoriferous labs, was the westernmost building on the campus. Beyond that, Lawson Hall was houses, the Wham Building a dry marsh, and the Northwest Annex was woods.

Itchy Jones and the rest of the Saluki baseball team played at Chautauqua Field, where the Communications Building is now. Between the baseball diamond and a state public health lab was a crawdad-laden ditch fed by a bug-infested drainage pipe large enough for an 8-year-old and his pals to crawl into. Beyond right field, Greek Row and Thompson Point dorms were construction sites where we had epic dirt clod fights.

Between U-School and my house was a densely wooded area with winding footpaths worn through the ivy. Where the Wham Building is now, the woods gave way to a muddy field filled with cattails and reeds taller than an 8-year-old. Parents forbade their children from going in the woods, so despite the poison ivy, ticks, pollen and chiggers, it was a forbidden pleasure. On the southeast edge of the woods, atop a steep hill fortified by thorn bushes, Virginia creepers and climbing ivy, was a burned-out house. With a basement, two floors, an attic, and rooftops to explore, there was plenty of room to play hide and seek, light fire crackers, and indulge in other risky behavior. We called it the haunted house, although it was mostly haunted by us kids. The authorities eventually got wind of the goings-on at the haunted house and tore it down.

On a more wholesome note, Sandy and I became Cub Scouts. For the regional Cub Scout Jamboree talent show competition at the Carbondale Armory, the town's all-white troop covered our faces with shoe polish and put on a minstrel show. Sandy got a solo, pantomiming Al Jolson singing "My Mammy." Even back then, the show was panned for being racially insensitive.

Most of the kids in my neighborhood attended grade school at Winkler Elementary, west of Oakland on Freeman Street. They went to middle school at Lincoln Junior High on South Washington Street, between Freeman and College streets, where the police department is now, and then to Carbondale Community High School, which was on North Springer Street. The black kids went to Attucks on the northeast side, across East Main Street from Woodlawn Cemetery. Like U-School, Attucks was both an elementary and high school, plus a community center.

The schools, my neighborhood and the west side in general were mostly white, except for Martha Johnson, our maid, who lived on the northeast side, but spent five days a week at our place, cleaning and corralling me and my brother. Back then, blacks were called colored people. We were one of the few families in the neighborhood to have a colored maid because our mom worked with our dad at Kay's, the dress shop they owned across from the (old) train station. (They later opened Kay's Campus Shop at Illinois and Freeman, above what was then Crazy Horse Billiards and Gatsby's bar.)

As a child, I can't say that I distinctly liked or disliked Martha, which is what we called her. She was the boss when my parents weren't around, and I respected her the same way I did my parents -- grudgingly. Martha was poor but she wasn't bitter. She was basically a decent person, and I love her now like a third parent.

When Martha was in her 50s and I was still in my single digits, she seemed ancient and intimidating. Her face was dark and wrinkly, and her body was short and wiry. She had rock-hard biceps from scrubbing our floors on her knees and wringing out our clothes by hand before pinning them to the clotheslines in our backyard. As well as cooking and cleaning, she bathed Sandy and me when we were little. She taught us Negro spirituals, like "Mary Had a Baby," and read us our *Jack & Jill* and *Humpty Dumpty* magazines. She'd smell up the house with collard "greens," watch her "stories" on our TV, and as she ironed she'd talk to herself about things that had happened at church, repeating conversations and cackling at the funny parts.

Martha lived in a nondescript home with asbestos siding on Wall Street, at the northeast edge of town, next to relatives who had a small farm with mules and chickens. There was a barber chair on her front porch where her former husband had cut hair. Most days Martha took a Yellow Cab to our house, but some evenings my parents would drive her home. Sitting in the backseat with Martha and my brother, I'd peer wide-eyed out the window as we crossed the railroad tracks and came upon sheds and clapboard houses with sagging porches. I remember the embarrassment all around the car when I stuck out my finger one evening and asked "what's that?" and my dad awkwardly tried to explain what an outhouse was for and that yes, Martha had one. At first I thought he was joking.

One summer, when I was about 10 years old and school was out, I fell in with some slightly older boys, some of whom were black, and we were sitting on the rocks at U-School's playground when I first reflected on the "n-word" I'd heard the term before, but it wasn't part of my vocabulary. (When John F. Kennedy was elected president in 1960, a politically incorrect limerick made the rounds that poked fun at the new president's diction and idealism, but today would simply be considered racist: "Do your work with great vigor, or you will be replaced by a N-word."

I don't recall how we got around to the subject, but one of the black kids said a nigger was a very bad person. I said something like, "well, isn't it a very bad colored person?" and he disagreed, saying anyone, black, white, blue or green, could be a "N-word" if they were evil.

Unfortunately, I didn't get the message. A day or two later, I was outside and Martha told me it was time to go inside, but I didn't want to go inside. Instead, I walked into our garage and hissed under my breath, the "N-word."

"What did you say?" Martha asked as she came in the garage after me, seeming more sad than angry. I don't recall what happened next, whether she bawled me out or if I apologized. I do recall feeling very ashamed, and I've never again used the word in anger.

Sports were a big part of our lives. We played baseball and football on the lawn in front of the state public health lab at Oakland and Chautauqua. We also played in front of the University Baptist Church at Oakland and Freeman, and in a neighbor's yard on Elizabeth Street. A year-older childhood friend, Tom Small -- a bad influence who turned me on to pinball and girlie mags -- dubbed it Sad Sack Field.

My next exposure to black people occurred when I joined Little League. My friend Tom was a gifted athlete, and my dad made sure I got on his team -- the Cubs. There were eight teams in the Atom League, which was the youngest division of Little League at the time. Seven of the teams were all white and one was all black -- the Sox. At the end of the season there was a tournament, and Tom pitched the Cubs to the championship game, where we met the Sox, who had just as talented a pitcher, Lester Taylor.

It was a tight game throughout, with Tom and Les matching each other strikeout for strikeout. For most of that season I had been frozen at the plate, never swinging, hoping for a walk, and I did the same thing in the championship game. But during my last at bat, I unaccountably took a swack at the ball and sent a squibber toward the mound. I saw Lester reach down for the ball, saw it dribble out of his glove, and realized I should be running to first base. I took off, but he recovered the ball and threw me out by a half-step.

In the seventh and final inning, Tom's arm gave out. He walked a batter, which in the Atom League was as good as a triple, because the batter soon stole second and third. Tom got a strikeout, but the next batter hit a grounder up the middle. From shortstop, I watched as the ball skipped over second base into center field. Game over. Tom stood on the pitcher's mound, crying. The rest of us threw our gloves in the air. Time for ice cream. I don't remember feeling upset that we'd been beaten by some colored kids, but it did occur to me that colored kids sure were good at sports.

A couple years later, when I was in the Bantam League and Tom had moved away, my new team played another black team -- well, pretty much the same team, except older -- and they were still good at sports. By this time I had come to seriously dislike playing the colored team, not because they were black, but because they all seemed to hit the ball to the shortstop, and I was the shortstop. One night we played the colored team on their home field on the northeast side, off Wall Street near the all-black Thomas Elementary, now Attucks Park. The diamond hadn't been graded, so before the game, we all went onto the infield to toss dirt clods into the outfield. But we couldn't get them all, and sure enough, midway through the game, a batter hit a grounder to short that ricocheted off a clump of clay and smacked me right on the schnoz.

I stood there for a second, stunned, as blood began to gush down my face, and then I just started bawling. My dad ran onto the field and carried me off. My only solace was that it had happened on the east side, where nobody I knew except my teammates had seen me crying in baseball. Until the next morning, when Martha arrived at our house and saw my shiner.

"I heard some white boy got hit in the face by a baseball last night and cried all the way home," she said. "That was you?"
What could I say?

In the early 1960s, the civil rights movement came to Carbondale in the form of SNCC, the Student Nonviolent Coordinating Committee, a chapter of which formed on the campus. One of SNCC's first actions, in 1965, was to picket the Family Fun restaurant on the east side, which had blacks working in the kitchen but none in the dining room. The faculty father of one of the three other Jewish kids in my class was in SNCC, as was his son, who was my friend. But I also had friends who were against integration, and my parents, although sympathetic to civil rights, didn't want anyone telling them who they had to hire. Many of the local Jewish families were of the merchant class, and after services at Beth Jacob Synagogue on a Sunday when SNCC was picketing, the congregation drove en masse to Family Fun, where we crossed the picket line to have lunch, except for my friend and his dad, who joined the protesters.

Soon SNCC was sending "salt and pepper teams" to apply for jobs at other businesses. If the owner didn't hire the black, SNCC would threaten to picket. My parents found a way around the problem -- they hired a colored woman. And they soon found that integration wasn't so bad, as other colored women began streaming into the store to buy clothes from the new colored saleslady.

There were just a few colored kids at U-School, and I didn't have much contact with them. That changed in 1968, when U-High was phased out and most of its students transferred to CCHS. Attucks had closed in 1964, so now everyone went to the same high school. (U-School's grade school closed in 1971, marking the end of neighborhood schools in Carbondale, as students were bused to achieve racial balance.) However, except for some of the sports teams and P.E. classes, high

133

school remained largely segregated. I still didn't have many blacks in my classes, and the races mostly socialized separately. My favorite teacher, English instructor Mary Sasse, started a human relations club to try to bring everyone together. I joined the club, as did my girlfriend, Kathy "Weegee" McNeill, but then I got jealous and made us quit. I was all for social equality, just not with my girlfriend.

In *Traces in the Dust*, Macklin observes that integration was a mixed blessing for Carbondale's black community. He says the closing of Attucks "spells an abrupt end to the close-knit, community structure Blacks had known for generations." He adds that desegregation, "for which Blacks had fought, ultimately proved to be a two edged sword. While it ushered in a supposedly 'new age of progress and opportunity for African Americans,' it also launched the Black community in Carbondale on a journey never witnessed before -- one which was to forever detract from the Black way of life."

During my last years at U-School, I entered the sphere of another precocious older boy, Jerry Magnus, who experimented with pot, went to protest rallies and put out underground newspapers. I transferred to CCHS in 1968 as a junior, but kept in contact with Jerry, who stayed at U-School and decided to do an underground newspaper on race, with an opinion survey, articles on local race relations, and other provocative stuff. He also wanted to write about the East Side Rangers, a group of young, black males who said they weren't a gang but a militant civil rights organization. Jerry invited me along to observe the group at their weekly meeting at City Hall, then located on East Main at Marion Street. I was apprehensive, and so were my parents, but I was as curious as I was scared, and my parents let me go on one condition -- that I park the family Buick on the west side of the tracks.

During study hall a few days later, I spotted someone I thought I'd seen at the Ranger meeting sitting at a table in the high school library. It was none other than my Little League nemesis Lester, who had become the star center on the Terriers basketball team. I timidly sat down across from him and asked if he would participate in a survey about race relations. Les glared at me but didn't say no, so I read the first question: "Do you think Teen Town should be integrated?" Without saying a word, he reached across the table, took my pencil from my hand, snapped it in half with his fingers, then stared at me as if I were the pencil.

We never finished the newspaper.

dedicated to Mary Sasse
(1932-2019)

CARBONDALE WAS MY PLAYGROUND

By Bill Byrne

Between the late 50's and the mid 70's, Carbondale was my playground.

From age 2-1/2 to 18, it was an ever-expanding home base, starting, literally, at my home but by age 4 expanding to the neighborhood. By 5th grade, my friends and I had a thorough knowledge of the rest of the town. And by high school, our universe expanded to all of Southern Illinois.

What made Carbondale unique, of course, was Southern Illinois University. SIU back then was about 25,000 students and faculty, which made up 50% the greater Carbondale's population. So it wasn't quite the tail wagging the dog....When we moved from New Jersey (born in Elizabeth, NJ and lived to talk about it) in the late 50's, my dad's job transfer was to Allen Industries in Herrin. He and my mom chose to move to Carbondale largely due to the quality of life in a large university town. It was the best decision they could have ever made for their children.

Looking back, Carbondale was an old town, and SIU for the most part, was very new. When you really think about it, comparing the two communities, it's quite a contrast.

Carbondale was not a wealthy town, at least by today's standards. I don't believe there were any mansions. We were a town established by railroad paths and access to coal. Hence Carbondale's name.

To be sure, there was a lot of poverty in Carbondale. For those my age, we saw almost on a daily basis Jeff January and his two horses and wagon, hauling away discarded items that he collected from various businesses and homes. Cars always respected his slow wagon, and gave him leeway. There were some of my friends that had tiny homes, some with dim lighting and all tattered furniture.

1957-1963

We moved to Linden St, a little house that backed up to the four ballparks in between Carbondale Community High School and the CCHS's Bleyer football field. Our house was 1040 square feet with 3 bedrooms, 1 bath.

My parents had one room, my sister the other, and the three boys shared the third bedroom. Bunkbeds were needed. We three boys were roommates from birth right up into high school.

Having two older brothers had pluses and minuses. I was the "hand-me-down" third boy......hand me down Sunday church suits (all identical, which made me look like I wore the same suit for eight years in a row), hand me down bikes, and even hand-me-down bath water (for a short while due to my mass protests).

The first movie I ever saw was around 1959 at the Varsity theater. It was *Attack of the Alligator People*. It was great only because it was on a giant screen, but even at pre-K, the banality of this cheesy movie made it hilarious.

We had great neighbors that included the Medlens, later Joe and Jay Boor, and my first girlfriend, Pam Feimester. Not far away Pat Brown became one of my best friends and is still in contact. And despite him talking me and others into "rock fights" at old Oakland Cemetery, and playing tackle football with no pads through the years, I survived. Pat survived too, though in one sandlot football game, a few of us gang tackled him and dislocated his hip. Then we collectively wised up.

My most interesting neighbor, two doors down, was Johnnie Paul. He turned out to be a serial killer. And he was a bad boy. Unfortunately, I spent more time with him than I wanted.

His poor mom was in and out of the Anna State Mental Hospital of those years lived in Carbondale. She'd come down to our house and for whatever reason would start reciting verses with the Bible in hand. I have a vivid memory of my mom ignoring her while vacuuming our carpet around her.

Johnnie Paul did so many bad things. He stole, he beat up kids, he hurt animals. Once he tried to hang our cat, with his belt, on the fence in our backyard that bordered the ball field. Thank goodness my brother Tim got to him before the cat died, undid the belt, and proceeded to beat JP up. That night at the dinner table, the family all agreed he was destined for a criminal life. He was responsible for multiple deaths of young women when he was in his 20's. He died while serving a life sentence at Menard prison.

In hindsight, we were crazy kids. We swam in storm drainage ponds, which were filled with leaches. No big deal.... we'd finish up our "refreshing swim" to get out and pull off one or two leaches. We rode our bikes behind the mosquito jeeps that pulled the exterminator's chemicals with giant plumes of white smoke. We did this multiple times per week in the summer, as all the parents waved to us with smiles. This was not just a phenomenon in our area of town, but my friend Mel tells me the northeast had the same tasty treat as did other areas of Carbondale. Other dangers that we didn't even really know about were all around us. We had two parents that smoked (my mom quit in fourth grade), no one even thought about wearing suntan lotion or sun screen in the summer. Quite the opposite- all the girls wore baby oil when tanning at the beach. Seat belts didn't exist. Alcohol and driving really weren't on adult radar screens, at least by today's views. .

Our area's grade school was Brush, which has long been razed and now a memory. The principal was Mrs. Swindell and my kindergarten teacher was Mrs. Toler. The only memory that stands out was that the boys and girls had to take turns for using the open bathrooms. In first grade, Mrs. Smith was a good teacher but sent anyone that was being rambunctious to go into the supply closet. I was ordered there a few times, but it wasn't that bad. There was a small window that brought in light and ALL the supplies were in there.... pencils, paper, scissors.... a smorgasbord of fun.

At Brush, a few times a year we'd go to the basement, line up in a long, dimly lit narrow hallway, and individually have our hair checked for lice, by sticking your head under a fluorescent black light and having the school nurse search your head with her gloved hands. I felt like a pet.

1964-1966

The summer in between third and fourth grade we moved to Meadow Lane, about a ½ mile behind Murdale Shopping Center. The house that my dad had built was a split level and was pretty cool. Still stuck with two other brothers in the bedroom. We had new neighbors.... the Ashbys's, the Rice's, Sasses', the Wham's, and the Dean's (whose chihuahua was cute but when he died, they buried him in a peach can. I guess that is a benefit of a tiny dog), ... a great neighborhood.

Back then our phones were all on party lines.... meaning that a handful of homes shared the same phone line. So I'd be on the phone, and someone from another house would pick up the line and say "Are you going to be much longer"? And my next-door neighbor from my class would always be listening in on our calls. We could hear her breathing. I guess this was the pre-curser to social media.

I was a good kid. I swear! Didn't steal, didn't vandalize.... but we snuck into and explored everything. The Varsity theater, SIU basketball and football games, churches, new construction of houses and buildings, the armory, and all retail shops. On non-school days, we left the house early, at 9-ish and came back for dinner. We'd bike all over the town. Almost every day we played sports- basketball, football, or baseball.

As we got older and bolder, my friends and I would bike up to SIU almost daily. We'd explore every building- Old Main, Altgeld Hall, Morris Library, U-School…you name it. Bikes were to walking as cars were to bikes.

Since our move, our new school was Winkler Elementary, on West Freeman. I attended there fourth grade through the beginning of sixth grade. The southwest section of C'dale was fun. We were very close to Murdale Shopping Center, which was not only one of the first strip malls we'd ever seen, but continued to add on stores and expand. Eventually they added Bresler's Ice Cream Shop, where I worked for two years. I once got a raise from 97 cents an hour to 98 cents. That penny raise dramatically affected my financial lifestyle. Another Murdale store added was "Go-Go Raceways"- a hobby store with two giant racetracks for kids with a little more money to race their model cars, and numerous other stores of our interest. Go-Go's had a pin ball machine that had some screws loose and we were able to slide down the glass and hold down the bonus lever so that we could rack up a million points and add as many free games as we wanted. THAT was more fun than just playing.

We were blessed to have woods behind our home. A bunch of our friends and I often played army out there for hours and knew every inch of the woods but not well enough to not to bring home poison ivy on a regular basis. Behind the woods was Colt Stables. Going into the stables was pretty neat as the owners didn't mind us kids at all. We didn't cause any problems with the horses. Colt Stables was on Chitaqua St. Further east on Chitaqua, was a steep cinder-covered hill known as Tar Hill. In fifth grade I rode down Tar Hill and the tire hit a cinder and threw me from the bike, and landing on my knees. It was a bad accident. My friend Danny looked down at my knee and he turned white, saying "I can see your knee cap". So that was 42 stitches…10 inside and 32 outside. By six grade the town had completed a new elementary school, Parrish, where we were transferred to after the beginning of sixth grade. Yet another change.

1967-1969: Lincoln Junior High School and Carbondale Community HS-East

It was tough times for our country, and Carbondale was right in the middle of it all. It was our introduction to junior high -- 7th and 8th grade, for the entire town and area around Carbondale, and to integration. The integration was multi-front: town folks and country folks, the U-school folks, and especially blacks and whites. This was the first time in all of our lives that we were meeting folks we were always aware of but never knew. Then throw gas on the fire-- we were at the peak of the Vietnam riots and the race rebellion against oppression across the country. And Carbondale was explosive with racial tensions and with the SIU students from the enormous upheaval about Vietnam. On a national basis, this didn't end in junior high….it lasted through high school.

In 7th grade, we met kids that had totally different views and upbringings. There were fights and there were close calls of getting your butt kicked if you were in the wrong place at the wrong time. Fast forward to Sophomore year and beyond and almost all of these folks were our friends. By my mid-junior year, DeWayne Kelley was my best friend. We laughed about the time we almost got into a fight in 7th grade. If there is any real meaningful paragraph in my one chapter here, it is here. Our country could learn from this.

Lincoln Junior High was crazy strict. Below is just one of 16 pages of rules:

Lincoln Junior High Building Rules

1. *Students are not to enter any classroom until the 8:25 a.m. bell in the mornings, and the 12:20 p.m. bell at noon, unless requested or permitted to do so by the principal or teacher.*
2. *Before school or during the noon hour, the junior high girls may use the rest room in the lower hall. Boys use the rest room at the end of the north corridor, near the boys' shower room.*
3. *No students will be permitted to remain in any class or practice room unsupervised morning, noon, or night.*
4. *Those students who must come to school early because of bus transportation may go to the gym upon arrival if the weather is bad. Girls use south side bleachers, boys north side. Boys are to enter the gym by the north-west door next to the Art room; girls the south-east door next to the girls' shower room. Students are to leave the gym by these doors at all times. The front doors to the gym are not to be used during the school day. All students must remain in the gym once they have entered.*
5. *Absolutely no talking in the halls while classes are passing, entering, or leaving the building.*
6. *No running in the halls or on the stairs at any time.*
7. *Boys and girls are not to loaf within the rest rooms at any time.*

The list goes on for pages. Mr. Patton was our principal and his right-hand assassin was Mr. Allen, a big, burly man that dished out the punishment for breaking any of these 1,248 rules. Mr. Allen had a LARGE paddle (were there spikes on the end of it??) and he was infamous for doling out punishment for breaking any one of these rules. I got busted for chewing gum and got sent there once. I met up with my classmate Mel Hughlett, who I believe got sent there for even a smaller infraction. I believe we both got off with a stern warning....as Mr. Allen held his paddle in hand...tapping it against his other hand, as a warning.

LJHS was so strict, it was worse than the military. We got yelled at for having our shirts outside and not tucked in. Our only reprieve was lunch hour. Most of us got the hell out of that building, away from the poor food of the cafeteria, but mainly just to get away...to anywhere.

We'd go to the Alabi, which had crappy food but great pin ball machines, or more likely go to the Moo & Cackle. Note the 20 cents burgers. They were worth every penny.... Friday at lunch time at Lincoln we had our weekly "social get-together" dancing hour in the school gym. Boys were on one side of the gym and girls on the other. They played current tunes ("Never My Love", by the Associations, comes to mind) and if a guy was brave enough, he'd walk, in socks, across the *long* gym floor, to request

a dance from one of the hundred girls on the other side. If she said yes, then they'd slow dance in front of everyone. If the girl rejected the boy's offer to dance, it was the walk of shame back across the floor, alone....to the laughter and to the humiliation of the entire gym. To me, it was a risk-reward issue, with the reward paling next to the possible humiliation. I experienced both success and the Walk of Shame back to the boy's side of the gym.

I had, like most kids, a ton of friends. Probably my best two friends were Harry Edelman and Chris Duckett. They shared all the experiences similar to mine at LJHS and CCHS. We took blood brother oaths on some of our adventures for those six years that I still plan to honor.

Another memory of my junior high was the discovery by my friends and me of the SIU Steam Tunnels. These tunnels were fascinating and made up a vast network of underground tunnels connecting almost all buildings at SIU. They varied in size, shape, lighting, temperature, and risk factor.... there were a few sudden drop-offs for example. We explored them all.

There were multiple entry points within a number of the buildings. In the Engineering building, next to the Arena, there was a basement tunnel that led to the steam tunnels. It was like being in a sci-fi movie. Our easiest point of entry was just outside of the SIU student union. Most entries were not locked but while exploring, we'd run into locked gates. We usually could squeeze through (we were in junior high) or we'd just go back and find another route. We got so familiar with them that we knew the

tunnels, better than the maintenance staffs that managed or patrolled the tunnels. We hand drew a few maps which in a way were exactly how modern-day video games map out your path for survival and how to get to the next level. I didn't save the maps we drew, but they were similar to the one here of the actual SIU steam tunnels I found online. This vastly understates all the side tunnels.

The most exciting parts were the chases. There were generally two to four of us, and we were all good athletes- at least compared to custodians. When we'd see them, they'd yell for us to stop and of course we took off. In their pursuit, they didn't have a chance. We way outran them every time, often having to re-squeeze through a locked gate that the older men had no chance of getting through nor finding the right key to unlock it.

Our closest call was a time when we were challenged by a young patrol guy that kept up with us pretty well. After a few minutes of pursuit, I took the gamble of scaling a ladder that I had no idea where it would lead. When I popped the manhole cover, (no easy feat but my adrenaline was 100%), it was right in the middle of Lincoln Drive…in the middle of the road, near the Campus Lake. There was traffic and fortunately no cars were going overhead. And the four of us made a lightening quick getaway. Those were wild times.

1969-1970

In 1969, the day we graduated from Lincoln Junior High Penitentiary, we boys were MARKED prey. The Carbondale annual ritual of hazing brand new freshmen boys by the new juniors in HS boys began. It was like a combination of the "Hunger Games" movie series and "The Purge" …. everywhere you went you risked a car full of juniors pulling up next to you, kidnapping you into their cars-taking you hostage, and then, through the rite of passage, they'd shave your head. Their options were to A) shave off all your hair, B) give you a mohawk, C) the reverse-shave down the middle of your head-hence the circus clown look, or D) random hair cutting either checkerboard style or even more random. It was called "Welcome to Your High School Initiation". The "games" ended the first day of high school class.

And the boy victims fell into three categories: A) the wimps that hid out all summer, B) the boys that gladly turned themselves over to the juniors and enjoyed the experience of abuse, and C) those of us that ran like hell and avoided being caught at all costs. We ran and out foxed dozens of attempted kidnappings, because some of us were on the on the track team and all of us played sports every day, and also we all had vast experience of escaping capture (see steam tunnels above}.

It was towards the end of that summer, going into our freshman year, that a few of us finally met our fate. We were at Murdale shopping center, in the drug store reading the magazines (we often were kicked out after standing there at the magazine rack, reading for 30 or more minutes without buying anything), when the juniors burst through the door. Since the magazine rack was right next to the front door, we had to be fast......we ran to the back of the store, through the pharmacy, through the storage area, and out the back door. We made it about a half a mile, *almost* back to my house, when the car came screeching to a stop next to us, and they nabbed us. We were shaved on the spot. Chris was with me, and we got a random buzz shave. We were within two weeks of the cut off for this silly tradition, almost to the finish line, but we failed. About 70% of our class got shaved, and we all did the same thing; we went home and had our heads fully shaved clean. Girls got initiated too. A number of them got "lip-sticked', or had their hair put in some ridiculous hair style, but no hair removal.

Freshman year started at the brand new CCHS -EAST campus, out on the fringes of eastern C'dale. We were isolated, far away from everything, and all of us had to take buses to and from the school. Worse, we were separated from CCHS Central which had all the sophomore to senior students.

Weekends we went to Crazy Horse Billiards, Teen Town, or got ourselves invited to any upper classman party we could find. We started driving some of my friend's parent's car without parental permission. My friend Pat took his mom's car, while she was at work, and we went joy riding to Murphysboro and around for 3-4 hours and then he dropped us off. On the way back to SIU where his mom parked her car, the police pulled him over, as his mom had reported her car stolen, and arrested him. His mom was thoroughly ticked off but the police let him go.

1970-1972: The Final Years in Carbondale

Everything changed when we became Sophomores. We finally got to CCHS Central and despite leaving a brand-new building in CCHS-East, everyone preferred the old Central campus. We could walk to restaurants at lunch. We could walk home after football practice. We could even eat junk food at "the store". We were no longer in isolation.

Most importantly we were with three classes and not just one. In 1970, my friends Harry and Chris and I became special friends with three senior girls-all were very popular and a blast. They let us drive their cars even though we were months away from getting our license. We learned how to drive with standard transmission and using the clutch pedal. Loved going with them to the spillway at night. It was the best of times.

One time my friend Pat pulled up in front of our house in a 1946 sports coupe. Pat paid $75 for it. You had to stomp on this pump to get the car started. It was one step better than the Model T. It was hysterical to drive in it but it was short lived. The car lasted two weeks before he had to sell it for scrap.

So much was happening in our country in 1970. Racial tensions were high, Vietnam war protests were near their peak, Jimmy Hendricks and Janis Joplin died of overdoses, and riots-both race and war protests were still raging. There was national news from Carbondale as there was a Black Panther shootout with police in November. The Chicago Tribune's headlines about the event were enormous.... like font 72. Yet, race relationships in our high school were getting better and we started to become friends with many folks who three years earlier were strangers.

By junior year, 1971, we all had our car licenses, and started to expand our wings to all sections of Southern Illinois, including other towns, Crab Orchard Lake, the Spillway, Giant City, and beyond. Athletes, the hippies, the "Store Gang", and our brothers all started to really co-exists and enjoy and respect each other. We went to concerts out by Makanda and Giant City. We started going to concerts at SIU and the DuQuoin State Fair that included big bands... Cream, Bread, Steppenwolf, amongst many others.

The spillway was a favorite for many at CCHS. It was fun during the day and even better at night, as it was a major make-out hangout.

Another favorite place was the Sunset Drive In Theater, out on Old Rt 13. Sometimes we snuck people in the trunk in to save us money. They had classic movies like, "The Undertaker and His Pals". One of the girls I dated my junior year was Gitta, a transfer student from Germany. She was beautiful, and I was proud to take her to her first drive-in movie ever.

We were also able to sneak into some of the SIU happening nightclubs, like Merlin's. Merlin's changed names a few times, to the Gauntlet, and other management changes before it folded. I dated three girls my junior year and the parties we experienced were all a blast. The poor party sponsors-ALL had parents out of town, were all faced with massive clean-ups the next morning.

A life altering event occurred one early evening during the Vietnam riots in downtown Carbondale. Students were mostly congregated down on south Illinois Ave in the 710 Bookstore area, at the beginning of the SIU turf. I was a junior HS kid and was anti-hippie & pro Vietnam at that time. Come on-what was wrong with these people? They didn't believe in Nixon and the direction of our country? My brother in law Tim was head of the SIU student police chapter that patrolled the campus. His group, along with real police were holding back angry SIU students,

Then the defining moment occurred. There was a wall of screaming hippies and on the other side was a wall of people yelling at the hippie protesters…. six feet dividing us. I was with my brother Mike and his friend Gus. Then Gus got into the face of one of the protesters. Gus was a tough kid and he had his finger pointed in this guy's face. Then suddenly the hippie dude shoved him back, and then HE took the offensive, and was in Gus' face…screaming. I could see the hippie's spittle forming on Gus' face. He had Gus frozen as he screamed that his brother died six months earlier in Vietnam…. shot in the head. He was so livid that he was willing to have Gus kick his butt, but he didn't let up. His brother's death was his rage. Gus looked defeated- and not because of physicality, but because he understood.... just like Mike and I did, that that guy was right- *the light bulb went off.*

In our senior year, the National Guard used our high school parking lot for stationing their riot armored vehicles. We felt like we were at war. One night during the riots, my brother in law Tim-the head of SIU student security had a brick thrown into his "boys". He was taken to the hospital and it was not a minor injury. There were major riots going on. A guy laid down on the railroad tracks in protest and a train ran over him. This is all true. Life in Carbondale.

My parents moved to a suburb of Detroit in December and I insisted that I spend my senior year in Carbondale and not move to a new school for my final six months. They relented. I moved in with my sister Nancy and her baby Amy, into Evergreen Terrace, on the edge of SIU. It was a wonderful short-lived experience but by February, Nancy and Amy were off to Tacoma WA to join Tim in the military and so I was passed off to my brother Mike and his wife Marilyn who lived in a tiny apt on S. Hays Street, just off a Cherry. It was in the SIU footprint, as all neighbors were students and the campus was right next door.

This apartment had to be 400 square feet and I slept on a pull-out couch. This changed quickly as Marilyn was pregnant and they all moved into her parents' home. So here I was, a senior in high school, living on my own. I could walk to CCHS, a short distance, and got around with the help of my girlfriend's car. Jan Carr was a saint. And my best buddy DeWayne carted my butt around a lot too.

Despite living by myself, I only missed one day of high school my senior year. I got strep throat. When I went to school the following day, the principal's assistant insisted I have an excused absence from my parents. I explained to her that they lived in Detroit and that wouldn't work. She called over the principal, Mr. Black. He too demanded an excuse from my legal guardian. This was like a comedy skit.... I explained to both of them that I WAS the legal guardian (I was 18 too). They stared at me, not knowing what to do, so I grabbed the pad and wrote on it "Please excuse Bill Byrne from school. He had strep throat. Signed, Bill Byrne". Mr. Black looked at me, grabbed the note, and stormed away. He didn't like me that day.

I had promised my parents that I'd move up to Detroit upon graduation. I lived by myself, had a beautiful girlfriend, and incredible friends. And actually, pretty good grades. I was the high school Dial yearbook sports editor both junior and senior year. DeWayne and I had a blast and along with many other friends, we partied on weekends but took school seriously.

There were actual riots outside of my apt complex on Hays St., tear gas and all. People pounded on my door; I could smell the tear gas coming through the doorway. My buddy DeWayne showed up, blown away by what was going on.

This was high school and my last days of living in Carbondale. Upon graduation.... that final night, we had a party of about 4 couples in my shoebox apartment, played music, and danced in tight quarters. It was a final goodbye, really, to all my friends, to my high school, and to Carbondale.

Postcript: My parents came down from Michigan for my graduation. The next day, I drove back with them, moving away from Carbondale for good. These were some of the most memorable years of my life.

NEW GIRL FROM FLORIDA WHO DRIVES A HEARSE

By, Louise Tolle Huffman

Arriving in Carbondale that summer of 1967 was not my choice. I mean who would choose to move for their junior year in high school? It would be my 3rd school in 3 years, a strange experience since I had not only grown up in St. Petersburg, FL, but lived within a 4 block radius from 9 weeks to 13 years old—suddenly moving around was not in my plans.

Regardless, I wanted to make the best of it. Thanks to Azile Winn (Sherry's mom), Sherry, Mary Lewis and Nancy Vogler (in her adorable pink Mustang convertible) were forced to show up at my house the day before school to "meet the new girl." Truly, I will always be grateful for those introductions which made going to the new school a bit easier with some familiar faces to look for—and as I soon learned, most Terriers were open and friendly.

But…there was another big hurdle to overcome before I would find a place in the class of '69.

CCHS was in the midst of some big changes that year—U School and CCHS were forced to become one entity. I found that students from CCHS assumed I was from USchool, and Ulies, assumed I was from CCHS—it was hard to break into the groups and get noticed. I finally announced in one of my first classes that I wasn't from any of the schools—I was new.

That helped, but it also helped that my car got me noticed—I was quickly identified as "the girl from Florida who drives a hearse!" My dad always bought used cars—but he felt that if he bought Cadillacs they would last longer. In this case he was right! The car was 'born' the same year as most of the class of '69—in 1951-- and it lived at my house until I was almost 20 years old. He had bought a Cadillac limousine that had been used as a funeral home limo that took families (NOT dead bodies!) to funerals. Truth is, it wasn't a hearse, but truth wasn't as important as its value as a catalyst for meeting people! On the whole, it was a great old car with lots of personality, but it also had a few famous "fails."

One night, I was driving a group of girls around when the brakes suddenly were gone. We coasted down the hill on Grand Ave. Hearts were pounding as we shot across traffic on Wall St. and ended safely coasting uphill to a stop at the gas station that used to be on that corner. On another day, the U-joint broke, and the car just stopped dead on Main St. in front of the hospital. I thought it had finally died for good, but again, good mechanics fixed it.

The "hearse" spent many a night driving through the McDonald's parking lot looking for the boys, and driving by friends' houses and honking—usually filled with up to a dozen passengers with the jump seats pulled out. Remember the days when everyone threw in a quarter to cover gas for the night? We also ran out to lunch, and IF we didn't cross the tracks to IV's, we were *almost* always on time getting back to school.

I remember during the summer '68, I was driving on Route 13 toward Murphysboro to a yearbook committee meeting. The car suddenly had a violent shimmy to the left and then back to the right. I thought, "good grief—is the U-joint going out again?" When I arrived at the house for the meeting, everyone was agitated and excited—Southern Illinois had just experienced a 5.4 Richter Scale earthquake. I patted the hearse and thanked her for great shock absorbers that allowed my earthquake experience to just be a shimmy!

At the time of moving to Illinois and leaving my lifelong Florida friends, I would not have said it was a good thing. In retrospect, I know I was so very lucky to have moved to such a special place as Carbondale where the student body was open and accepting of new people moving in. I was able to develop great friendships that have endured for a lifetime and make me excited to return to our reunion 50 years later.

PLAYIN' THE GAME...

By Eric Beyer

"I'll bet I can jump farther out on that branch than you..."

He was right. When I tried to jump and grab farther out I missed, fell, and broke my arm. I never could beat my brother at games, especially in that summer before third grade. We had just moved to Carbondale. Knowing nobody else, naturally we played together. I tried to compete with him even though he was (and still is) 3-and-a-half years older. Good humility lessons.

When the new kid showed up at Brush for third grade with a broken arm in a cast... well, that was an attention-getter this kid really didn't want. When you want to fit in it doesn't help to stand out like that. Then, in one of our playground games of chase I rounded a corner at full speed and head-butted Scotty Williams giving him a minor concussion (and me a minor lump). His Mom was surprised when she came to get him – apparently he had a reputation as the hard-headed kid in the family. Go figure. On top of it all, in New Jersey (where we moved from) they taught cursive in third grade. Here it was taught in second grade. So, this broken-armed, iron-skulled, behind-the-writing-curve newcomer didn't fit in all that well.

In those days and the years that followed sports were key for guys to fit in. Especially the All American game of baseball. Whether it was sandlot games in the vacant fields near the Food Shop by Van Horn's house or the organized youth little league – this was my chance. Joining wiffle ball games with Beastie, Van Horn, Westberg, and the rest of the

Cherry-Forest-Schwartz neighborhood gang could have been my ticket. Alas, too bad my baseball/wiffle ball skills were mediocre at best. However I was passable at the Wolfman and Kick-the-can games we played until the street lights came on. Ultimately playin' the games led to hanging out with Westberg on his back porch drinking cokes and having burping contests after he'd waxed my butt shooting hoops in his driveway. Nothing but class!

Well, Brush led to Winkler led to U School. Different kids and games each time. It helped to have an athletic older brother leading the way. As a freshman at U School of course I went out for football, following in his footsteps. I vividly remember a one-on-one tackling drill where I was steamrolled by a Senior running back. That one hurt, both physically and emotionally. As luck would have it our coaches were first rate. They taught us the fundamentals and emphasized teamwork. I even got to play in a varsity game and by following my blocking (I was too small to be seen behind them) got to score a touchdown. On the JV squad I got the opportunity to start as QB. I found that football provided a real feeling of being an accepted part of a group of peers – a team. So I worked hard at weight lifting and running so I'd be in shape to play. I also worked at learning the fundamentals of blocking, juking, tackling, following blockers, and taking hand-offs. These were critical skills for a little guy like me in order to survive and succeed.

Then it happened – the University decided to close U school. Wouldn't you know it? The close date would be at the end of my Junior year. Was I ready to graduate a year early and go off to college? No way. So I transferred to CCHS for my Junior and Senior years. Talk about jumping from the little pond into the big lake. I knew most all my classmates at U School and lots of kids in the upper classes too. At CCHS there were all the different clicks – the jocks, the brains, the artsy-types, the cheerleaders, the store-gangers, etc. And now the Uoolies had to mix and mingle as best they could. Where would I fit in? Well, maybe football? Given my size and skills the best match would have been the offensive backfield. But those positions were well-filled by the Seniors and back-filled by the up-and-coming guys who had played the previous year in JV. It must have been a challenge for the coaches to figure out what to do with me. But they found a support role that was right for me.

There was a different game at CCHS being played that had an unexpectedly large role in inclusion/fitting-in. *Paddles. Pumpkin-chucker. Nose & toes. Horn Dog. Dooba-baby.* Being tagged with a nickname was a sign of acceptance. I caught my *Perhaps .009* nickname (later shortened to just *Perhaps* or *double-oh-nine*) from LeFevre based on an answer I gave in our physics class. On the surface it was a bit of a slam and a tease, but getting it was kind of cool. LeFevre was particularly adept at tagging guys.

Senior year football is still a blur for me. Unlike LeFevre who 30 years later could give a detailed play-by-play of the Cahokia game including descriptions of the cops patrolling the stands, I don't remember many details. I do remember a great set of coaches. Curiously, I mostly recall my screw-ups like dropped punts and losing a fumble in the mud of the Mount Vernon game. Why is it those stick out in my memories? Fortunately I have newspaper clippings from the school paper and the Southern Illinoisan to supplement my failing memory. Regardless, those guys are the brotherhood with whom I grew up and I appreciate and value them to this day. It was a privilege and an honor to be a part of all that team.

Carbondale was an unusual place to grow up in back in those days. A mixture of socioeconomic classes with a university student population the same size as the town. Us HS kids were influenced by the drugs and alcohol culture of the college kids. It was a racially segregated community struggling with integration. All this was against the backdrop of the Vietnam war, the draft, and the protests. Growing up then probably prepared us for surviving the changes and struggles our country has endured over these last 50 years. Certainly my experiences shaped the person I have become. Especially the games we played.

COUNTRY BOY: LAST OF A BREED

By Russ Mayer

I wouldn't trade my childhood with anyone I know! It's been said "It's not a sin to be poor but it sure is unhandy." I would know.

I consider it a privilege to have grown up in the 50s and 60s in Southern Illinois. Some experiences are as such to truly "get it" you would have had to have been there. My family moved to the area in 1953 when I was only three years old. Dad bought 80 acres of land and an old, run down two-story farmhouse from my great-grandfather Mr. Alva Nance. Alva had 13 children and rented the old farmhouse to his son, James, who had 10 children. Because of all the activity with so many kids, the house came with a four-foot wide bare ground path all the way around the house. Grass couldn't grow there for years.

In the early days, indoor plumbing was still a few years away. We ran out to the well by the barn where we manually had to turn the crank on the pump, filling a two and a half gallon bucket. Then we had to carry the bucket back to the house. The barn and water pump were almost fifty yards from the back door of the old farm house! Fortunately, my mother was a woman of vision. I can vividly remember her saying to my dad "Bob, if I just had running water I would never ask for anything else." Now, when a woman says something like that you better perk up and get to work. So the digging began. The ditch was dug, the water pipe laid, and we had running water to the old farmhouse. It should come as no surprise, considering we didn't even have running water for a long time, that the heating system lacked a little to be desired.

I remember those cold mornings, gathering close to the front feed coal stove that sat in the middle room. A kitchen was to one side, the bedroom on the other. My brothers and I slept upstairs. Our bedroom was one big open room with a window on each end. In the middle was a heater vent that was directly above the morning coal burner. The only heat that reached us was what came through that small, one-foot, heat vent. Needless to say it didn't take long for us three boys to get downstairs and gather around the coal stove.

My two brothers and I all slept in the same bed. It really benefited us during the winter. Three can stay a lot warmer than one! Not so surprisingly, as we grew older the bed seemed to get smaller. King and queen size beds weren't really popular yet, so I grew accustomed to sleeping with a leg, an arm, or even my head hanging off the mattress. It took several years of sleeping alone before I could sleep without a body part dangling off the edge of the bed.

The coal burning stove required a seemingly never ending supply of coal. There was always a full bucket of coal at the foot of the burner. My younger brother, Bobby, and I made good use of the coal before it was put into the stove. We would entertain ourselves for hours playing with small plastic cowboy and Indian figures. The chunks of coal were perfect rocks for our men to hide behind. As strange as it may seem, we truly enjoyed playing with the coal, letting our imaginations run wild. The only downfall was how messy we were afterwards. That's where the #2 galvanized wash tub came into use. Every Saturday night (whether we needed it or not) we took turns taking a bath in the wash tub. The water was heated on the coal stove. After the bath, the water was carried and dumped outside. Even after we had running water into the house there was no plumbing to carry it away. A five gallon bucket sat under the kitchen sink to catch the dishwater. When it was full, we carried it outside and emptied it. Since plumbing was nonexistent in my home, an outhouse was a necessity. And did we have a good one! It was a two-holer with a crescent moon cut in the door. And the door had a lock on it! Things were looking up.

One of our favorite pastimes in the summer months was swimming. Oh how we loved to go swimming. But there was a price to pay. When my mom made a rule she stuck to it! "If you boys want to go swimming, you must first work in the garden." So that's exactly what we did.

Mom taught us boys how to swim in a pond that dad had dug for the cows. Back then bulldozer work was pretty reasonable. Dad paid $80 to have the pond dug. We even had a water slide! Actually, it was more like a mudslide. We would throw water up on the bank to make it slick.

Then all that we needed was a little run. When you hit the slide you would zoom down into the murky water. We had to take a shower outside with a water hose to get mud from our body and out of our hair.

Before we were able to get a license, our main mode of transportation was a bicycle. You had to be sixteen years old to drive, but you could ride a bicycle at any age as long as you could reach the pedals. Poplar Camp Hill was always a challenge to ride your bicycle up, but a real adventure to ride down. What is now the beach at Cedar Lake used to be where Poplar Camp Road crossed Poplar Camp Creek. It was a one lane, wooden bridge that crossed the creek. Our neighbors, the Richard boys, lived half way up the south side of Poplar Camp hill.

One fateful day we were southbound, going down the long gradual sloping gravel road that led to the bottom of the hill. There were four of us on one bicycle. I was sitting on the crossbar that attaches the handlebars to the seat. Roger was on the seat and had control of the bike. His younger brother and my younger brother were on the luggage rack. Four people on one bicycle is not a good idea. Riding was usually better than walking, but not on that particular day. The closer we got to the bottom of the hill, the faster we were going. The bicycle began to wobble. My foot got caught between the fender and the downtube. Roger lost control. The bike lurched in the deep gravel in the middle of the road, sending us boys flying ahead of the bike.

When I hit the gravel road, I had three boys on top of me. We were all mangled together and instantly sore. Since I was up front, I received the blunt force. Blood was streaming down from my forehead and dripping from my chin. I couldn't even see, so much blood was pouring from the wounds above my brow. To this day most of my family believes I still have rocks in my head. I'm certain that was the first of many head concussions to come. I have lost track of how many concussions I have had but I remember they came from bicycles, car crashes, horses (that put me in the hospital for 5 days once!), falling from trees, and football.

How I loved football.

As time went by, things began to slowly change. After graduating from 8th grade it was time to think about high school. Mostly, time to think about football. My desire to play football helped me overcome a lot of fear and apprehension about moving up to the "big school." Not only did I have to overcome the fear of the unknown, but also the reality that I lived approximately 8 miles south of Carbondale. As a freshman without a driver's license or any form of transportation, that quickly became a problem. But I was willing to do anything. I wanted to play football. I *had* to play football. So I often hitchhiked to make it happen.

*Russ Mayer was the starting fullback on the 1967
All Conference Terrier Football Team*

After I turned 16 and got my driver's license, getting around got easier. But my life was far from easy.

Sometimes life throws you a curve. When that happens you have to stay in the batter's box and knock it out of the park. I got married on May 11th, 1966 to my longtime girlfriend Joyce "Squeaky" Hill. In case you're wondering, yes we are still married 53 years later. Now that I was married with a family, I had all the responsibility of a full blown adult, but still had two years of high school left to get under my belt and lots of football practices. Did I mention I loved to play football? Thankfully, I was 16 with a license. I didn't need to hitchhike anymore. But I needed a vehicle.

It was two toned, black and rust. A standard shift 1955 Plymouth with mermaid decals on the fenders and on the inside dash. My first car. I bought it in 1966 from Tex Roy Rogers Richards, the same neighbor boy who wrecked the bicycle with me on Poplar Camp hill years earlier. I paid $35.00 cash for that nice ride. The starter was bad on it, but the compression in the motor was so low I just had to get it rolling a little bit, jump in and pop the clutch. It would start right up. The first time I discovered this way of starting my car was a little unusual. It was completely by chance. I was stuck in the middle of the road, the car was dead and I couldn't do anything about it. Thankfully my brother-in-law was working his horse nearby and came by to help me. He put a rope around the front bumper and got me moving. I popped the clutch and —

ah ha! — she started right up. From then on I parked on a slight decline when I could. No worries. If I could get rolling, she would start!

One afternoon in 1967, I was watching television with my father-in-law. A Chevy commercial came on. A sleek, beautiful vehicle appeared on the screen. They called it a Camaro. It was love at first sight! I casually mentioned to my father-in-law how much I would love to have a car like that. I wasn't even thinking as I said it. Just a young boy dreaming about a

passing fancy. At that time I headed to football practice as soon as that last school bell rang and to work directly after. I worked at the DX service station on the corner of route 13 and University Avenue in Carbondale.

Back then we had what we called "full service" gas stations. An attendant would pump the gas for you, wash your windshield, and check your tires and oil if needed. I was working in the grease rack when the bell rang to let me know someone was needing gas. When I looked up, I could see the front end of a canary yellow car with black pinstripes waiting for my service. It was a Camaro! And even more shocking than that — my wife was behind the wheel! It was the first Camaro I saw up close and personal and somehow my wife was driving it! If it had been any other woman I would have assumed she had stolen it! But not my Joyce. She was — and still is — an honest, God-fearing gal that would never steal a car, but there she was in the driver's seat. Her dad had gone down to Jim Pearl's Chevrolet in Vienna and bought a brand new Chevy Camaro because I mentioned how much I would love to have a car like that. My father-in-law really liked me. I'm honestly not sure why. Just glad he did! He was willing to take a chance on me. I hasten to add that I made all the payments. It was not a gift. He signed the paperwork. I didn't have "bad" credit, I didn't have *any* credit. So I made the loop from a 1955 Plymouth that had seen better days to a brand new, never been used, 1967 Chevy Camaro all in one short year!

The last two years at CCHS were somewhat a blur. Going to school full time and working every night until 10:00 pm, plus twelve to fourteen hours on the weekend, keeps a guy fairly busy. It was especially rough during football season. School, practice, and then work.

Except Friday nights under the lights.

I knew how important it was to have a high school diploma. My education almost got derailed once because of a fight. Fighting at school for any reason was not tolerated and rightly so. The price you paid for fighting at school was automatic three-day suspension. Sometimes you just have to stand up for what's right regardless of the consequences. The young man I fought any myself both got "kicked out" of school for three days. I have often been asked who won the fight? Nobody wins a fight like that. Lessons can be learned. I think the best lesson to learn is to avoid fighting if at all possible.

The somewhat embarrassing part of being suspended from school was that my mother had to come to school to get me back in. That in itself was not so bad, but I was married and had a year and a half old daughter. But mamma got me back in school. Mr. Diamond, the former agriculture teacher, was the acting truant officer at the time. In the remarks as to the reason for the absence, he wrote "fist-a-cuffs." I still have that blue slip stored away somewhere after all these years.

It would have been so easy for me to drop out once I was expelled. I was plain exhausted.

Honestly, it seemed almost more appealing to be another dropout rather than to continue being bone tired every day. But somehow I persevered. I knew how important it was to have a high school diploma and I wasn't willing to give up yet. Plus, there was football to think of. My friend John Oliver really helped me get through the last two years. John and I had most of our classes together. So, like a zombie, I followed John from one class to the next. I would have been a high school drop out if it hadn't been for John and my desire to play football. Did I mention how much I loved football? I walked across the stage, shook the principal's hand and received my diploma. Thank you John and the Carbondale Terriers football team for making that happen.

Sometimes life can get a little difficult, but with faith, patience, and perseverance, God will see you through. My nearly two-year-old daughter, Tammy Lynn, attended my high school graduation. Now let that sink in for a minute. I thank God and my wife for standing beside me to make my life what it is today. Thank God I'm a country boy! Last of a breed!

A TRIBUTE TO COACH WALT MOORE

By Dr. Mike Given, Ph.D.

From An Email to Floyd Debow and Bob Pankey:

Thank you so much for the note about Coach Moore, and thanks to Floyd and Bob for their memories. I hadn't heard the news and even though I'm saddened, I feel lucky to have learned some important lessons from Coach Moore. He was also our freshman football and JV basketball coach and the first black teacher I ever had. It was a very bad time in America in terms of racial divisions, but Coach Moore did not allow race to become a factor in our practices, during games, or even on the buses and restaurants we shared on our road trips. When there were problems-and of course there were problems with teen-age jocks-Coach dealt with us as individuals, not as black or white kids.

On the day he was hired to replace Mr. John Cherry, Coach Moore actually called me at home to tell me the news. How many coaches would call a 16-year old student to share such a moment? Unfortunately, by the end of our senior season, I had turned sour. I didn't feel like I was getting enough playing time and so I sulked and pouted, getting increasingly lazy in practice and going through the motions when he did put me into a game. Before the regional tournament he called me aside and told me that I would not get to dress or play in the tournament, but I could continue to practice and if we won the tournament, I could return for the sectionals. But I was a jackass and instead decided to quit. I walked out and missed my chance to participate with my friends in the most important part of the season. The important thing was that Coach Moore gave me the choice. He didn't make the decision for me but allowed me to make this important decision. Even though I made the wrong decision, he never coerced me or made our discussion public. In fact, at our senior banquet, he not only presented me with a varsity letter for the season, he very graciously mentioned that I was accepting a football scholarship to Western Illinois (his alma mater where he later became head basketball coach) and wished me good luck.

Many years later I returned to Carbondale to attend graduate school. One day I was walking across a parking lot to my office at SIU when I saw Coach Moore getting out of a state car. I walked up to him and introduced myself because I didn't think he would remember me after all those years. Coach Moore was, by that time, an Athletic Administrator at Western Illinois University and was in Carbondale for a conference meeting of some sort. We stood in the parking lot and talked for a long time and I finally got a chance to apologize for my adolescent behaviors and tell him how much his lessons had meant to me in my life after CCHS. He smiled as I had seen him smile so many times, and it was as if all those years and the bad times had never intervened..

I was preparing for my British Literature class today when I got the news that Walt Moore had passed away. That day we were to be discussing Wordsworth's Ode: Intimations of Immortality. There are a few lines that I think are fitting as we look back at those times and remember Walt Moore.

What though the radiance which was once so bright
Be now for ever taken from my sight,
Though nothing can bring back the hour
Of splendor in the grass, of glory in the flower We will grieve not, rather find
Strength in what remains behind;
In the primal sympathy
Which having been must ever be;
In the soothing thoughts that spring
Out of human suffering;
In the faith that looks through death,
In years that bring the philosophic mind.

1933 - 2004

Obituary By Jeremy Hall

Ray Shelton, like many of his classmates, was in awe of Walt
Moore when the Mt. Vernon Rams basketball star walked the halls of the
high school in the late 1940s and early 50s. But when he shared a
physical education class with Moore and saw him step aside to let others
have a turn at bat, or serve as an umpire to make room for one more
participant, Shelton gained a deeper appreciation for the standout athlete.

He was an outstanding basketball player, said Shelton, a 1952
graduate of Mt. Vernon Township High School. But he was a fine
gentleman, too. He was well-respected.

Moore, 71, died early Wednesday morning at McDonough District
Hospital in Macomb. Moore was a starting guard on the Rams, back-to-
back state championship team that finished the 1949-50 season
undefeated. He was a first-team all-state selection three times.

Walter was highly respected, said Max Hooper, a Rams teammate of
Moore. (He was) just a true friend. I,m going to miss him. Hooper said
he spoke with Moore about a week-and-a-half ago. "I was going to go up
and see him, and he talked me out of it," Hooper said. "Walt was a good,
close friend and a fine man, added. John Riley, another member of the
championship teams. "There were a lot of times during the season we
were completely inseparable, and that was both on and off of the court."
Teammate Eddie King recalls playing against Moore when the two were
on different grade-school teams. "He was a year younger than I,‰ said
King. We played them in the Casey tournament, and I had to guard Walt
at that time. He was one of the quickest guys I ever played against."
Later, when King was a high school sophomore, he sought advice from

Moore when the freshman had made the varsity squad. "I was really challenged by Walt,‰ King said." He told me, "You,ve just got to keep working." He and I became very close friends. We were roommates at the state tournament. I tried to persuade him to come to Bradley with me. Instead, Moore attended the University of Illinois and Tennessee State University before graduating from Western Illinois with a degree in physical education.

He started at forward for the No. 2 ranked Western Illinois University basketball team in 1957; he was selected to the Little All-American team that same year. Moore taught and coached at Carbondale Central High School, Carbondale Attucks High School and Macomb High School. In 1968, he was named Coach of the Year by the Evansville (Ind.) Courier, Southern Illinois Coaches Association and WJPF Radio. Two years later, Carbondale declared June 20, 1970, as Walt Moore Day. The Walt Moore Trophy is presented each year to the most outstanding basketball player at Carbondale Community High School. Moore worked as an assistant coach at Western Illinois from 1970-73 before serving as head coach for the Leathernecks from 1973-77. Later, he worked as an admissions counselor at the school. Additionally, he served in the U.S. Army from 1952-53. In Mt. Vernon, Moore will be remembered for his lifetime of success that started here. "He was someone people could look up to," said Larry Goldman of Dix, "Growing up in Mt. Vernon, he was the first basketball player I heard of, said WMIX basketball announcer Dave Farley. "I knew there was something special about him." Circuit Judge Terry Gamber, a former Rams star himself, said he will cherish a visit he had with Moore during his senior year at Western Illinois. Gamber,s father was in charge of the Mt. Vernon Kiwanis basketball banquet that year and arranged for Moore to speak with his son while he was in town. "I was 12 years old, Gamber said. "It was really neat. What I remember is he was such a soft-spoken, nice guy. Moore is the second player from the 1949-50 team to die recently; Bobby Brown died earlier this spring, and that has been hard for a group that Riley said came through Mt. Vernon in an era that produced a tight group of classmates. "The fact of the matter is, we became a very close-knit group, he said. There was a special closeness, a special feeling, that over the years never diminished. Moore was laid to rest at Memorial Gardens, Mt. Vernon.

DANCING THE SHUFFLE BALL CHANGE

By Dr. Donna L. Manering

I was a transplant. A term that was more meaningful in the 1960s than it is now in times of global awareness and migration. As a young girl, my experiences in a small rural southern Illinois town were probably similar to those of kids growing up in Carbondale. Catching fireflies, riding bikes, chatting with friends, swimming in pools and ponds and exploring the neighborhood provided lasting memories for many of us born in the 1950s. My dream of dancing one day kept my parents busy and their billfolds empty. Dancing would later play somewhat of a role in my life choices.

During the elementary years, I attended a small parochial school where my class consisted of twelve girls and two boys-people I had known from the very beginning. The entire class was our clique. With fourteen in a class and nuns in control of the school, the students found various ways to explore their independence. I recall a particular antic that is cringe worthy. One male student became skilled at climbing out the window of the second story building and walking on the ledge around the building while the rest of the class cheered. Obviously, there was no authority figure present at the time. As an educator, it is difficult to believe what we did in those days and my willingness to participate!

I never could quite understand some things that occurred during those days. The practice of getting under our desks in a duck and cover maneuver seemed interesting and a bit frightening. The warning of a nuclear attack was never fully explained to the students. All we knew was that it could be awful and that we needed to be prepared and that getting under our desks would save us. Hmmmm....

There was a Dairy Queen in our small town but it wasn't the franchised kind. This DQ served things like hot tamales, hamburgers and green river drinks. Students often walked from the school to the DQ for lunch and sometimes those lunches ended up as afternoon snacks eaten under the lift top desks in the classroom. Luckily, the nuns either ignored the munching or didn't notice. That was often the highlight of the day!

During the 1950s and 60s in the absence of cell phones, there were other ways to stay connected and to socialize. Since the town was small and that era seemed safer, the best way to connect was through bike riding. Before the end of the school day, neighborhood kids would decide where and when to meet and that was the plan. The younger kids would put clothespins and a piece of cardboard into the spokes of the bike tire to produce a motor like sound. Then they could fly down the hills and sound very imposing. Only a disciplinary action from one of the parents could disrupt the evening's activities. Riding, gossiping and generally feeling free could last until dark or dinnertime.

When we weren't outside we were watching TV which was very limited in time and in selection. The Mouseketeers were to be admired and emulated but the Lone Ranger was one of my favorites. I would often sit on a toy saddle and ride along with the Lone Ranger and Tonto. That is a secret I haven't shared with many. A cowgirl skirt and boots were my favorite attire in those days.

Prank calls could be made when parents weren't listening. Calling a random number and asking, "Is your refrigerator running?" was a favorite. The recipient would respond "Yes" which offered the opportunity to say "Then you better go chase it!" Seemed funny at the time. Phone calls have gotten more sinister recently and kids have found other ways to prank.

4-H played an important role for those in the rural community. The 4-H leader was invested in keeping kids involved and there were many activities and projects if one chose to participate. Most students didn't live on farms but had access to animals if that was of interest. Horses were one of my projects but I could also demonstrate how to make various foods or give oral presentations on a variety of topics. The year that I demonstrated the fine art of making stuffed pork chops at the Illinois State Fair, my family and friends nearly overdosed on pork after my numerous rehearsals! Another activity was "Share the Fun" where a group of 4-H'ers performed a play or musical. The songs from "Oklahoma" still haunt me. 4-H provided a lot of fun but was also instrumental in shaping children from our town to be leaders and not to be fearful of displaying their talents.

When my parents bought a business in Carbondale, I was thrilled to be moving to the "big city" and to branch out from the parochial days. To deny that it was initially a culture shock would be disingenuous. A CCHS student who was a friend of a friend was supposed to be a support for me but I quickly discovered that she wasn't all that interested in introducing me or showing me around, so I was on my own!

Walking onto the CCHS campus that first day and seeing so many unfamiliar faces was a bit daunting. I recall the front lawn and sidewalk of the school being crowded and noisy that day. Walk onto a campus and stand around and listen to people chatting and being so excited about the beginning of a school year and plop! there you are in the middle with no one to recognize or acknowledge your existence. What an unusual situation for a young fourteen-year-old who had only experienced a small town rural school where she was known by everyone.

Not many specifics come to mind about the first days and weeks of school after that. Initially, I was "friended" by a young lady who I soon discovered had a lot more personal experiences with life than I had. She was a bit older and had an even older boyfriend. She took me under her care and I was grateful for that but often perplexed by the differences between us. During that time I remember thinking that I was merely a little girl plunked into a school with students much more advanced in their personal lives than I was. My strict parochial background provided solid academics but a socially isolated environment.

Months later a few of the freshmen girls approached me and as we talked I realized that they were more compatible with my maturity level. They enjoyed boys their own age, clothes, shoes and hanging out. They were involved in school activities and enjoyed their studies and making decent grades. They didn't seem to smoke or drink (too much) and enjoyed slumber parties and just being with friends. They were my kind of people.

During my freshman year I was oblivious to segregation, integration and anything in between. I grew up in a community where everyone seemed very much alike. I recall that we had one black family in the town and the parents and children were welcomed but probably not well known by many of the other families. Coming to Carbondale in 1965, I didn't realize that the high schools were just integrated. I found it exciting and fulfilling to meet people from different backgrounds with varying ideas. As I put on my little blue romper and prepared for PE, getting to play ball or walk around the track while chatting with classmates became one of my favorite classes! Well, I enjoyed English,

Math and French with Madame Treece, but students didn't get a chance to chat as much as in PE.

I loved and still love being a student and learning. I loved Science in high school but I especially loved Mr. Borger. He was young and handsome and kind of quiet but someone that I found to be inspiring. Mr. Borger was the homeroom teacher during my sophomore year. The school decided to have a talent show and someone from the homeroom needed to perform. Somehow Mr. Borger (and perhaps some of the students) found out that I had dancing experience. Mr. Borger asked me to perform during the talent show and to represent the homeroom. I couldn't refuse a request from this teacher and so I said that I would do it. During the month before the talent show I contemplated various ways to break a leg, a foot or to somehow become incapacitated. I had made friends but I didn't feel comfortable performing in front of the entire school in a dance costume. Also, the boys in my class tended to make fun of people who did anything different or just anything and still feeling like a "new girl" I couldn't picture getting on that stage and suffering the catcalls and humiliation that might be forthcoming from the bullies. I wasn't able to get sick or break a leg or do anything to stall my performance and the show went on. I don't remember the specifics but I know that I made it and lived through it. Also, several years later when I started dating my husband to be, he shared that he recalled me dancing and that he was somewhat "impressed". You never know how things are perceived by others! Ha!

Don't judge a book by its cover would not describe the attitude of most high schoolers and it didn't in the 60s. Bass Weejuns and wooden box Collins purses were all important in making a look complete. The most popular Weejuns had tassels and were cordovan color and needed to be highly polished. The box purse typically had jewels glued on to enhance an animal or flower design. The more jewels, the more costly the purse. Pair those with a short, short jumper and tights and you were set. The dress length seemed risqué then but nothing compared to the scanty outfits of today. A friend still has her high school Weejuns and my closet still holds two box purses and a jumper. The purses still fit!

Living in a university town provided interesting opportunities for meeting college kids-guys! Unknown to our parents some of the class of '69 females were intrigued by college boys. The guys were minimally intrigued with the girls but mostly excited about having townies with cars. The relationships were typically short-termed and not all that interesting.

One of my best summers was probably that of my junior year. The freedom of a car and fewer restrictions from parents allowed some of us to enjoy places outside of Carbondale. Some of the junior class girls were co-conspirators in those activities. The strip mine north of town and a float gave us many hours of enjoyment and sun. Put a little iodine into some baby oil to accelerate a tan and we were set. The junior year probably damaged my skin more than any other. The sunspots that I am continually trying to find lotions to camouflage are a testament to how tan we were that year!

The females of the class of '69 might be envious of the opportunities available to girls in 2019. Although it is often noted that the expansion of women's rights began in the 60s, there were still a lot of limitations for girls graduating in 1969. I was recently asked what sports I was involved in while attending high school. If there was an opportunity to be involved in sports it was unknown to me. That is a striking difference with today's teenage females who are provided a plethora of selections. Miss Cox and Mrs. Buzbee tried to involve girls in PE class in a variety of activities but hair, clothing and social events often dominated the hour. Career selection seemed to be somewhat limited as well. When it was time to select a major for college, many graduates of our class chose to teach. Although it is an honorable profession, some of us that are talented in math or science or other areas didn't explore beyond that of imparting our wisdom to others in a classroom. These are positive changes from the good old days!

My profession has generally been education along with serving as a director for a labor union. One year life took me to a small, rural school in southern Illinois to serve as a high school principal. Basically, my only experience with high school was being a high school student so the position was a challenge but one that I totally embraced. I felt empathy for the students in that high school and how it felt to walk onto a campus where either you didn't know anyone or you felt "left out". My own experiences as a high schooler turned out to be positive and left me with many good memories but also with compassion and understanding of all students. I still remember how one of the prettiest and smartest girls in the high school suffered throughout that year. One would not typically expect that someone of that caliber would sometimes feel out of place, bullied or encounter any of the other negative situations that can occur at that stage of life, but she did! So did the student that wasn't as handsome or as bright. I probably wasn't as analytical in my younger days but now I understand how important it is to be accepted and especially in the high school years to be part of "the group" or any group.

At the age of 68, I find that specific memories of high school years are somewhat blurred. Happily, I am in contact with several high school friends. One friend and I talk on the phone daily with our cell phones on speaker so that we can go about our daily activities. Not sure what we discuss but it is always of importance. Sometimes we talk for hours. Another friend is one who visits Carbondale on a regular basis and lunch and chatting are often on the agenda. A renewed friend from high school and I enjoy bocce and wine with friends on a regular basis. We all understand that although our pasts didn't make or break us we were definitely shaped by our high school days.

I regret that I didn't journal during those years. What fun and what great insight it would be to read the thoughts of that 14-18-year-old girl! I encourage my grandchildren to journal, but like me, they don't take the time to jot down their daily activities and thoughts.

I married and had children at a young age-a decision I would not necessarily encourage for teenagers today but something that worked for me. I am a fairly rare commodity since I went to high school in Carbondale and remained during my adult life. Marrying a guy from Carbondale who didn't want to leave settled that question. Both of our sons attended the same high school as we did. The education that all four of us received at CCHS was solid and shaped us for integrating into the wider world both academically and socially.

I don't recall the dance routine or the outfit from that fated talent show but I can still remember some of the basic dance steps and in a private moment might break into a little soft shoe or do a quick shuffle ball change. My goal is to keep dancing-figuratively speaking!

MAKANDA COUNTRY MOUSE

By Connie Childers Cooley

Hel-looo…I called loudly out of the 3- inch wire opening. Naked bodies flashed by the window. The City of Carbondale had blocked off Illinois Avenue to allow for streaking along the strip. As the night grew later, and with greater alcohol consumption, the streakers grew braver. Walking up to the window of Dairy Queen, one said, "I will have a chocolate Sunday," "I'll have a 10-cent cone," said another. Shrieks of laughter could be heard when one man proclaimed, "I don't have any place to put my change!" Hmm, diverting my eyes to only look at his face, I wonder where he had been keeping the dollar bill, he had just handed me? How had a country girl like me, ended up in this situation?

At 15, I felt as if could take on the world. I wanted a job. Well, actually, I wanted money, and the only way to money, was a job. My parents provided us with a nice, if not slightly small, 3-bedroom house. We never went to bed hungry. Christmas was always nice and we took summer vacations. We did not do Disney, (we drove past it once), but we had a lot of fun. However, there wasn't a lot above and beyond. Therefore, when I wanted more, I went to work.

The Death Slide and Happy Plates

My childhood was similar to most, who were being raised in the Unity Point school system. We went to school, we made new friends, we tried to learn something, and we all looked forward to summer vacation. I attended Pleasant Hill school the first 3 years. The playground looked like something out of Little House on the Prairie, except we had a death slide. It was a very tall metal structure. Our teacher would help us climb the 20 or so stairs with gaps in between each stair, taller than our little legs. She stood below with her arms outstretched, as if she could catch us if we fell. Then, because we girls had to wear dresses, we wouldn't slide, just scoot and squeak all the way down.

Our teacher, taught us in class and in addition, watched us on the playground. She taught us all the old yard games: The Flying Dutchman, circle dodge ball, Duck, Duck, Goose, farmer in the Dell (I aspired to be the farmer, but alas, a boy was always chosen), and so many more outside games! I assume the teacher did not get a break all day, because she even ate lunch with us.

Lunch was served in the basement. In order to be able to go to the playground you first had to have a HAPPY PLATE. Oh, how I hated the Happy Plate. Apparently, the plates were happy when all the little compartments were free of food. The rules followed five-minute intervals. One item left, one had to wait five minutes, before going outside, two items equaled 10 and so on. Sometimes one would barely get outside before the bell would ring announcing the end of recess, especially if spinach or lima beans was on the menu.

A large square jungle gym sat by the driveway where the busses stopped to take us home. I have a very vivid memory of Linda Harris saying to me, "HI, I'm Linda, do you want to be my friend." In which I answered, "sure!" Six decades later, we continue to be friends.

The Man in The Moon

Our family lived in an old, old farmhouse, referred to as Newberry's Place. This was a kid's dream home. Long vines had been cut to swing out over the long gravel driveway. A great big porch was the perfect place to spend a hot afternoon. The huge yard had mature trees. But mom, HATED living there! A pump stood in the kitchen for water. There was an out-house, and bathes were taken in a galvanized tub, by the big stove in the living room. Looking back, I can see it was a lot of work for mom. But Curt and I loved it! We stayed home a lot, as the one car went to work with dad. In the summertime, mom would throw bucket after bucket of water on a dirt spot, making it a perfect mud slide. It was at this house, standing in the yard, I saw the Man in the Moon! My dad had told me all about him. I ran to the house to have him come look. While we were looking at the sky, a light moved slowly against the dark. Thinking it was an airplane, I pointed it out to dad. He said, "no, that's not a plane, that is a satellite." I truly had no idea what he was talking about, but when I would look to the sky, I would see them often. Who knew, I was witnessing the future, when all I had wanted was to see the Man in the Moon.

Hopscotch and Jacks

Fourth grade took us back to the main school. I was in awe of the chalk boards which wrapped all the way around the room, except for the bank of windows along the back wall. The room was bright and inviting. Fourth grade introduced me to Hopscotch and Jacks. Hopscotch proved to be a very competitive sport! We started with rocks to mark our space. Then, someone showed up to a game with a little rubber disc. I begged to order one! When mine came in the mail, I was so relieved. I had felt shamed to keep using a rock.

When it was too cold to play outside, we played Jacks. This too was very competitive. There were many arguments about the *red ball*. Some of us had to use the spongy one that came in the set. Others had purchased a small red super ball. The super ball was defiantly an advantage. During forth grade, we did not have a television at home. So, we played games, sang songs with dad as he played his guitar, and Curtis and I bickered a lot. One cold winter month, dad suggested we have a Jacks tournament. It truly was a lot of fun. Who knows who won, but Curt, two years older, had big hands and long fingers, I'm guessing he took the prize? As way of most Jacks, the first-time dad stepped on one barefoot, in the dark he admonished us to keep them picked up. The second time, they went into the trash. Years later, I understood exactly how he felt, when my bare foot found a single Lego in the dark.

Big Ole Incinerator

On our playground, yes, right smack dab in the middle of our playground, stood a big ole incinerator. Gee golly, how that thing could stink! We played around it as it was blistering hot and coughing out thick smoke. The teachers would warn us not to get too close! Dick and Jane had served their purpose in the school system. Our Think and Do books still had images of Dick and Jane, but no more stories. Daydreaming out

of my classroom window one day, I witnessed the janitor with boxes of
Dick and Jane books. He was feeding them into the incinerator a handful
at a time. I felt very sad for some reason. However, years later, when I
owned a used bookstore, Dick and Jane books were rare! I had a smile on
my face, when the occasional one came across my counter. Apparently,
janitors had made Dick and Jane books a valuable antique by feeding
them into incinerators across the country as well.

The Neighborhood

I was eight when we moved into the house, which my parents would
spend the next fifty years of their lives. We lived on a couple of Acres,
the Neiderbrocks lived beside us with their young son Mark. The Tulies
lived behind them, and the Moons were on down the road a bit. Our yard
became a gathering place to play ball, we did not have trees. The Moon
kids, and Mark would come over, we would play 500 and catch. Dad
would set up a badminton net and we would slap those birdies around,
until they ended up on top of the house. Then we had to wait for a stiff
breeze to play again. We played Evie- Ivey -Over and croquet. Croquet
was the favorite for a long time. We would even have tournaments to
determine the best player.

I have always loved to sing. Brenda Moon could play a mean piano
from the time she was about 10 years old. Some of my fondest memories
are of sitting on the piano bench and singing while she played, a fan
humming in time at my feet in her living room. The fan was small, made
of metal. The cover had such a wide gap, a grown man could put his
hand though them. It was kept on the landing where Brenda had her
piano and organ. I was careful not to let my feet dangle, I am quite sure I
would have lost a toe!

It is HOT and Humid in Southern Illinois!

For some reason, my dad did not care for air-conditioning, Something
about his sinuses. I hated it! I would lay in bed at night, vowing to never
marry a man who did not like air-conditioning. Fortunately, I did, most
days one could hang meat in our living room, and it would not spoil.
Living at home, the heat would run us out of doors early on summer
mornings. If I rode my bike fast enough downhill, I could convince
myself I was cooler, except, riding back uphill was HOT. Hanging ones
head out of the car window helped some. If I happened to fall asleep, my
face would feel stiff, and dried drool had to be washed off clear to my

ear. We spent a lot of time at home. Dad took our only car to work.

On some days in the summer, mom would scrounge up enough change to send Curtis to Herter's market. She would always admonish him to wait around and let Mary slice our bologna. She had witnessed Gobby, yes, he was called Gobby, wiping sweat from his brow and then slicing meat. Curt would take a backpack and head off on his bike. It was a long way, about 3 miles. Going there was great! Man, could one fly down Herter's hill!! But going up was a different story. Herter's hill is one of those hills where you will think you are at the top, but there is an additional hill added to the top. Gary Darnell owned a mini-bike and would come flying by just about at the top of the first hill. "Wish I could give you a ride!" he would yell as he flew by.

Curt would come home pretty tired, the bologna would be quite warm and the one soda we shared, would need ice. Herters Market was the last of the old-time markets of an era gone by, they had the coke bottle cooler filled with ice and made sandwiches for semi-truck drivers. They allowed people to buy on credit. I thought that was the coolest thing ever when Brenda Ragsdale and I went to Herters and she bought chips and two sodas, telling Mary to put it on her mom's credit. The first time I had tasted Taco chips, was with Brenda. Mom said she would ground me for a month if I bought on credit. When a new highway was built, it bypassed Herters, and sadly they closed.

A five-mile radius social life

Even though we stayed close to home, I still had a very busy social life. I belonged to the Boskydell Hustlers 4-H club. Rose Lipe was our leader. She had been a 4-H leader for years and years and years. I still cannot believe my parents would let me climb up in the back of her old rickety red pick-up truck, and ride to soft-ball games in Murphysboro. She had wooden sides on the truck, and there would be so many of us, we would all stand. Oh, how I loved to play 4-H ball!

Girl Scouts took a lot of my time. I enjoyed earning the badges. Mom was our leader; she went above and beyond to make it a fun experience. About the only time we went "to town," was for church, on Sundays. Everything else happened with-in a five-mile radius from home.

Sometimes, grandma would come get us and we would go visiting. She loved to visit with Mary Forgoshe. Mary and her husband Steve had immigrated from Hungary many years earlier. I couldn't understand much of what Mary said. My great-grandmother had helped her learn to speak English. Unfortunately, my great-grandmother swore like a sailor, so Mary had a colorful vocabulary. Mom was relieved I couldn't understand her. They were very nice people. Quite old by the time I came along. They had worked very hard as farmers their whole lives. I'm not sure they bought anything from the grocery store, if they didn't grow it, raise it, pluck it or milk it, they didn't eat it. I am very proud to be the owner of a Mary Forgosh, 100-year-old quilt. (shhh, please don't tell my sister I have it).

Sunday, it's NOT Sunday

Mom would go to town to buy groceries. If she could, she would leave us at home! She shopped at A&P until they made her mad, and then she moved to IGA. She liked to stop at the Ben Franklin and buy ¼ pound of Bridge Mix. She could make it last almost whole week. Her hiding place must have been the freezer, because we didn't know this for years! Occasionally, we would go to the Varsity theater for matinees and walk over to Dairy Queen to sit on the little crooked concrete wall. Dad would say, "you can have anything you want for a dime!" If we asked for a Sunday, he would say, "a Sunday? It's not Sunday!" The names of the treats were so fun to hear. A Jack and Jill Sunday, (chocolate and marshmallow), a mister Malty, (frozen chocolate ice cream in a little cup), Mister Misty Kisses, (frozen misty in a plastic tube). However, there was always a huge selection of 10-cent items, it was hard to choose!

Finally: Junior High

After what felt like years and years, more than six years for sure, we made it to Jr. High. Which was in the same building as the other grades. Sixth grade was a hoot. Our teacher was somewhat of a hippie. He had his hair cut, wore appropriate clothing, but thought like a hippie. We all loved him. He told me years later, his theory: he hated giving students grades. He wanted to write a letter to each parent and express the good points of each child. Then discuss how all could work together to improve in the area's the child was lacking in. I would have been all over that! Please, somebody say something good about my performance! He would take us outside on a regular basis. He felt young brains needed more sunshine than they were able to get day after day in a classroom. He would take us on "field trips," to a creek that ran at the back of the school's property. He called it Science, we called it FUN!

Seven and eight grades were designed to prepare us for high school. As a result, we moved from classroom to classroom, because we would be doing that in high school. We walked across the hall.

Jr High introduced us to boy/girl dances and sleepovers almost every weekend. We would rotate from house to house. My friend, Linda found an old note in her mother's belongings after she passed away. It said, "Happy Mother's Day mom. I won't be here; I'm going to Connie's."

Boy/girl dances were the most awkward situations ever. Some were in the gym at school, which resulted with the boys finding a basketball, and the girls standing around while music played. However, Lori Lambert had several dances at her house. Lori always had a boyfriend. She was pretty and a cheerleader, she looked good in her cheerleading outfit. She was friendly and fun to be around. We would congregate in her basement and the music would start. "Cherish is word I use to describe...." All of us would stand by the wall hoping someone would cherish a dance with us. The boys would go home, and we girls would spend the night. So many giggles and rehashing of who danced with whom. And who might have almost gotten kissed. Which boy we would never think of kissing and so on and so on. When we would get too loud, Lori's dad would bang on the floor with his wooden leg, which usually made us howl louder.

One piece or two?

Junior High allowed me more freedom to wander. I was allowed to walk to Susan Louge's house through the woods to Midland Hills. My dad had installed a buzzer on the side of our house. All the neighbors knew when we were being called home; us and all the dogs. I could hear the buzzer at Susan's, probably a mile or so away. Freedom or not, mom knew exactly how long it should take me to get home. Susan's mom had a conch shell in which, she would blow when Susan was at my house. Who needed a cell phone? Midland Hills was a really great place to hang out. They had built a dock a distance from the shore of the lake. Susan and I spent many happy afternoons swimming back and forth. We would finish the day with a camp-out. Our little tent set up a just far enough from her house to feel we were on our own, yet safe at the same time. I was meeting a new boyfriend at the lake one afternoon. I called Susan to ask if I should wear my one piece or my two piece? It was the beginning of realizing how naive I had been raised when she snorted and said "Connie, the two-piece!"

One year, the lake was drained, leaving about 3 inches of water. We had a winter to remember, when the water froze. Day after day, my brother and I trudged in the cold, through the woods to play. We played until there was only mud left, or until the buzzer buzzed.

Ponyboy and Sodapop

Books have always ruled in of my life. In my minds eye, I can close my eyes and see myself sitting on the couch reading. I can also hear mom speaking loudly saying, "Connie, put down that book and come help me with dinner!' Curtis had of course moved on to high school when I was left behind in the seventh grade. When he left his copy of The Outsiders laying out, of course I picked it up and was instantly intrigued. When he caught me, he yelled, "mom, Connie is reading a book meant for high school students." By that time, I had read the majority of the book. Mom asked me if I thought it was appropriate reading for a seventh grader. Well of course it was. Who wouldn't want to dream, I mean read about bad boys named, Ponyboy and Sodapop. Who didn't want to cry buckets when Johnnie didn't make it? Who did not memorize Robert Frosts poem?

'Nothing Gold Can Stay
Nature's first green is gold,
Her hardest hue to hold.
Her early Leaf's a flower;
But only so an hour.
Then leaf subsides to leaf
So Eden sank to Greif.
So dawn goes down to day,
Nothing gold can stay.'
Robert Frost

Music and Television

Music was a big part of the late 60's. Lori had a little record player; she would bring to school with a stack of 45's. We all loved those afternoons when we couldn't go outside, singing along with current artists. Even now, on an oldies station, I can usually get most of the words correct. I cannot always recall what I had for lunch, but I remember songs from fifty years ago! Some of the singers who come to mind are; Bobby Sherman, David Cassidy, The Osmond's, The Jackson 5 and of course, everyone loved the Monkey's! It would be a couple of more years before the songs became anti-war and anti-establishment. It seemed just for a little while longer, we could be innocent.

The Partridge Family, Dark Shadows, The Big Valley, Gunsmoke (could you out-draw Matt Dillon?), The Brady Bunch, The Beverly Hillbillies, Twilight Zone, Mission Impossible and The Wonderful World of Disney, played on our T.V. Happy little shows to brighten our evenings.

East

And then the big day arrived. We loaded up busses and traveled to town to tour East high school. (talk about Hillbillies!) Curt's class was the first class to attend East. The building was huge in comparison to our country school. We saw kids from all the other feeder schools. The schools ranked in size as follows; Lincoln Jr. high, Unity Point, Giant City, and finally, but certainly not least, Desoto. The building was very MOD, orange carpet, a sunken circle in the library with circular seats along the inside, new desks, and a very nice cafeteria. Although we from Unity Point knew the cafeteria was not going to measure up. We had the absolute best school cooks to ever stir a pot!

Home Economics

East High School was a nice starting point, Central was a little intimidating. Home Economics was not something we had experienced at Unity Point. Holy Cow! What a beautiful kitchen! Miss Boone was an interesting teacher. Many times, it felt as if she didn't even realize we were there. We did cook a few things, learned about measurements and how to pack down brown sugar. We chose between two pattern styles for the dress we wanted to learn to sew on. I chose a princess bodice and was very excited to start. Mom and I purchased all the items needed, off to school I went with a vision of how wonderful my dress was going to look when it was finished. My grandmother sewed most of my clothing, I just knew I would make her proud! Let's just say, sewing class was not the butterflies and rainbows I thought it would be. My thread kept getting tangled, I mean really knotted and everything, including the fabric was tangled, and stuck in the sewing machine. Miss Boone would come over to look and tell me to figure it out. When I finally worked my way to the zipper, I knew I was in trouble. There was NO WAY that tiny zipper was getting sewn in there by me. We were not allowed to take our dresses home, but I snuck mine into my backpack and took it directly to my grandma's. She offered to teach me how to do it, but by that point I was so sick of it, I didn't care. I no longer cared if she was proud of me. I snuck it back in class and waited to receive a perfect score. My grandmother earned a B on her zipper. She was so angry; I could hardly keep her from charging the school in protest! I think the only time I ever had that dress on, was the day we had to model them. I hated it. My grandma never forgave Miss Boone for giving her a B.

Miss Cox and Miss Cox

Even though I hated my gym suit, I loved P.E. at East. Miss Phoebe Cox was a very good gym teacher. She had already taught a million years before our class arrived. Her sister, Miss Jane Cox, had taught English at Unity Point. One time I was not working up to my full potential. Which is a nice way of saying, I had a D in English. She took me into the hall and said, "Connie, I am not going to call your mom. I know you can do this work. I'm going to give you a chance to show me you can." At the end of the semester I took home a very proud B. She stopped me in the hall, winked and said, "I knew you could do it!"

Both she and her sister did not pull any punches. No one even thought about talking back, or not participating. Both were outstanding examples of professional women. Many of us came from homes in which our mothers stayed home. They sat around and ate Bonbons and watched Soap Operas. Actually, my mom worked her tail off. Some of us who lived in the country, did not realize women could have careers. The Women's libbers were just getting started after all. Miss Cox made P.E. fun. She taught us many techniques and games we had not learned in our smaller schools. At Unity Point, I had been considered one of the better athletes. However, the Giant City girls were a force to be reckoned with. Vurla Cox would steal the basketball every time I had it! We did become great lifetime friends. But, I'm still jealous she could out play me

Seventeenth Summer

The summer after Freshman year, brought a summer romance into my life. Brenda Moon had loaned me the book Seventeenth Summer. I was smitten. The storyline was a young woman, seventeen years old, who has a summer romance. But how could something that beautiful happen so far out in the country? I knew all the boys in the neighborhood, and I

178

knew it just wasn't going to happen. One day, I had walked over to Linda's house to play whiffle ball. She only lived about a quarter of a mile away. As I walked up to Linda's yard, I could see the game had already started and there were two rather tall young men in the yard playing. They both had long blond hair, did I mention they were both very tall? Who were they? Where had they come from?

They were brothers who had just moved to the neighborhood while their mom went to southern Illinois University. They were California boys and looked the part and looked out of place in our country neighborhood. I suddenly wished I had spent a little more time on my appearance. Craig, the older of the two, didn't seem to mind. We became fast friends. He began spending more and more time at my house. Mom and dad liked him, but holy cow, he was a big boy and hungry all the time. It was a beautiful summer. We would take walks in the woods, sit on the porch swing, and swim at Midland Hills (do I hear birds singing?) Craig was quite intrigued by fireflies. Illinois may not have an ocean, but we had fireflies over California. My father had several bales of straw stacked 4 or 5 bales high by our garden area. We would climb up on top and talk about our future together. He wanted to have children and wanted to name a daughter Jessica. Years later I learned he did have a daughter, and he did name her Jessica. He was the first boy to ever buy me flowers. He made me feel pretty, for the first time I didn't feel like such a Tom-boy. For the whole summer, I felt pretty special. Then school started and he discovered CCHS offered a lot of girls to choose from. And so, our time together ended. I still thought he was tall and handsome, and it did hurt just a little. But somehow, I knew it was just a Seventeenth Summer… even though I was 15.

Life moves on

A few weeks after breaking up with Craig, the boy who would become my husband made a trip to Dairy Queen to check me out. He wasn't tall and he wasn't from California, but he had long blond hair and drove a cool car. A 1969 green fastback mustang. How could I not be interested?

Many, many years later I had the opportunity to talk to Craig's daughter, Jessica. Craig had joined the Marines when he left Illinois. He met her mother at a disco, go figure. But their marriage did not last very long. He was engaged to be married a second time, but sadly, on a beautiful California day he drove his new motorcycle in front of an oncoming truck. He was only 34 years old. Jessica asked me why we hadn't stayed in touch. I was still in high school and he had moved on to Marine life. Besides, in 1972 people didn't just pick up the phone and make long distance phone calls. I was happy with my local boy; and never looked back!

Vacations with the Childers and the Dunkel's

Our Family vacations mostly consisted of loading canoes on the top of cars and throwing belongings in the bed of an old truck, converted to be our pull behind "camper." We slept in tents and canoed rivers, such as the Current and Jacks Fork Rivers. Lakes were not as much fun to canoe on, but on a lot of Sunday afternoons; we would take the canoes down to Cedar Lake, paddle out a certain distance, picnic, and play swamp the canoe. The Dunkel family were usually with us. Mom and dad let me bring Susan along, so I wasn't outnumbered by my brother and the four Dunkel boys. My parents bought each of us our own paddle, mom painted our names on them. Susan rated her own paddle. It hung on the wall at my parents' house for many years. A few years ago, Susan happened by the house and dad gave her the paddle. The Dunkel's and the Childers had some great adventures together; including almost getting arrested, all 13 of us!

Florida here we come

Carbondale was having a huge snowstorm. Which was exciting because So. Illinois doesn't see a lot of snow. But of course, The Childers and the Dunkel's were headed to Florida for Christmas. Life had changed drastically at our house. Sweet 16 had finally happened! Driver's license and car dates were finally a part of my repertoire. Monte was born during my freshman year, making us a family of six. Lorie, is seven years younger than me. Curtis had joined the Marines. He had just finished boot camp and had come home on leave to join us on the Florida trip. My preference would have been to stay home, as opposed to traveling twelve hours in a Galaxy 500 with six people. I do not think Monte sat on a seat the whole trip, he just climbed from one lap to another (pre-car seats).

This was the year there was a supposable gas shortage. Every time we stopped for gas, we would wait and wait in line. Some stations would only allow a certain number of gallons to be sold at one time. Resulting in having to driving across the street to wait in yet another very long line. Just across the Florida boarder, we were waiting in one such line. Someone would wait in the car while the others stretched their legs, so as not to lose our place in line. As usual, I was in the middle of a book, so I stayed in the car with monte. He sat on my lap, fell to sleep and promptly peed on me. It seemed to be a very long time until someone came back to check on us. When dad came to move the car forward, he was clearly angry. Apparently, a Florida Highway Patrolman was just sure Curt was AWOL. What? Really? AWOL and traveling with his family? When the car was fueled, we all went in to see if we could find a solution to the problem. There I stood, 16, didn't want to be there, looking like I was the one who had peed my pants. All of us just wanted to get back on the road. Curtis had presented his leave papers, not good enough. His commanding officer was called, who verified he was authorized to be there, not good enough. Finally, Bill Dunkel informed the Florida State Officer that if he was going to arrest Curt, then he had to arrest all of us. There were thirteen of us, including Bills 82-year-old mother. She had not spoken through this whole ordeal, but caught Bills attention and worriedly said, "Bill, I haven't ever been arrested before." The look on her face prompted Bill to try one more thing to satisfy the officer. He called a friend who was a U.S. Senator, who vouched for us and finally, we were back on our way. By then my pants were dry.

Paychecks are nice!

My parents had taken a couple of weeks to decide if I could work at Dairy Queen. My dad knew Joe Waicukauski and knew him to be a great guy. When the school allowed me to get a work permit, they relented and said yes. Dad would drive me to work in the early evening and pick me up at closing time. Usually all he would get for his efforts was a vanilla malt.

Having a little money really opened my eyes. I had never heard of a sidewalk sale. In the 1970's there were several clothing stores on the strip. But, the first thing I bought was a fan for my bedroom window! Paychecks felt pretty good! I enjoyed my time at Dairy Queen. It was as if, I was slowly introduced to town living. I met people, (including my future husband, local boy Kem Cooley), through that 3-inch screen. I was safely behind the glass, with Mr. Waicukauski watching over my shoulder. He was a big dude; I do not think anyone would mess with him!

I learned several lessons working at Dairy Queen. Aside from, not touching my face and washing my hands. I learned what marijuana smelled like. Apparently, the munchies could be satisfied with ice cream. I learned African Americans tan and sunburn. Unity Point School is a very diverse school now, but during the sixties, having an African American attend was unheard of. The young woman who trained me, brought me up to speed. She showed me how she had forgotten to take her watch off over the weekend resulting in a tan line. She taught me; people are people no matter their color. I really liked her; she paved the way for me and my future of making friends because of who they were, not because of their skin color. I learned some people called chopped nuts, nut meats. I learned a paycheck didn't always go as far as you would like for it to. I learned my future husband did not want the 10-cent cone he purchased from me. He handed it to his sister, who promptly threw it out of the window. Apparently, he liked what he saw, and I became a passenger in his cool car. His sister refused to be put in the back seat, (nobody puts Gaytha in the backseat!), so I sat on the hump in the middle. The exhaust pipes along the sides would burn little burn circles on my legs. But it was worth it. I had a boyfriend!

College Students can be Scary

Even though I was feeling grown -up, there were times when I still felt like a country mouse. A college student who frequented the Dairy Queen often, started asking me out. He just looked so old. I kept telling him no. One night, in the pouring rain, he walked the seven miles to my house from Carbondale. I felt bad, but not bad enough to come out of my room. Besides, Kem was there. My dad felt really sorry for him but respected my wishes of not seeing him. He left me a bracelet and a matching necklace. I'm sure my parents thought, this guy is in college, and this guy works at a gas station...which one would you choose for your daughter?

Don't Look Ethel

I survived the night streakers' took over Illinois avenue. There are no longer clothing stores on the strip. A few bars are still there, after 50 years, PK's, is still thriving. But, after the owner, who I understand was the heart of the place passed, the family is selling. Restaurants have come and gone, Pagliai's pizza is in a new location, yet it is for sale as well.

The train station closed the old station and built a new one several years ago. The varsity no longer shows movies but is a center for plays and musical performances. Recently, the crooked concrete wall by Dairy Queen was restructured and sits straight.

Dairy Queen is still the heart of downtown Carbondale. It sits in its shining white and red glory the same place it has always been. Generations come to its window children ordering something new, parents ordering a trip to the past with an old favorite. The days of "anything for a dime," are long gone as well as the fun names of the treats. If I am visiting Carbondale, Mark Waicukauski will let me slip in the side door and put a curl on my own cone. Not much has changed inside. The cups are still stored on a high shelf, just inside the door. It still smells fresh and clean. The window is the same, however there are now cash registers as opposed to the 1970's when everything was added in our heads. Instead of the money being put in a wooden drawer under the counter, a drawer pops open under the machine. Mark is not as large looming as his father. But I doubt there is anyone who would challenge him either.

I have lived in several locations since I left Carbondale in 1976. I have traveled many places in the United States. It was a privilege to travel to Europe and see places some people only read about. Being fifteen was a long time ago, and I am no longer embarrassed by the sight of a naked man. But, when I leave my parents house seven miles South of Carbondale, I drive on old 51 for a couple of miles. It brings me back; I catch a glimpse of Linda's house in the rear-view mirror. The little house we lived in on the top of a dangerous hill. Our dog Snowball is buried on the peak of the hill so he can look out over the traffic. Herter's hill is still a killer, I would not try to ride a bike on it now, nor would Curtis, I suppose. Herter's Market stood for as long as it could. Vines and weeds overtook it, until a bulldozer became its fate. Sitting at the 4-way stop, while the light is red, I can see my grandparents' house tucked in behind trees grandma planted shortly before it became my Uncle Jack's house. When the light is green, I could choose to continue on Old 51 with its curvy old concrete road. But, turning left at the stop light is New 51, is the faster route to town. The highway feels unfamiliar, even though I have traveled it many times. As Arnold's Market comes into view, I can still feel like a Makanda Country Mouse going to town.

OTHER MOTHERS: MRS. E, MRS. K & MRS. F

By Dr. Steven Lewis, M.D.

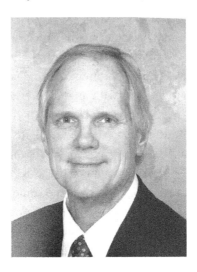

Mrs. E

There was no one in my neighborhood that I more admired, more wanted to be like, and therefore more wanted to be friends with than Peter . In some way he was everything that I wanted to be and knew I wasn't. I was only in grade school, so I didn't even know what this meant. I only knew that it was true. I realize now that I could have resented it, objected to it, or avoided it, and no doubt at times I did, but mostly my response was that I wanted to be part of it.

Peter's house and yard were the social center of the neighborhood. The adults drifted over there in the evening for food, beer, cigars, and conversation. The kids came to play. Some of this I simply could not understand. When his mother Mrs. E cut into the juicy red pulp of a giant green watermelon on a summer evening, dozens of people would show up to get a piece. It was as though her watermelons were different that everyone else's. I knew they came from the grocery store or farm stand just like ours did, but something about the way she cut it up and offered it made you want it.

Mrs. E was always nice to me. She was greeted my arrival in a direct and personal manner, and responded to my presence, even if just briefly. Of course, everyone else got her attention too, but each as individuals, so naturally I took it personally. The immediate consequence of getting Mrs. E' attention was to get instruction on what would happen next, and the first order of business was food. Always food. I loved that part. Any time of the day or night she would open up the kitchen and make sure I had something to eat. Things I never had at home. Sardines in mustard sauce. Cream cheese. Challah. Sweet little strawberries crushed with sugar. Plums, pears, or peaches picked twenty minutes ago from trees in the back yard. Hamburgers grilled up in the middle of the day. I took this personally too.

We were a university community. Life was stable and decent, but there wasn't a lot of extra. And one of the occasional household questions in a neighborhood like mine was what to do when there was something extra. Peter's family went to Europe. All of them. For almost the entire summer. A lot of university families did this. At that time I still thought of Europe as a destination rather than a loose term for a large number of cities and countries that are the actual places people go. Eventually, Peter and I were best friends, but there was a long purgatory period when I was just a neighborhood kid. And that was when they went to Europe.

In their absence that summer, their back yard remained the center of social life for the kids who did not go to Europe. We would gather there under the tall shade of the tall pin oaks in the comfortable and familiar surround of the deserted back yard. The normal social drive of whiffle ball and watermelon had gone to Europe. Lacking social order, we made up games. To the side of the back yard, behind the grapevines, was a huge sandbox. We took to gathering in the sandbox where we could sit on the boards around the sides and dig in the sand as we talked and decided what to do next. And gradually digging in the sand became what we did next. Every day. The usual tunnels and hills and crude castles gave way to a big hole. And with several kids digging every day, the hole soon went through the sand into the dirt. And every day the hole got deeper. We became enchanted by the size of the hole and talked constantly about how big we could make it. A fox hole. A secret underground room. An underground house. An underground city. As the hole got bigger and the dirt piled up, we realized that we had to obscure the scope of our activity. The dirt had to be hidden. So we resorted to hauling the dirt away in buckets, and covering the hole with a sheet of plywood, then putting sand on top of that. And every day we removed the sand and the plywood cover, dug the hole bigger, and took away the dirt. The summer passed peacefully in this seemingly purposeful undertaking. Except that when it got to where it took two people to pull one up out of the hole, I started having dreams of cave-ins and suffocation. And since our end-point was fantasy, who knows where this might have ended if someone had not mentioned that their mother had mentioned that they were coming back from Europe. Tomorrow.

Tomorrow?

Tomorrow.

We have to fill the hole!

With what?

We regarded our creation now with new vision and saw that its size was shocking. The dirt had been scattered all over the neighborhood a bucket at a time and could not be recovered. With what was piled nearby, we could fill no more than a third of the enormous hole. Of all the things we had thought of in digging this hole, filling it up again was not one of them. After much panicked discussion it became clear that it would have to be filled up with something else.

What else?

Anything else.

The stack of bricks by the garage that matched the house. The tricycle left on the side yard. Garden tools kept in a small outdoor shed. A spare tire held in reserve on the side porch. Doormats from the front and back doors. Buckets, brooms, mops, and outdoor shoes and clothing from the back porch. Anything we could find that would take up space and fill a hole. Fortunately they had had the presence of mind to lock the house. Then the dirt we had went on top of that, and the sand on top of that, and we went home for a few days. We understood that when people get home from Europe, you leave them alone for a while. They need to rest.

Eventually it was whiffle ball and strawberries and watermelon again. In time I sat after school at Mrs. E's kitchen table being fed sardines in mustard sauce and cream cheese on challah and sliced nectarines. And I looked out the picture window past the plum trees and the grapevines into the back yard. And as though I were capable of seeing through the earth I could clearly see a minor museum of mid-century household items buried secretly just so many feet away while I answered Mrs. Es perpetually interested questions about my class, my teacher, my test result or any immediate business of my day. And though she offered me an inclusion that I hungrily accepted, I nonetheless felt a sense of other. I had secretly violated the privilege of her abundance and gone undetected, and now continued to profit from her ignorance of my guilt. As we grew to be more familiar and better friends, it seemed impossible to go back and straighten this little bend in our mutual road. Regarding the missing objects, nothing was ever said.

The first time I was aware I felt bad about this offense was when I should have told the simple truth. Mrs. E, while you and your family were in Europe, we buried most of your possessions in the back yard. I offer no satisfactory explanation of this behavior. But now at least you don't have to wonder what happened to all your stuff, or feel violated that it was taken by some stranger intruding upon the sanctity of your home. And now I won't have to feel ill at ease accepting your undeserved attention and generosity, because I no longer harbor in my heart the secret thorn of my transgression. No doubt she would just smile knowingly, hinting that perhaps she had buried a few in her time. Of course, I could tell her now. She still lives in the same house with the same back yard. But I think it's too late to dig all that stuff up now. Let some future generation dig it up in surprise. Let some distant descendent unknowingly study their great-great-great grandfather's tricycle in a photograph of domestic artifacts in a future anthropology textbook.

Mrs. K

We knew an older boy who was into pornography. Well, what he was into wouldn't be called pornography these days. It was just black and white nudity. But what made it pornography was that he had it delivered to a P.O. box in a brown paper envelope. Harold and I were not into pornography. We were only 12 years old. We were just young and curious. Harold's parents, Mr. And Mrs. K, had an unexpected black and white 8mm movie of their honeymoon. He showed it to me once, hilarious in its depiction of them as impossibly young people frolicking on a Florida beach. Mr. K carried Mrs. K in his arms while they both laughed. But it wasn't the movie that was significant, it was the projector. Movie cameras and projectors were not common household items. And this older boy had started getting stiff yellow envelopes containing small metal reels of 8mm film of uncertain content. It was filled with mystery, intrigue and interest. So I borrowed one of these mysterious metal reels in its stiff yellow envelope, took it to school in my blue denim three-ring notebook, and after school took it to Harold's. Mr. And Mrs. K had a store. A women's clothing store. Actually, a women's fashion store. Or shop. Or shoppe. Which meant that they were never home until after 5:30. And we were out of school and home by 3:30. We had privacy and time. We set up the projector on one side of the living room and unfurled the screen on the other side. We were going to get the big picture. I got the movie out of my notebook and we threaded it carefully, pulled the curtains, turned out the lights, and let it roll. It was a black and white film of two young women playing catch with a ball and then sitting on a swing. Nude. Like I said, this would not be considered pornographic now. In fact, it had an ambience of innocence that was more like the nudity of early childhood. Much later I learned that there was name for this genre of art film, but then later still I forgot the name. None of which is the point. The point is that in the middle of this little seven-minute black and white naked frolic the garage door started up. Harold was the first person I knew to have a garage door opener, which meant we had about ninety seconds to turn off the projector, turn on the lights, open the curtains, rewind the film, remove it from the projector, unplug the projector, take down the screen and put it all away in three locations before the door opened and Audrey and Julius inexplicably walked in the door. They were home early for the first time in their long and reliable working lives. We started to do this, immediately understood that it was simply not possible, and in a moment of Haroldian inspiration, grabbed everything and ran into the bathroom and locked the door.

In a few moments, there was a knock at the bathroom door.
Are you in there?
Mrs. K's voice.
Yes.
Are you alone?
Long pause.
No.
Who is with you?
Short pause.
Steve.
Steve?
Yeah, Steve.
Who's Steve?
My friend.
What friend?
MY friend. From school.
I don't know Steve.
That's Ok. I do.
What are you and your friend Steve doing in the bathroom? Together.
Long pause.
Washing our hands.
Washing your hands?
Yes. Washing our hands.
Sounds of vigorous washing of hands in sink.
Long pause.
Oh.
Footsteps receded from the door.

It was Mrs K.'s voice at the door. Her presence on the other side of the closed door was so intense that I could feel her inside the bathroom. I was astounded by the conversation that my friend had just had with his mother on my behalf – "Washing our hands?" – I could never have taken on my mother that way for twenty-some good reasons. Decades later, when I had children of my own, I understood that there are times as a parent when you are presented a choice of prosecuting for the truth, or accepting your child's judgment that you don't need to know. Looking back at that last silence on the other side of the door, Audrey was having such a moment. She really didn't need to know, and accepted that. Not understanding this at the time, I couldn't believe that she just walked away from it. I was greatly relieved to escape so easily. Except that she was still home and we were still in the bathroom, and eventually we would have to come out of the bathroom with clean hands and she would be in the kitchen. We did and she was, and nothing more was said. And that is how I met Mrs. K. It was the beginning of a long relationship predicated on doubt and non-disclosure. I always felt more at home in Harold's house than in my own. Unless it was 5:30 and Mrs. K was walking in the door. Then I felt like I shouldn't be there at all. Like there was something dubious about me that I had to keep hidden in her presence, except I didn't know what it was.

Rather than feel that way about it, it might have been better at the time, or perhaps shortly after, to just tell the truth and resolve everything once and for all. Mrs. K., we were just watching some pornographic movies in your living room while you were at work. I'm just telling you this so you won't be concerned about what we might have been doing in the bathroom together, and so that you won't have to worry about what we are up to while you're at work in the future. I'm certain she would have appreciated this candor. Then no one would have to feel uncomfortable, and it would have been the beginning of a better relationship with more potential. I guess I could tell her that now, but I think she moved to Florida.

Mrs. F

Gerald was older than I was, but nonetheless we were friends. Gerald's parents traveled out of the country a lot. And sometimes Gerald went with them. They had house pets. The pets did not go with them. And even though I was younger, his mother, Mrs. F, regarded me as a responsible young person, and addressed me in an adult-like manner. I was a responsible young person. Around her I was. And so when they were going on a long trip, she entrusted to me the care of their pets. A poodle named "Duke" that would stay in the fenced yard, and a shelf in the basement of small round bowls containing Betas. Siamese fighting fish. I was to come once a day and play with Duke, put out food and water for him, and go in the basement and feed the fish. Don't let the dog in the house, and don't go in the house other than the basement to feed the fish. I was to be paid, and in my world any money was a lot because I didn't have any and because I didn't seem to need any.

This was presented to me as agreed upon, so I agreed upon it. I was happy to do it. It's just that they didn't live in my neighborhood. In fact, they didn't really live in my town. They lived out at the edge of town where new houses were being built, and I could ride my bike. I had a third generation JC Higgins balloon tire bike that was operational, but their house required passage down and up a geological wonder known as Tar Hill. This requires no explanation. The trip down was life threatening for the opposite reason that the trip back up was life threatening. But I was a responsible young person, and I would do it.

It went pretty well for the first week. I thought poodles were little dogs in rhinestone collars. This was a standard poodle, and this dog was bigger than I was, and stronger too. He was always enthusiastically happy to see me, jumping all over me and knocking me down just to say hello. I had experience with beagles, little dogs that always run the other way, so this was something new. The fighting fish were less interesting than their name. They don't fight much on their own. But they also weren't much trouble. It was a long way out there just to turn around and come back. So I started hanging around a little just to make the trip more worthwhile. And then I got to thinking about how Gerald had told me how much he liked beer. A lot he said, especially with sausage. He had been to Germany. I had never been permitted this pleasure, but he made it sound like something that I would like. If they drank beer, there had to be some in the house. I went up the stairs to the kitchen. I had never been in the house part of the house. Geralds's room was in the basement, so that's where I had been. But I wasn't going into the house. Just the kitchen. There was no beer in the refrigerator. But there had to be some someplace. If you're going to be in the kitchen, you might as well be in the hall closet and that's where the beer was. Meister Brau. It wasn't cold, but Gerald said they didn't really drink it cold in Germany. I opened it and took a sip. I had no idea what to expect. Bitter. Sour. Maybe it should be in a glass. I poured it into a glass. Bitter. Sour. Maybe the sausage was more important than I had realized. I went through the refrigerator again. I was starting to feel comfortable in the kitchen. There was some old salami wrapped in tin foil. I sliced some pieces off and sat at the kitchen table waiting for my enjoyment to commence.

Abruptly the giant dog came crashing up the stairs into the kitchen. I had left the doors open. He lunged at me happily and dumped me over onto the floor, chair, glass, beer and all. Then he lunged onto the table, grabbed the sausage and disappeared into the house. I got the mop from the beer closet – I knew where it was now – and mopped up the floor and washed the floor and mop again and again to get rid of the rank smell of the beer. I threw away the beer can, washed and replaced the glass, and started whistling and calling for the dog. He didn't respond.

I no longer felt comfortable. I really didn't want to go into the house. I really wasn't supposed to go in the house. But the dog was in there some place, and I would have to go in and get him. I started down the hall I already knew. I had never seen a house like this. Everywhere were objects from far away places. Glass, ceramic, wood. Rugs, wall hangings, paintings, sculptures. Beautiful. And no dog. I walked cautiously as if afraid to injure something, calling and whistling. He wasn't responding to me at all. I went down the hall, looking in each beautiful room as I went, and then turned to go through the study and dining room into the family room. The family room had a large stone fireplace surrounded by facing sofas, and in the space between the sofas and fireplace was an exotic rug from where I could never imagine. The whole room was arranged to appreciate the rug, which gave a luminous glow that rose to the vaulted ceiling above. I heard Duke in the kitchen now. He had been moving ahead of me and I heard him now clatter down the stairs and shortly appear out in the yard again. Now all I had to do was leave. Passing quickly through the living room, I saw what he had been up to, piled high on the rug in front of the fireplace between the facing sofas. Eating the forbidden sausage had triggered him to perform the forbidden act in the forbidden place. I was overwhelmed.

It would not be possible for me to clean this up. In the first place, I just couldn't. It was too big. In the second place, the carpet was basically white, and it was obvious from across the room that no matter how ardent my effort there was going to be substantial evidence left behind. And if I cleaned it up mostly, I would have to explain it mostly. If I cleaned it up, that meant I knew it was there. And if I knew it was there, that meant I was in the house. And what was I doing in the house? But if I didn't clean it up at all, it could only be because I didn't know about it. And I didn't know about it because I was responsible and hadn't come in the house. I don't know exactly what the final elements of my decision were, but I do know that I left and never went in the house again. Ever. Even without going in the house, I could clearly picture what was evolving on the rug in front of the fireplace. And the worse it got, the less I dared go in. It was another ten days before they came home.

When they returned, the dog was happy, the fish were healthy, and Mrs. F was pleased. She thanked me for my reliable effort, shook my hand, and gave me the promised money and a little more. She was then once again the mother of my friend, no longer my employer. Nothing at all was said about the rug and its abuse by the dog. How could I be responsible for what I didn't know about, and how could I have known about it if I hadn't gone in the house? And since I wasn't supposed to go in the house, obviously I hadn't. This was entirely too easy. I felt ill. I can still see what the mess must have looked like when they finally got to it, and what vile oaths were sworn by the person who had to clean it up. And who was that? I never even heard about that part. Mrs. F was protecting my innocent feelings from the unpleasant knowledge of something beyond my capacity. It didn't involve me.

I realize now that I could have done my best to clean it up and then just told the important part of the story. The dog got away from me and bolted up the stairs. I did my best. But I wasn't being called upon to do my best. I was being called upon to be responsible. Having failed at that, I could later have unburdened myself. Mrs. F, while I was relaxing with a beer in your kitchen, resting from my labors on Tar Hill and glad simply to be alive, the dog did something nasty on that beautiful carpet in the living room. But since I was not supposed to go in there, I didn't clean it up. But I also hadn't been called upon to be unburdened. It was my place to be responsible. So I guess I was.

THE FOUNTAIN OF YOUTH

By Larry Eastwood

If someone were to ask me now that I am in the autumn of my years, what was your favorite year; I would answer 1959. I say this not because of historical events, although there were several. For example, there were Eisenhower, Khrushchev, and the Cold War; Castro seizes power in Cuba; Buddy Holly and the music died; NASA announces the Mercury Seven astronauts; the Dodgers beat the White Sox in the World Series; and Alaska and Hawaii become the forty-ninth and fiftieth United States.

This particular year stuck to me because I was an eight year old boy, who had completed one full season as a player on the Jets Little League Baseball Team and I was looking forward to the next games at Oakland Field where I would be wearing a new pair of rubber spikes. It also happened to be when I was on the receiving end of the best Christmas ever.

I acquired a lifelong passion for movies and television then, probably because my dad allowed me to go to the Varsity Theater almost every Saturday afternoon and since his job was repairing televisions and radios, we seemed to have a TV and music in every room of our house .

There were two extraordinary movies produced in 1959, I particularly enjoyed "Ben-Hur" and "Journey To The Center Of The Earth." As far as television, these were the days before cable, satellite dish, and video streaming. We had three channels represented by the major networks. My dad was a techie and very knowledgeable of the newest electronics. We had a tower antenna on our roof that turned in any direction by means of a rotor motor. We could tune in independent KPLR channel 11 in St. Louis. That was the big time. I was on top of all the good shows like <u>Bonanza,</u> <u>Twilight Zone</u>, and <u>Rawhide.</u> My cousin and I were fierce fans of <u>Rawhide,</u> because one of the stars had our same surname and we thought somehow we might be related notwithstanding he went on to become a superstar actor, producer, and director and an American icon even to this day. I watched these shows religiously and always studied the credits to learn who the regulars were and even the guest stars. Explaining all this might make you wonder where am I going. What's the point?

Let me digress a bit further. One of my favorite singer/songwriters is John Hiatt. His body of work is prolific and just pure genius. In 2003 he wrote a song called <u>Circle Back</u> from the <u>Beneath This Rough Exterior</u> album. In the very first verse he writes Ward Bond/ Was his sidekick Rowdy Yates? It was as if he were asking me. Now the song is about nostalgia and sometimes we have to relive our past to better understand ourselves, just like I am attempting to do here. But back to the song; was Rowdy Yates Ward Bond's sidekick? Absolutely not! Ward Bond played a character called Major Seth Adams in a TV series called <u>Wagon Train</u>. Rowdy Yates was the ramrod for Gil Favor in <u>Rawhide</u>. Now you can only be savvy of this kind of trivia by knowing your " Westerns" from the late 1950's.

More importantly it was at this time that I decided I liked school. After all I was already a veteran student at Springmore Elementary, if you count kindergarten, first, and second grades. Learning was fun and I liked eating in the cafeteria and I had really nice teachers, especially Mrs. Zimney my second grade mentor. She always told me I was a good student and she liked my sense of humor, which made me feel like a star. Also did I mention she was young and very pretty?

All that school is a bowl of cherries stuff came to a grinding halt the day after Labor Day 1959. It was when I walked into the third grade classroom of Doris Bevis. I could tell by her visage this woman was going to be no nonsense. In all my years at Springmore, Giant City Consolidated, and Carbondale Community High School; I knew of only three teachers, who were tough disciplinarians and did not suffer fools lightly. They were all strong willed women, Hester Cavaness, Margaret Crowe, and Doris Bevis.

I knew Ms. Cavaness mostly by reputation as told by Bob Striegel. He said one day while sitting in freshman English on the second floor of the old building that ran parallel with High street. He was going to end his struggle with her and his somewhat low class standing. So he walked up to her desk and before he could utter a sound she said, " What do YOU want?"

"Miss Cavaness, I would like..."

" Bob Striegel, you know what I would like? I would like you and Wally Crane to quit enticing that gang down at Mac's Store to yell obscenities and shoot spit wads through the windows?"

"But...."

"Is that all you can say?"

"I want to ask you if I can learn how to study and become a better student."

"Go back to your desk, sit down, open a book, and be quiet!!"

I was fortunate to have had Margaret Crowe for English III and IV at CCHS. She was battle hardened and could not stand wasted talent. I watched the "Old Crowe" spar with Mike Given almost daily for two years. I remember most her requesting he use his intellect in a positive direction. He rebelled and tried his best to disrupt her class. She saw something more than a bad attitude and now he is a professor of English at Stephen F. Austin State University going toe to toe with the same type of exasperating punks.

First day of third grade and I knew this was not going to be a walk in the park. Ms. Bevis ruled with a heavy hand. She was obsessed with classroom rules and etiquette. However, she was fair and a knowledgeable instructor. Everyone in our class seemed to adhere to this structure, except for one individual. He was by name, Miles Fletcher. Miles was not a rebel or trouble maker. He simply went his own way and Doris Bevis did not care for it at all. There were two rules she lectured us on a daily basis. The first one was, if you needed to go to the restroom; then ask for her permission, which usually was always given. The second rule was, if you are sick and especially if you are nauseous; get up and go straight to the bathroom.

Then one day in early November, 1959, Miles walked slowly up to Ms. B's desk and then in ultraslow motion he arched his back and pitched forward. Out of his mouth came a torrent of brownish green and chunky liquid. It covered her hair, glasses and face and splattered her desk and papers. The miasma left behind by the effluent made us cover our mouths and noses. The look on her face was of apoplectic horror. "What have I told you kids over and over?" If you're going to be sick, go quickly to the restroom!", she said quietly.

We were let out for an early recess, which was welcomed by all of us. And when we came back to our classroom, there was our janitor spreading the ubiquitous red sawdust that supposedly soaked up the bilious liquid, but just could not absorb the smell.

We did not speak of the incident anymore and far as I remember, there were no similar accidents that year. I have wondered often what Miss Bevis took from such an experience. I am sure it was not the only mishap that occurred in a long career of nurturing young people. I do know this, it was not evidence of Ponce De Leon's fabled elixir of immortality we witnessed, but we had our own fountain of youth in third grade during my favorite year.

THOSE WERE THE DAYS, MY FRIEND

By Emily Stafford

What a time it was to be starting high school. So much was happening, across the country, and I was barely aware of a fraction of it, at 14. And yet here we are, some fifty years later, having collectively taken steps both forward and backward, and wondering just what sort of legacy we'll be leaving for the generations that follow.

Early September, 1966, still hot and humid in southern Illinois, but with a tiny hint of Fall in the air. We were sweating, standing outside the old high school that morning, across the side street from the infamous "little store." Partially shaded by an old oak tree, we were waiting for the first bell to ring, books clutched tightly to our chests. Trying to look cool, but with feet shuffling back and forth and furtive glances this way and that--long before I understood the meaning of the word "anxiety."

So, freshman year, and 14 years old. Trying to figure things out, socially, academically, and in every other way. Night time dreams of being lost in the hallways, searching endlessly for the assigned locker. Lots of kids, especially older kids . . .a lot to take in. Freshman girls had assigned "older sisters," seniors appointed to offer some transitional guidance. Mine wasn't very talkative, as I recall. I doubt her role had been particularly well-defined, or that she had received much "how to" coaching. I may not have offered much to work with, myself, not being the most outgoing of kids at that point.

A memory that surfaces immediately when I think of that first year involved a Friday night dance in the smaller girls' gym on the northeast side of the campus. What I remember most about that night was the violence that occurred as the music ended and students were leaving the building. There were stairs leading down from the elevated doorways to the sidewalk. Hearing some commotion below, along the north side of the building, I stopped to peer over a concrete ledge. Curled up against the side of the building, trying to shield himself from the blows raining down upon him, was a young African American male student. He was surrounded by three white male students, who were hitting and kicking him. I didn't recognize any of them. I was terrified, although it's doubtful I had anything to fear, and ran quickly with the crowd down the steps toward the street and away from the violence. I never heard what happened to that young man. I hoped that some of the teachers supervising the dance became aware of the assault and intervened before he was badly hurt. Regardless, the feelings of guilt and shame for my cowardice that night have never left me, and I consider them healthy reminders. To whoever that young man was, and to all of the other African American students who experienced similar violence and disrespect during those early years of school desegregation, my humblest and most sincere apology.

As many readers will recall, those years were tumultuous times, on many fronts. Just the year before, the 1965 Watts riots had left 34 dead and many more injured. The Selma to Montgomery marches, in defiance of segregationist repression, were part of a broader voting rights movement underway throughout the American South. Despite the passage of the Voting Rights Act that same year, a landmark achievement of the Civil Rights Movement, many hearts and minds remained unchanged—as evidenced by that Friday night in 1966 outside the CCHS girls' gym in Carbondale. The previous closure of Attucks High School now required all African American students to attend CCHS. The atmosphere was racially charged, and that tension found its way into the classrooms and hallways. I have since realized how much more acutely our African American peers must have felt this, and the anxiety with which they likely walked around, never knowing just what might happen next--and when they might be personally targeted.

In response to incidents like the one I witnessed, and the obvious racial tension on campus, the CCHS administration and faculty established an appointed group of African American and Anglo students called the "Junior Human Relations Board" (JHRB). I have no idea how students were selected for participation in this group, but I was fortunate to have been one of them. By this time, CCHS also had some remarkable African American faculty, staff and coaches, including Arthur Black, who facilitated and sponsored this JHRB group. My recall about what we discussed during the student meetings that took place is poor, as is any memory of what we may or may not have actually accomplished. A classmate recalls once seeing banners in the hallways that read "Black and White Unite!"--but neither of us can say whether those banners had to do with an upcoming school dance theme, or were the work of this student group, or both. I do remember a heightened sense of personal responsibility regarding my own behavior, partly related to what I had witnessed as a freshman. I also recall thinking that it was important to model positive social behavior for my peers, as best I could. I began to develop a strong resolve to never again run from manifestations of hatred or "look the other way." I credit the CCHS faculty/staff leadership for attempting to involve students in coming together to seek solutions, and for setting the stage for some direct dialogue to occur. We also clearly benefited from being part of an even more diverse and vibrant university community. Opportunities exited, on and around the SIU campus, to help us begin to see beyond the racist thinking and behavior to which all of us (Anglo kids) had been amply exposed, whether we were aware of it at the time, or not. The more comprehensive social constructs of white privilege and institutionalized racism would not be written about—or spoken of—for many years still to come.

By school year '68-'69, all Carbondale high school students were attending CCHS, as by that time both Attucks High School and University High School had closed their doors. My class—the Class of '70—clearly grew in diversity, academic strength and athletic skill, as a result. Our opportunities for expanded learning, social and political challenge and understanding of each other increased. Clearly, our boys' sports teams benefited enormously, with two consecutive trips to the state basketball championships during those years. . . and one second place trophy! Some refer to sports as the "great equalizer." It would be hard to argue with that, given what we witnessed at CCHS during those years. Those who played so well together as team members, and those of us who cheered them on as spectators, benefited from this example of teamwork and camaraderie. We owe a huge debt to those student athletes, and to their progressive coaches, for their leadership and accomplishments, of which we were all very proud. If only girls' athletics had not been lagging so far behind during those years! The times they were a changin', but not fast enough for many of us.

I would be remiss not to take a moment to acknowledge a special thanks to some of the exceptional teachers who were influential in my growth and development: teachers like Theodora Bach (Speech/Humanities), William Anderson (Geometry), Zoe Lightfoot

(Science/Chemistry), Gladys Sullivan (Science/Biology), Charles Lemming (History) and Margaret Crowe (English), to name a few. Big kudos, as well, to Art Black, for being the coolest dude around--even when I accidentally backed into his car in the parking lot one weekend, while he was dutifully overseeing the student dismantling of some dance decorations in the girls' gym. Mr. Black was a "well regulated" person (long before modern psychology coined the term) and totally kept his cool. His response meant a lot to me, and to everyone who witnessed it, as well.

All around us, so much was happening during these years, in addition to the previously mentioned Civil Rights Movement--the Vietnam War and protest movement, the Gay Rights Movement, and the Women's Liberation Movement--to cite the most obvious. The assassinations of both Dr. Martin Luther King, Jr. and Sen. Robert Kennedy, the Stonewall Riots in NYC, the founding of the Black Panther Party in Oakland, and the Kent State shootings are potent reminders of the times. And then there was the tragic burning of Old Main at SIU, right in our own back yards—a lot for a high school student to assimilate.

Lest the reader think that these high school years were fraught only with social, racial and political unrest, let me also reflect on some of the high points and other things that took place. There were, indeed, many good times. I've already mentioned the "sports highs" that our talented athletes dished out. And the music--OMG. It really couldn't have been any better. For instance: Woodstock, summer of '69. Three days of fabulous music and the demonstration that non-violent interaction was possible in a group of near 500,000 young people (despite adverse weather conditions and food shortages) was a remarkable thing, indeed. Unfortunately, although most of my peers knew how to drive by 1969, no one I knew--myself, included--had the financial resources, parental support, guts or planning savvy to take off to upstate NY. We paid close attention to what little media coverage of it there was, though, and fantasized about being there.

I have often said that The Beatles helped raise me, in terms of values and behavior--but there were so many other influential artists and groups, as well. It was a very rich time in the world of music--from the British Invasion to Motown to Bob Dylan, Simon and Garfunkel and Joan Baez--to Janis Joplin, Jimmy Hendrix and Jim Morrison--and all of the other American rockers, Blues musicians and singer/songwriters--the list is endless. And there were some great local groups, like Big Twist and the Mellow Fellows, who were my favorites. There were first loves, first drinks and smokes, escapades, rebelliousness, first jobs and first earned money (!!), getting a driver's license (and occasional use of the family car), school dances (without racial violence), friends, parties, Teen Town, building class floats and constructing school dance decorations together, Student Council activities, summers spent swimming in nearby lakes . .. . .it was a challenging time, but also a very rich environment in which to grow up, in so many ways.

I remember one prevailing question present my mind, throughout those high school years: I often wondered why so much cruelty and violence existed in our own country and around the world. Why were human beings, despite our "big brains," so challenged to be kinder, more cooperative and more compassionate toward one another? I'm sure that nagging question had a lot to do with moving me initially toward the study of behavioral psychology and the mental health field, and then later toward legislative advocacy, as my career path unfolded. Here's hoping that some lasting change and progress has been made, although the challenges facing the coming generations are certainly no less daunting than those we faced. The thought never crossed our minds that someone with a gun might enter our school intent on mass murder, for instance. With that sort of fear, we didn't have to live . . . nor that our planet might one day irreparably suffer from the effects of our environmental abuse. All of this said, I wouldn't trade growing up in Carbondale, and my high school years at CCHS, for any other place. I will always consider C'dale to be my home, although I've not lived there in almost 35 years now. I'm grateful to have grown up in a university community with so many interesting, diverse and wonderful classmates—as well as others in the student body--many of whom have stayed in touch and continue to reach out and maintain connections with one another. We're a lucky bunch, in so many ways. I'm humbled to have had this kind of thought-provoking, and largely supportive, start on life in Carbondale. I'll always be proud to be a Terrier, and continue to get by with a little help from my friends.

WHY I NEVER GRADUATED FROM CCHS

By Matt Rendleman

I hated high school. So one day in 1969, in the middle of our senior year, Eric McGowan and I took off for California, first by train, then by thumb. In California, I imagined, people knew what life was all about. For some reason we journeyed by way of Florida. We ran out of money in Benton, Arkansas.

With no funds to move the trip forward, we went to work for a local contractor named Bobby. He was a good-old-boy with two bulldozers, a backhoe, a truck and trailer to haul them, and a dapple gray stud horse named Booger. Eric and I became part of a team that made all these things work. One of the dozers was an ancient International TD18. It started on gasoline then, with the engine spinning, would switch to diesel blowing giant smoke rings up toward the clouds until it warmed up. The International had a flat triangular blade in front, lined with huge saw teeth. The blade ran along the ground like a filet knife severing trees right at the soil line. The dozer driver was protected by a cage, but he still had to be careful since there was no telling which way the trees would fall. A tree once fell on a hydraulic line delaying work for a few hours. The other dozer was a smaller Case with controls similar to one of today's zero-turn mowers, except there were four levers instead of two. When business was slack we did odd jobs like digging post holes (there are lots of rocks in Arkansas) and anything else that came up.

I remember Arkansas as a place defined by its odd denizens. Bobby's usual backhoe operator was Glen. Glen's bride, who had grown rather plump since matrimony, came home one day to find Glen bedding another – in their own trailer's bedroom. She left him, but it was all a joke to Glen. Boorish behavior was common. Despite being no better myself, I still felt like an outsider. Glen took Eric into the roadhouse to drink and meet women, but I had to stay in the truck because I looked too young.

Another occasional worker, whose name I've forgotten, seemed more stable than Glen. He had converted his pickup truck to run on bottled gas, which he got at a discount or maybe free. He was building his own barn and for a hobby raised wolves. There were other characters too, ranging on the danger scale from about five to ten.

Bobby paid us sporadically until he finally quit paying us altogether. At least we had a place to stay in an abandoned house on his property. We broke the tie the gas company put on the meter so we could cook or warm ourselves. We stole groceries. Occasionally Bobby's wife would feed us. Eric had had enough of this "freedom" before I had and went back to Carbondale. A few weeks later, I followed. California seemed farther away than ever.

"Why begin such an Ill-fated adventure in the first place?" you ask. I had become ever more isolated through high school. One by one I began to jettison the things that I was involved with and finally the people I knew.

Things that I threw overboard:

Academics did not captivate me. Math was interesting for a little while, but I gave up on that. I found it preferable to be a know-nothing smart ass in class.

Sports: I genuinely loved basketball, but I knew I couldn't make the Carbondale high school team. Eventually I dropped out of athletics; first football (the coaches had no idea what talent they had on their hands), and finally track too, a sport I could actually compete in. None of it seemed worth the effort.

Religious faith: I did the Presbyterian members class for young people at the First Presbyterian Church in Carbondale. As a graduation highlight, we answered some simple questions as a group from Reverend Howe. The class, like so many things I did, did not seem to have a point. By the time I finally did finish high school I had developed an eighteen-year-old sophisticate's view of Christianity. Religious faith, I had decided, was a carryover from mankind's primitive past and would probably soon vanish altogether. "There may be a God," I told my father one time, "but I'm sure he's not a Big-Man-in-the-Sky." What I meant, of course, was that any god that existed could not be concerned with me, and certainly didn't have an opinion about the way I lived. Any god that did exist would have to fit my conceptions if he wished to retain the title of God.

Friends and drugs: The recreational drug of choice (or necessity) for my buddies and me was marijuana. At first it was exhilarating; a mildly hallucinogenic joy ride. (Once an upperclassmen sold me a "nickel bag" of horse manure. I want that five dollars back.) After the first few episodes I ceased to enjoy even that. The experience seemed to make it plain that I was absolutely exposed to the world. It only intensified a feeling of spiritual nakedness. If I dared to speak I only opened a window to my soul for everyone to peer into. So I preferred to stay quiet or alone. I didn't want others to see that I was hollow and inadequate. Nobody else felt that way, I was sure – only me. (More than forty years later I realized that such an experience in some form is common. Note Adam and his wife hiding and covering themselves with fig leaves.)

Eventually I even jettisoned my friends. Life was unhappy, but in my mind there was still California.

Having burned most of my bridges in Carbondale, I didn't graduate from CCHS. Instead I finished high school in Edwardsville with my Dad and his family. I didn't join any clubs. I didn't participate in any sports. I had one friend, a boy my father dubbed "Crazy Rick." I just held my nose and got through senior year. But this depressing story does have an epilog.

Back in the groove (or rut), I signed up for college – after all, that was the next step in life. Senior year plus. But my father, who got me enrolled in the first place, must have seen the slow-motion train wreck of mediocrity coming down the tracks and asked if I would not like to join the work force for a while before furthering my education. Wise idea. And a relief.

I spent a year working on the river; more specifically the Illinois, Ohio, and Mississippi River system including the Atchafalaya and Intercostal Canal to Port Arthur and once to Brownsville, Texas. I started as a deck hand for the Gladders Towing Company, and after an appropriate apprenticeship, and Coast Guard supervised examination, graduated to Tankerman – class B. That meant I was officially qualified to pump anything up to, and including, gasoline (just not anhydrous ammonia) on and off of barges. My license stated that I was "validated for emergency service" – an official endorsement that always worried me a bit.

If there were characters in Arkansas, there were more on the river.

Captain Simpson probably had the highest IQ of the lot. He was the only one who could work the autopilot on the newer boats. He once enlisted me in an elaborate hoax perpetrated on our cook, Zella Doom. Zella was a Christian woman of good will and without guile. To involve her in our scheme, I enlisted her help in hiding giant wads of "cash" that had suddenly, and to her mysteriously, come into my possession. This "cash" consisted of five or ten dollar bills wrapped around newspaper dummy bills meticulously cut out by Simpson on one of his six-hour watches in the pilot house. I hid the pretend fortune somewhere in the boat's large pantry. Simpson came down to dinner in a dramatically dark mood. He vowed to kill anyone who had robbed him. I've forgotten how it all played out, but we had Zella going for a while.

Simpson once told me that a lot of young guys think that they can "come right into the pilot house," without the proper vetting or something. Being even more tone deaf then than I am now, I hadn't realized that he was considering training me to be a pilot. Making money as a highly-paid pilot did not have much appeal anyway. I was still dreaming of California. A few years after leaving the life on the river I heard that Captain Simpson, who had become Port Captain, died in a helicopter crash inspecting ice on the Mississippi River in St. Louis. Holland was an engineer. The chief engineer is the next in charge in succession following the captain. Holland spoke slowly, but in such a way that you could not find an opening to either speak or escape.

Wanda was the cook who introduced me to gumbo – one of my life's greatest culinary delights. We had a captain who sang hymns in the pilot hours, one who smoked cigars and left an incredible mess, and one who collided with a Cajun boat in Morgan City affording me the opportunity to testify before a Coast Guard hearing in New Orleans. In sum, the river had its exciting moments, punctuated by long periods of boredom, but nothing to hold me for long.

After a year working the Mississippi and intercostal waterways along the Gulf, I finally set out on my own for California, the place where, I was sure, the answers to life lay. In a way that I didn't expect, I actually got that right. I hitchhiked all the way to Big Sur.

California was not to be outdone by Arkansas or the river in its panoply of characters. One of them was "Doc" – not his real name. He once told me what his real name was, but I have long forgotten it. I'll always remember him as Doc. Doc had been a biker and had changed his name for legal reasons. (I think he was wanted for something.)

In Big Sur I met other like-minded souls where we found a place to abide on a wooded mountainside. We set up camp and commenced to live. There was a stream that provided drinking water and water to clean the dishes. (We had to warn visitors to do their business AWAY from the stream.) I was always guarded, but there was a family-type atmosphere at our camp.

Doc's woman was Cathy, a lovely woman who once disrobed by the fire where many of us guys were watching the flames. Nothing wrong with that. This was the age of Aquarius. We pretended to be disinterested. Doc suggested that she might want to spare us in the future.

Many of the hippies we met warned us to watch out for "Jesus freaks." They had the power to make you uncomfortable. But before we could take the advice to heart we had invited a couple of them to our encampment. They engaged us in extended conversation with Doc in the lead. It seems that Doc had read some version of the New Testament.

I, however, was not going to be taken by these Elmer Gantries and I registered my disapproval by glaring at the one engaged with Doc. To my surprise he was unfazed by my disapproval. I had never seen – or at least noticed – this in anyone before and it impressed me beyond words. What I saw in him was a freedom from judgment, the judgment of others that had always made me a slave. The peace that he so evidently enjoyed came from somewhere else, a place I was not familiar with. I quickly went from critic to fan boy. I was so awed that I gushed: "I want what you have." "Anytime you're ready," was his answer. Resistance was futile.

The next night Doc seemed intensely fixated on the fire. Finally, overcome with the thoughts consuming him he said, "Can you dig it man… a God that loves you so f******g much that he sent his son to die for you." Now that was an earthy testimony that I wouldn't dare try in church. He was overawed by a God who would love him. I began to rethink my assumptions. The next night by the same fire I had an encounter that changed my life forever. Finding out I had been wrong about most everything was actually quite a relief. My world – the world that existed between my two ears – sucked anyway. California had not disappointed. I came back to Carbondale with a buddy, Patrick Tuten, partly by hoboing a freight train from California to St. Louis.

That trip is a story in itself. Tuten and I had gotten as far as Barstow, California, where old Route 66 would once take you east. Barstow now joined the Interstate at either end of town. The entrance ramps to the Interstate were separated by a miles-long, 100-plus degree strip of commercial sprawl; and we were at the wrong end it seemed. Few cars passed us hopeful hitchhikers, and so after a few hours we decided to make the exhausting trek to the other end of town where we were sure more cars would see us. When we arrived there may have been more cars, but they were overwhelmed by countless more hitchhikers. If any motorist slowed down to pick someone up, dozens of other would-be riders would descend on the car and scare the potential ride away. The day was waning, we were exhausted, and we were far back in a queue that seemed only to be getting longer.

"Look," some enterprising community organizer said, "There's a train track right over there. We can all get out of here. I've done it lots of times." Our desperation made us vulnerable to the appeal, so after actually asking the engineer of a slowly passing train which way it was going, we boarded another stationary train. Our chosen vessel was a piggy back car, a flatcar with a rail down the middle to secure the trailers of over-the-road rigs. There must have been more than thirty of us sitting on this open-air conveyance in the California desert as the sun began to set. As discouragement took its toll potential passengers got off a few at a time until night fell and only about half remained. Still the train hadn't moved.

Sometime after nightfall the train began to move. Eventually it was rocketing at what must have been an incredible speed. I say "must have been" because it was too dark to see what we were passing or how fast it flew past. We only knew that it was shaking like a roller coaster as we hung on to the center rail for dear life. I had no idea where we were going.

The next morning all our faces were black from diesel soot. We looked like Al Jolson in blackface. When the train stopped we found an open boxcar and got inside. Someone had a road atlas, and for the rest of the trip to Kansas City members of our cohort would jump off, one-by-one, when they reached a road on their east-west coordinate and then head north or south to their eventual destination.

Once at some out-of-the-way grain elevator in Arizona or New Mexico we were discovered by an employee of the Santa Fe Railroad and ordered to exit the train. As a new destination the place would have been worse than Barstow. The only road we could see was one-lane and gravel and there were more than a dozen of us still on the car. I begged for mercy and it was granted – he let us stay onboard.

Finally, as we approached Kansas City the Santa Fe line's mercy ran out. Peeking out the doors we could see a giant complex of tracks, a huge railyard drawing near. More ominously, two men, in suits jumped onto platforms on either side of our boxcar. They each had their coats tucked back to give them quick access to their side arms. We thought it best to do whatever they asked.

Our rag-tag group was escorted to the offices of some executive who first asked if we had broken into any other cars. We assured him we hadn't. (We had. During one of the train's stops, hoping to find something to eat and supposing we had found oranges – you couldn't be sure in the dark – we got back to our boxcar only to discover we had pilfered a case of lemons.) Our supervising executive then gave us an appropriately stern lecture on the gravity of what we had done and made us promise not to do it again. We again assured him that we wouldn't.

Then, after a brief pause, someone in back asked where we might catch a train to St. Louis. There were some giggles. Our executive blanched, then with a kind of dumfounded expression said, "Well, you might try Rock Island across town." Kansas City was as far east as the Santa Fe went. Tuten and I did indeed find the Rock Island, and rode it clear to St. Louis. A ride or two later and we were back in Carbondale.

I had found what I didn't know I was looking for. Life was no longer as bleak, and I didn't have to hide. Marijuana was fun once again. (I know what you're thinking – no, I quit nearly 50 years ago.) The adventure continues to this day, but I think that if I had to go back to high school now I'd enjoy it a lot more.

ILLINOIS AVENUE

By Bill Leebens

1966

The sign said: WARNING: You are entering a congested motorcycle area. Proceed with caution. "What the hell does *that* mean?" my father said.

Soon enough, we knew: we were swarmed by Vespas, step-through Honda scooters, screaming two-stroke Suzukis, and all manner of 'cycles and scooters.
Congested, all right.

The road into town turned into Illinois Avenue. The swarm went both ways; there was no sensible one-way traffic, yet. That would come years later.

Along with the bikes, I saw the train station, what seemed like a million people on the sidewalks, the Dairy Queen, and my first glimpse of the green campus of SIU.
I liked it. And in spite of tumult, unrest, and the angst of teen years--- that feeling has never changed.

1967

My early years revolved around comic books. My memories of pre-Carbondale life, back in Austin, Minnesota, are tied to the comics I was reading when events occurred.

Shopping with my Mom at Austin Drugs, August, 1962? *Journey Into Mystery* #83, the introduction of Thor.

Ross Johnson's death, me sitting in the back of the car as my Dad visited the widow, some time after December, 1963? *Batman # 160*, "The Alien Boss of Gotham City".

One of my first tasks upon hitting Carbondale was to find sellers of comic books. Aside from a few grocery stores at either end of the city, most were along Illinois Avenue.

Hewitt's Drugs and University Drugs were the best sources, and as I became familiar with the city, I often rode my bike between the two, up and down Illinois, looking for the latest releases. My new pal Dave Sulzer was a fellow comic junkie. We snobbishly ignored the Superman world at DC Comics, reading only Marvel Comics titles, and we would call one another with news of our latest finds.

That summer, I took a morning class in German at Quigley Hall, which then housed the Home Ec department. After class, my pal/classmate Dan Morgan and I often went to the museum in Old Main, or would cruise the stores along Illinois Avenue.

Kaleidoscope, the quirky gift shop, was always a fun time-killer. One small purchase from there that I remember was a tiny soft-cover book printed in Japan on crinkly paper, *How To Play Go Game*. I never mastered Go, but the wording of the book's title always made me laugh. That was a quiet, idyllic time.

Things change.

1968-1970

Kids are always upset at missing excitement, no matter how much it might've put them at risk. I saw this years later in Florida, when my kids were upset by not being in the middle of Hurricane Charley. Oh, well.

During the late '60s and early '70s, I frequently rode my bike down Illinois Avenue and passed by Old Main on the way to Morris Library. My father's faculty card gave me unlimited access to the million-volume library, and I took advantage of that.

I became adept at loading my baskets with books, strapping a Jenga pile of them across the baskets and fender, and carefully riding home. It was a time of turmoil. As a junior high student, I knew that, but I wasn't actively involved in anti-war protests. I mostly agreed with them...until they did stupid things.

Like bombing the Agriculture Building. And setting fires. And opening gas jets---to what effect?---at the Chemistry Building. I'd read *The Autobiography in Malcolm X* in 8th grade, but that didn't mean that I believed in "by any means necessary." Besides, this stuff was totally *un*necessary. A year later, my beloved Old Main was gone. For no reason. Totally unnecessary.

We'd always been able to see the tower of the building from our backyard; now we saw it go up in flames, and collapse. Years later I'd experience déjà vu as Notre Dame went the same way.

Another year later, and peaceful protests on Illinois Avenue following the Kent State deaths turned violent. Tear gas, nightsticks, the whole Chicago '68 experience, followed by the shutdown of SIU.

I didn't witness any of it. I felt left out. Oh, well. For months and months afterward, businesses on Illinois Avenue sported plywood where windows had been. Totally unnecessary.

Every time my Dad and I drove down Illinois, he would rant about the damage. He was *pissed*, in a major way. I rarely agreed with him in those days, but in that case--- I did.

1973

Dave Brown was the first of my friends to move out on his own. While still at CCHS, he did graphic design for an ad agency that had offices above Atwood Drugs on Illinois Avenue. Dave managed to find a cool apartment on the other side of South Illinois above a bakery, with a patio, no less. From there we could watch whatever chaos was unfolding on the street below.

Part of that chaos was periodic street parties that shut down Illinois. Regarding this, I channeled my Dad: I also thought it was "pampering a buncha goddamn drunks". Those drunks were only a little older than me, and I would sometimes hang around those street parties--- not to participate, but to sneer disdainfully at their behavior. And look at girls. I was a snob, but I was still a teenage guy.

One such night, my friend Brian Baggett wandered through the chaos with me. We knew that Dave was working alone upstairs at his office, as he often did, and we thought we'd pay him a visit. The glass-paneled door at street level led to the office on the second floor. Being teens, we amused ourselves by banging on the door and shouting, "DAVE! DAVE!"

No response.

We banged louder, and riffed on Cheech and Chong: "DAVE!! C'mon, man, I NEED A FIX! DAVE!!"
Eventually, we heard Dave running down the stairs, and he unlocked the door and looked out, looking both annoyed and bewildered. Oddly, he was looking past the two of us.
"What's going on??"
A voice behind us said, "yes, WHAT IS going on??" The person Dave was staring at.

Brian and I turned to see an angry-looking guy in aviator glasses and a tan windbreaker, holding up a badge.
"umm…"

Talking very fast, I tried to explain that we knew our buddy was working tonight, we just came by to say hi, and be stupid and loudly make drug references while the downtown was, apparently, crawling with undercover cops. Sorry, we were just kidding around. Really. Didn't mean any harm. Heh.

He was not amused. After glaring at us for what felt like an hour, he shook his head, scolded us, and wandered off into the fray.
I have no recollection of what we did after that. It's funny how stark terror can mess with your memory.

Another night, another street party. On this particular night, I wandered farther north on Illinois, and passed a uniformed cop standing at the head of the cobblestoned alleyway next to Hewitt's. I was heading down the alley towards my truck, parked in the back, jittery from being around the crowd.

Startled by a shuffling noise behind me, I turned, and saw a young guy. A very, very *drunk* young guy. He swayed and wobbled around the alley, then stopped and looked back at the cop.
I had a feeling this wasn't good.

Sure enough. After staring at the cop, he leaned down, wobbling, and began to pry a brick out of the pavement.
Now I was *sure* it wasn't good.
He managed to lever the brick out, and turned back towards the cop. As his arm pulled back to heave the brick at the oblivious cop, I grabbed his shoulder and spun him around.
"Don't do it."
He tried to focus on me, still wobbling. He screamed, "you're NOT MY FATHER! You CAN'T TELL ME WHAT TO DO!!"

I had no idea what drunken Freudian nightmare I'd wandered into, but I didn't care. I held onto his shoulder.
After a minute or so, he dropped the brick, shook my hand off, and wandered back towards the street, cursing the whole way.
I watched to make sure he wasn't going after the cop. He seemed to have run out of rage, and just blended back into the crowd.
I put the brick back in the pavement, stepped it down, and went on to my truck.

1973-1974

That truck? It was a 1954 Chevy half-ton that I'd bought from a neighbor of Tony Troutman's, down by Makanda. At some point in its hard life---there were a number of dents, the wooden bed was well-worn, and there was a good bit of rust---someone had painted it bottle green, seemingly using a brush. Also brush-painted on the doors was a sign of sorts:
H.B. Downs

Makanda Ill
GVW 3100

In earlier times, farm and commercial trucks had to display the owner's name, city, and gross vehicle weight. This truck came from earlier times. Much earlier.

I talked the affable Henry Downs down from $200 to $165, and we had the title signed over and witnessed by a notary in a Makanda store. My partner in crime and ride there, Russ House, followed me as I drove the truck home. We were both a little uneasy about its ability to make it there.

But make it, it did. I dubbed the truck "Arrow" because of its pointy arrowhead grille and my love of Harry Nilsson, who had a song, "Me and My Arrow". In the months that followed I drove the truck to school, expecting disdain from status-conscious classmates. To my great joy and astonishment, a girl I loved told me, "I like your truck. It's cool."

It made no difference, though. I still couldn't work up to asking her out, much less express my potentially-scary maybe-obsessive love, or confess that I often drove past her house at night. Multiple times.

The term "stalker" wasn't yet in common usage, but I guess I was one. A benevolent, lovesick one, mind you.

The truck hauled my similarly-dateless stag group around C'dale, too many of us crammed into the cab, more in the bed of the truck. The usual weekend routes were followed: out Main, down University, back up Illinois. Eat pizza, and repeat.

Senior year came and went without much drama other than my unannounced and unrequited love, accompanied by my GPA plummeting from 3.800 to 1.625.

With time, I kinda sorta got over my first love. Mostly.
My friends had plans for college, which I had doggedly dodged. My parents planned a move to Memphis, as Dad retired from SIU and was going to teach at the UT Dental school. I had no idea what I was doing.

But one sunny summer day, as I looped down University and hit Illinois Avenue and headed south on Highway 51, none of that mattered. I didn't know where I was going. But at least for the moment, I was free.

ROCK AND ROLL HOOTCHIE KOO

By Chuck Cochran

Part 1: Four Squires And A Bride

Before moving to Carbondale, playing the guitar was not my dream as a kid -- it was my father's big idea. I wanted to be a scientist. When I was 10 years old, I got a microscope and a chemistry set for Christmas, and I thought I was prepared to tackle my future. But my dad suggested that I learn to play the guitar during that same year, talked me into it and bought me a used 1959 Gibson Les Paul Junior and a Supro Amp. He found a place where my across-the-street best friend Johnnie Winfield and I could take lessons and so we started in at the National School Of Music in Granite City.

At the time, I didn't appreciate the gear my dad bought me, because: a) it was used, dusty, had ancient, rusty, broken strings, and b) Johnnie's dad bought him a brand-new, shiny-red Rickenbacher guitar and silver Tolex Rickenbacher amp from National. The school was really just a music-lesson front created to sell parents on purchasing new Rickenbachers for their "incredibly talented" children. My dad didn't fall for the pitch, but Johnnie's did. His guitar was breathtakingly perfect with its flat-wound strings and new-car smell every time you opened the blue velveteen-lined guitar case. It glistened like a chrome-plated Christmas-morning Schwinn bike. I made peace with my brown Gibson, learned to change the strings, learned to polish it to a bright finish, but at the time, I thought it looked "less than." Thankfully, I kept those feelings to myself.

Sadly, the tobacco sunburst Gibson Les Paul and Supro pieces would get sold off, because --how shall I put it? I was stupid! Alas, I was unable to look into the future and have the foresight to keep them. Too bad, as both the guitar and the amplifier are nowadays highly sought after by collectors...yes, very expensive classics today -- way more coveted than the sexy Richenbacher! I still loved all things pertaining to science, but now I was hooked on music.

I wasn't born in Carbondale. I was born in Granite City, Illinois, just over the Mississippi River from St. Louis, and lived for a little while in a tiny burg situated between Alton and Granite named Mitchell, a blink of an eye as one passes through the middle of town on Route 66. I attended Mitchell Elementary School through the 6th grade, coincidentally, with Derrick Dean.

The National School of Music was located in a 1920's-era, two-story brick building that looked like a doctor's office. Even in 1962 it appeared old, and musty, not unlike the elementary school I attended, but smaller - same look as the original CCHS main building - high ceilings, hardwood floors, wide staircases, etc. Johnnie and I went there every week, sat in rooms with spiritless teachers, and were taught how to sight read standard melodies such as "Mary Had A Little Lamb" and "The Yellow Rose Of Texas." At the time, I couldn't articulate why the music lessons were so boring and unsatisfying, but I had a hard time practicing at home -- exactly because the lessons were indeed so boring and unsatisfying. At home, in private, I worked out the melodies to songs that captured my imagination like "The Stripper" by David Rose & Orchestra (1962) and "Moon River" by Andy Williams (1961), hits that were currently playing on the radio. And meanwhile, I learned the hillbilly favorite "Wildwood Flower" as taught to me by my hillbilly Uncle Joe Whitecotton, who was a clever, storytelling, self-taught musician who could play guitar, bass, and piano, and who played in country bands, and -- had nice gear.

We moved from Granite City to Carbondale -- that's mom, dad and four kids -- during the summer following completion of my 6th-grade year after I had been taking guitar lessons for about a year. We inhabited a tiny two-bedroom house in Tatum Heights, where I met and became friends with David Cox, Art Schoolcraft, Debbie Nelson, Emily Stafford and the Olmsted brothers, Gordon (Gordie) and David.

At this time, our family had no "stereo." We listened to music on the radio, but we certainly didn't buy records. My older sister had a record player, but she wasn't much interested in buying records, and if I touched it, she would scream and hit me :) (Love you, Pam!)

This would have been 1965, I was 13 and The Beatles were so

popular that ABC-TV had a new cartoon show called "The Beatles." This happened at a time when I was hungry to learn new songs, but had no means to listen to them, so when this cartoon show appeared, I took advantage of it. At ten o'clock on Saturday mornings, the show would air, and it followed the same format in each episode. You'd get a few minutes of the cartoon, then one of the Beatles' hits would play while the cartoon images flitted around. Then there would be more chicanery and buffoonery, and then a second song would play. I found that if I sat in front of our portable black-and-white TV on it's own rolling chrome stand, with my guitar, paper, pencil, and intense focus, I could learn an entire song as it played through just once. I only had one shot at it, so I had to be ready. After the song played, I'd shut off the tube and write down the chords I'd just learned in time to be ready for song number two. This was gold. I learned TWO Beatles songs every Saturday at 10AM. And I learned how to listen. And I learned to scream at my siblings to "SHUT THE HELL UP!" so I could focus on my newly crafted private guitar tutoring session, compliments of ABC-TV.

It wasn't long before David Cox and I discovered that we both could play a little and so became besties over music. We would play in his basement and work out the parts to all the songs on "High Tide And Green Grass" by the Stones, of course. They were perfect songs to learn on and we were mesmerized. "Last Time," "As Tears Go By," "Satisfaction," "Good Times, Bad Times," "19th Nervous Breakdown," we tried to learn them all.

After the summer that I moved to C'dale and met David, we began our middle-school boy life at Lincoln Junior High School and it was utter culture shock! On my first day of school, a very large 8th grader "loogied" in my face as I was stepping through the glass doors in the front! (WHAT?) My 7th-grade year was spent playing music with David, and sometimes David Olmsted, who also played, but he was much older and kinda scary.

But during the summer after 7th grade I got a call from John Potts, who was organizing a band with Eric McGowan and Mike Dillow. I'd gone to some sort of "jam session" at a house north of Main Street and think Potts was there. That's how he knew that I played. So when John contacted me, he gave me Eric's address and said to meet them there on a certain Saturday, which I did. John had specific ideas about which songs we should learn, but I was better at working out the chords and such (remember the cartoon show?!!). He had all of the 45rpm records, so I borrowed them, took them home and learned the parts. I remembered we had stored away high in a closet, a scratchy little 45rpm record player with an actual steel "needle" on which I used to play "The Battle Of

New Orleans" when I was five. I used it to play (and by "play" I mean "destroy" with the steel-needled record-eating machine) Potts' 45s so I could learn the solo to "You Really Got Me" by The Kinks. It was the same routine - Saturday mornings, after school, whenever I could get in front of the record player. Then I would come back the next Saturday afternoon and show the parts I learned to the band. This went on throughout the entirety of our 8th-grade year, during which time we learned 15 songs or so, and during the summer before we started our freshman year at CCHS (by the way, ours -Class of '70 -- would be the last class to start high school in the "Old Main" building).

Then Potts announced he'd just booked our first gig! It would be at Ye Olde Squire Shoppe in Murdale Shopping Center -- slated for a Saturday afternoon in the fall of 1966, just prior to the start of school. I was happy. And petrified. It's so weird how the universe works! If anyone had told me that I would perform in the presence of my future wife, who would have been not quite 12 years old, at the very first time that I would play music in a public setting, I don't think I would've believed it, but it turned out to be true.

Mr. Haege, who owned The Squire Shop (as we called it - I mean who's gonna say, "Ye Olde Squier Shoppe?!") was nobody's fool, and apparently not squeamish about taking financial advantage of 14-year-old boys. So when Potts negotiated our payment, Mr. Haege made what appeared to be a great deal for himself, but in the end would turn out not to be. At that moment in time, the fad in clothing was "Mod," direct from Carnaby Street in London. Mr. Haege sold cheaply made Mod hiphuggers with Mod polka-dot wide (fabric-wrapped cardboard) belts, and Mod shirts with Mod polka-dot ties and Mod everything. It was kinda pre-hippie, but I don't think that word had been coined yet, so it was "Mod." And he insisted that we dress in his gear in order to promote the gig and his store. So here's the deal that Potts made: We would play for two sets, and in return, we would get a DISCOUNT on the clothing that we would be obliged to purchase from him. So in the end, we each paid Mr. Haege $12.50 for the outfits as well as the opportunity to play in his store. We all knew it was a stinky deal, but we didn't care. We were going to play out! (More petrified now.)

So we got our Mod outfits and we paid Mr. Haege his money, and he took Polaroid photos of us and put them up in the store window to promote his Grand Opening...and he told us that our name would be "The Four Squires." If you were to look at those Polaroids, you would notice that all four of us -- Dillow, McGowan, Potts and Cochran -had shaved heads.

That summer, right before we became high school freshmen, David

Cox announced to me that freshmen boys would be "initiated" into high school. "What does that mean?" says I. "It means that the upperclassmen boys will kidnap you and shave off your hair and who knows what else?!" says David. This idea terrified us. We were obsessed with it. So, what else are a couple of paranoid 14-year-old boys going to do? We concocted a plan to avert the crisis, of course! We decided we would make a preemptive trip to the barber shop and calmly get our own hair shaved off, and then the upperclassmen would think we had already been initiated! Problem solved!

So Potts, McGowan and Dillow actually were initiated by upperclassmen and had their hair shaved off. Conversely, my head shaving was self-inflicted, as was David's. Little did I realize at the time, that only "popular" boys got initiated -- the cool cats...and David and I were on no one's radar. The good news is, though, that The Four Squires all matched in their Mr.Haege-Mod-attired-shaved-head-Polaroid store promotion photos!

On the day of the gig, Uncle Joe generously lent me a large-ish combo amplifier with 2 12" speakers, which was the biggest amp I'd ever seen, and which we used as our PA system. I talked Dad into buying a Shure microphone from the Radio Shack catalog for $38.50, and then I plugged it into Uncle Joe's super-cool amp.

The gig was a great success as all the cool older kids turned out. Cyndi McGowan was there for sure, lots of CCHS tanned blondes, surely Janice Senkosky, Wendy and Janie Meyer, some others. As my wife Anne would point out 53 years later, all of the big-ticket girls from CCHS were there dancing right in front of me and regretfully, I don't think I noticed...Anne certainly did notice and took careful notes.

But hey, speaking of my wife...she was a little girl all of 11 years old, who rode her daddy-was-too-tight-to-buy-one-so-he-built-it-from-a-2x4-and-repurposed-roller-skatewheels-and-painted-it-red homemade skateboard all the way from her house at 1208 W. Freeman to Murdale Shopping Center to see a real live rock band. Her name was Anne Westfall and I didn't have the pleasure of actually meeting her that day. She was feeling good (enough) with her new Beatle-bob haircut, but was naturally too intimidated by older high school kids to make her presence known to anyone thus stood against the wall by the front door and quietly observed. One day in the future, I would discover that the day was one she deemed to be special. She was indeed a dyed-in-the-wool rocker from birth, so I've concluded as years have passed. Nothing would've stopped her from being present at such a momentous occasion as a live rock band actually playing at Murdale.

We played "Little Red Riding Hood" and "Wooly Bully" by Sam

The Sham & The Pharoahs, "Paint It Black" and "Satisfaction" by The Rolling Stones, "Louie Louie" by the Kingsmen, "You Really Got Me" and "All Day And All Of The Night" by The Kinks, "Wild Thing" by the Troggs, "Mustang Sally" by Wilson Pickett, "Heart Full Of Soul" by the Yardbirds, "House Of The Rising Sun" by The Animals, and "I'm A Long Tall Texan" by Murray Kellum. I'm sure there were others, but you get the idea. Once we ran through our limited set list, we just started over. No one cared that we repeated the songs. It was magical. Everyone loved those songs. We could have played any one of them over and over.

Of course, I was oblivious. It's just who I am -- kind of a geek, good at math and music, bad at social graces. I was oblivious to Anne's little-girl presence as well as that of the high-beamed girls which, if you had known me then, is perfectly understandable.

The irony of a 100-pound, five-foot-six-inch, pre-pubescent 14-year-old with a shaved head in a Mod outfit replete with a too-long and too-wide polka-dot tie singing "Long Tall Texan" in the rear of a clothing store was lost on me. I told you I was oblivious. But it was not at all lost on John Wham.

John Wham was a character, even at 15...no, especially at 15. These days, after having taught music for the last five years in a charter high school I helped Anne start, I have come to know that type of kid. He is loud, boisterous, impulsive, more than a little likely to be a class clown, takes unnecessary risks and is beloved by his friends for his irreverent sense of humor and no-holds-barred sense of street justice - which is really funny because it's accurate. Like a long rifle - great! - as long as it's not pointed at you! He might have been a bit of a bully, but I kinda miss it nonetheless.

So when the band started up the vamp to "Long Tall Texan" with all of its audacious in-your-face 7th-chord guitar champs and quirky two-beat groove and I began to sing, it was a perfect storm of a slightly Asperger's, bald, skinny kid singing a crazy, out-of-character, popular song, running head-on into an older hyper-strung, irreverent class clown. It was like a Canadian cold front running into the remnants of a warm Gulf hurricane and colliding over Southern Illinois. That's the kind of stuff the Tri-State Tornado was made of. And it was more than John Wham could handle.

As I sang the words, "I'm a lo-ong tall Texan," his head snapped toward me like a ventriloquist's dummy, with a "Oh-my-God,-I've-got-you-now!" maniacal look on his face, not unlike Jack Nicholson in "The Shining." Sooner than my vocal sound waves of the first phrase of the song had escaped my mouth into the transducer of the Radio Shack microphone and down the wire into Uncle Joe's hotrod amp, he began delightedly mocking my squeaky delivery of the tune. With arms waving, pogo jumping, he ecstatically delivered his teenaged tirade as I attempted to squeal out the John Potts-mandated song to the Squire Shop audience and he did not cease to humiliate me until I graduated from high school.

God bless you, John Wham! Who knows what kind of egregious ego I could have developed in subsequent Hollywood years if you hadn't kept me grounded like an angel with a difficult mandate from the big guy upstairs. That's the stuff of which memories are made and stories are told.

What I remember most about my happiest childhood days in Carbondale is that live music was everywhere. And it was exciting! One of the first moments I encountered it was in the summer of 1965 when I was thirteen. It was a time when the Carbondale Park District would lovingly and innovatively engage its youth by sponsoring live outdoor concerts around town, usually on a fold-up rolling stage that was hauled to the site like a mobile home behind a truck. This one particular concert of my memory was staged on the CCHS tennis courts across the street from Bowen Gym. I don't remember the name of the band, but they had horns, played R&B, and were effing hot! So on that sweltering summer evening in '65, for the first time in my life, I heard from blocks away the exquisitely compressed sound of a cracking snare drum and it drew me in like a Star Trek tractor beam. It was powerless to resist and it made my heart race. The sound was a sexy siren that made my heart ache and I didn't know why...like when you're too young to fall in love or understand emotions of desire, but you kiss a girl anyway and it leaves your head reeling, and you don't know how to process what just happened. It's like you are about to be happier and free-er than you have ever been - with life's limitless possibilities still intact and waiting for your next move.

And so it was, throughout my time in Carbondale. There were live bands at every turn, at every school dance, at every Teen Town, at every summertime concert. There were Coal Kitchen and The Viscounts, and bands from St. Louis, and Wayne Cochran, and REO Speedwagon, and well, the list is endless. There were outside concerts at Giant City State Park, on SIU's campus, at Campus Lake, for frat parties. There were inside concerts at the SIU Student Center, Shryock Auditorium, Bowen Gym foyer, the "Girls" gym, SIU Arena. And there were live venues/bars all over Southern Illinois. Bonaparte's Retreat, The Golden Gauntlet aka Merlin's, Pizza King or PKs. And by the time I was 15 years old, I was playing all of them in bands like The Sound Experience and Payge III.

Even before one was old enough to walk into a bar, live music was available for teens as well. And while I didn't know it at the time, I now know that live bands are way more exciting that any recorded music --a crappy band is more exciting than a good deejay. And that's the way it worked that fall Saturday in '66 at The Squire Shop. We couldn't have been very good. But we were a live band. And there's something to be said about that.

So I told you I was socially oblivious? While I was focused on picking out the chords of songs, John Potts, Eric McGowan and Mike Dillow were focused on the more social aspects of being popular and scoring chicks. It worked out. I did the heavy lifting on the musical end -- they were the marketing team. So we played our first set of tunes at the Squire Shop and took a break. Remember I told you the deal Mr. Haege struck turned out not to be so good? That's because Potts, Dillow and McGowan loaded up the back of their amps and drum cases with merchandise from the rear of the store where we were set up. I guess poor Mr. Haege didn't count on teens who matched his small-town ruthlessness.

So the rockin' post-hippie-era culture of Carbondale supported my rock-'n-roll dreams...actually rocked and cradled me like a wild child of its own. Once McGowan, Potts and Dillow moved onto other pursuits, I played throughout the earlier part of high school with schoolmates such as Gus Pappelius, Walter Bottje...and drummer Charlie Scott, who was a highly social cat, a people collector, a leader of his own posse. Oddly enough, I never did play in those days with obvious people such as the Bunten brothers, Charlie Morrill or Robbie Stokes. I've actually become better acquainted with Charlie
Morrill in our current golden years and he's nowadays kind enough to invite me to sit in on his excellent and enjoyable band gigs in and around Carbondale and Cape Girardeau whenever Anne and I go back for class reunions and such.

So Charlie Scott led me to bands of older guys with whom we comprised The Sound Experience and later, Payge III -- the tail end of that period is when Anne and I became a late-'71-Christmastime Carbondale couple. Playing music on a nightly basis with these older guys, most of whom were solely supporting themselves through local bar gigs, was exciting for sure and even what I'd call peculiarly addictive...the music, the energy, the equipment, the girls, oh my God the music, the boy-style humor, the late late nights and early mornings, the drunks...I was a goner as far as my college ambitions went. I'd always thought I'd someday become an electrical engineer. But those stiff and serious calculus classes proved to be pretty tough during my junior year.

I was so busy with playing four sets every night out in some roadside Southern Illinois honky tonk -gas up the Stepvan loaded with heavy band equipment, drive to some God-Only-Knows-Where bar with a gravel parking lot and bare lightbulbs out on some two-lane highway, unload the Stepvan, haul all of the stuff up some rickety-thin staircase to a wood-floored vomit bar, wire up everything of mine and everyone else's, fix the technical problems that always happened, start the first of four sets at 9:00 pm of ear-splitting rock 'n roll, throw-back cheap beer and Boone's Farm from plastic cups, end the fourth set with a raucous rendition of "It's Alright" at 1:00 am, tear apart the setup and carry ALL of the heavy equipment down the skinny stairs and out to the frigid parking lot, load in, drive at least an hour back to Carbondale, head hitting the pillow in my parents' house -- if I was lucky -- at 3 am. An 8:00 am calculus class didn't really work out so well under such life conditions.

This particular lifestyle of nightly gigging started at about age 15. Looking back, it's interesting how loose parenting styles were within Carbondale's child-rearing culture. I mean, I was playing gigs every night in college bars, frat houses, brothel-like roadhouses...and in the worlds of my folks as well as Charlie's, well, all of it was normal and fine, even supported. Not once did anyone in my household ever say "Hey...what about your homework?" "What about sleep?' I think the truth about our household was that my mom loved Elvis Presley, so my early signs of showing musical talent was exciting to her, much the same way a young and promising athlete thrills his parents with the possibilities of pride and greatness. Come to think of it, my folks' loose-handed parenting style existed not only within my family's household, but within those of so many others. But tell you what, I'll bet it wouldn't have flown in houses of Carbondale's better-heeled/higher consciousness-for-education families with last names such as Vogler, Goss, Simonds, Stotlar. Those teens wouldn't have been running the streets and hanging around in bars, especially on school nights. Wouldn't have happened on my watch as a parent years later in Los Angeles, for better or worse.

So in high school, it's the truth that I was out all night and then getting up and hitting those first-period classes at CCHS. I always loved school from the earliest days of it, loved learning for learning's sake, and some school administrators along the way make a point of reporting to my mom that I was academically gifted and that she should've taken action to make sure I would receive whatever it was I would need in order to carry that particular ball. But it's no wonder I never was one of the decorated academic stars at CCHS. How could I have been? I was a kid by day, and working an energy- and at-times-soul-draining adult's job at night. And sometimes the adult-level lessons were hurled at me whether I wanted to receive them or not...such as one time at age 16, in the middle of my guitar solo during "Evil Ways" at Carbondale's Golden Gauntlet on Illinois Avenue, a bouncer was shot and killed right in front of me.

Another thing I've realized in looking back was that I was swallowed up into a vortex of sorts, a national trend of which I had no way to recognize or gauge. What I was doing was also being carried out in similar ways all across the nation -- perhaps for the first time ever in history, especially at that magnitude. Thinking of the biggest and best of them who shared this lifestyle...Tom Petty was doing it in the Florida Panhandle, John Cougar Mellancamp was mirroring that teenaged existence only one state over in Indiana, Bob Seeger was running all over Michigan and Michael McDonald in St. Louis, doing the same thing. I feel a connection with such individuals as later in life I ended up crossing paths with a number of them. I met and played in bands with all kinds of kids from all kinds of cities and tiny towns, one was even a tiny 13-year-old runaway who played a killer Hammond B-3 organ. All of us -- the famous ones and the nobodies, had three things in common. First, we couldn't imagine doing anything else. Second, nearly all of us could trace back our fixation to watching The Beatles perform on the Ed Sullivan Show and being blown sky high by it. Finally, the lifestyle in and of itself truly was the only "Rock-and-Roll University." There was no college major to take us there or gentle cushy way of introducing us into the fray through, say, an internship or summer camp program. A School of Hard Knocks model was the one and only way to get there, wherever "there" was, and each of us had no choice but to take that route if we were truly going to live in that world. It was hard yet magical, a huge high-stakes gamble, a specific attitude and mindset that had quickly become universal ones amongst those of us who were bitten by that bug. Most of us in this contemporary brotherhood came from meager households...not true of a few, such as Elvin Bishop, who was highly educated and reared within a wealthy household; Bonnie Raitt, whose father was a successful Broadway star and Hollywood actor, and of course, James Taylor, who came from a highly privileged east-coast background...more on him later as well.

Payge III gave way to meeting more accomplished fellow musicians, and soon I was playing, singing and arranging within somewhat higher-profile local bands I started such as Mule and Mother Goose. All the while, Anne desperately tried to keep me grounded and engaged in college, exercising the little-known future part of her brain that was oriented towards college counseling and helping teens. She led me out of the mess I'd made of my engineering studies at SIU and into ill-fated experimental coursework in interpretive dance, TV production, theatre...but it was too little too late, the die was already cast. Completion of a college degree seemed pointless and distracting to me. I had music to play.

Throughout these times from about age 15 until I finally stopped the college part of things at about age 21, these various bands of mine would spend summers playing all night -- seven sets from 9:00 pm to 4:00 am -- on Rush Street in Chicago while crashing all morning and afternoon in some fleabag rented motels and apartments, exhausted...and then getting up at 4:00 pm, heading into the Loop back to Rush Street and doing it again and again, six nights in a row. Later in this period, we'd summer in Milwaukee and one year we skipped fall quarter at SIU and didn't come back until the winter months, lived in dilapidated Victorian-style hippie crash-pad houses near the Milwaukee River on the east side, and played in all of the Milwaukee beer bars and clubs with names like The Stone Toad, Someplace Else, Teddy's, and in the crazy-cold months, drove up and down two-lane snowed-under roads to places in Appleton, Ripon, Beloit, Osh Kosh, Green Bay...same routine followed...huge PAs, B-3 organs, Leslie amps, guitars, wires, widgets, drums, microphones...carried in and out of rooms, up and down stairs, holding parts together with tape and ingenuity. It's no wonder my now-67-year-old ankles are shot and now my right hip is worrisome. I was a dedicated soldier of rock and roll. It's a wonder I never really took to drinking or drugging. Did my fair share of experimenting with those activities, but always maintained enough of a healthy fear of that side of life to treat it with utmost distance. All I really cared about was the music.

Part 2: What A Long Strange Trip It's Been...

During my last Carbondale band's tenure as well as the last-ditch immersion into exploration of arts-side coursework as prescribed by Anne, I received a call from a musician I knew in Milwaukee to move back up there and join a band that had some hits during my high school years, but was now living on nickels and dimes, doing the gypsy-style travels to all of the nightclubs throughout the entire Midwest. The band was The Ohio Express, which in its NY-based infancy had some smart business people backing it during the (thankfully) brief bubblegum music period, and it had churned out such hits as "Quick Joey Small," "Yummy Yummy Yummy," "Down At Lulu's," "Chewy, Chewy." Well, those glory days were over and now the remnants of that enterprise were still squeezing the remaining life out of that one, hitting farmers' daughter-attracting sorts of places in Ohio, Muskegon, Michigan (looniest town I've ever experienced...everyone we met acted as though they were high on acid, but weren't), Iowa, Michigan's upper peninsula, Minnesota.

Attempting to move with the time, The Ohio Express morphed into a glitter-rock copy band a la David Bowie called Silver Street, and we wore a lot of rhinestones, arched eyebrows, gleaming-glam makeup and high-heeled shoes. This display of femininity and mockery of traditional male roles was sometimes too much for the venues' local-color customers. One night in some one-horse club in frigid Superior, Wisconsin, I sat down between sets at the bar and ordered a Coke while I rested for a few. I arbitrarily occupied a seat next to a girl with a drunken boyfriend who didn't appreciate our frilly ways. He hollered out while smashing a wine bottle over the back of a chair "YOU F***ING F****OT! YOU GET AWAY FROM MY GIRLFRIEND! I'll SLIT YOUR F***ING THROAT!!" Oh, feets, don't fail me now! And he proceeded to chase me all over the room, wildly waving his jagged wine bottle while I jumped, tripped, flew over tables and chairs, bobbing and weaving in my glitter shoes and lipstick, running for my life until some bigger male types tackled him.

So...all the while this lifestyle was moving along, Anne was (remarkably) still in the front-and-center picture. She figured out how to wrap up her SIU degree one year early and moved to Milwaukee to live with me while she attended grad school at UW, and together we built a serious relationship in the midst of loose women and crazy low lives who drugged, dealt, drank -- and we negotiated our way into a young marriage as she didn't want to disappoint her mother by living with me outside of matrimony. She was 20 and I was still 22 when we walked down the aisle of her mother's Methodist church on Main Street in Carbondale on Saturday afternoon, June 14, 1975. We honeymooned at Devil's Kitchen Lake for two nights in an old tent my hippie friend lent us for the occasion, and then the following Monday, we tore down the campsite, returned my Dad's fishing boat to him, and headed eight hours' back to Milwaukee, straight up the 57 through Chicago. Anne was finishing her M.A. degree at UW and starting a full-time job in advertising. I continued the nightly beer-bar music cycle. And then one day the phone rang and on the other end was Amy Madigan and some of her musician compatriots -- the same Amy Madigan who later became a well-known actress in Hollywood, starring in "Field Of Dreams" and other movies. I'd been music chums with her whole rock band in Milwaukee, one they built during their years in college together at Marquette University. So Amy and company invited me to move to Los Angeles and play on their first album. They'd just been signed to

Electra/Asylum Records and would be cutting the record in the company's in-house studio, which was located in an old ranch house deep in the San Fernando Valley. It's as though it was meant to happen, deemed possible by God and the Universe as Anne was easily able to get her new corporate job transferred to LA, so we packed up the van, drove down to Carbondale to say our goodbyes, drove across the country, landed in LA, never left.

In Los Angeles, it was a different music scene from what I'd known...faster track, meaner and crazier people, crooked producers, a far-tougher hill to climb. I slowly learned the ropes and developed bigger- and bigger-ticket connections. Anne became a Hollywood publicist for a lot of years and moved up the chain in that world of activity. But at one memorable point in early '86, as I worked on the first house we bought, located in LA's Silverlake District, I noticed that I was starting to consistently turn down high-prestige music offers left and right for no reason that was obvious to me. Anne noticed it once or twice and inquired, and I wasn't exactly certain what I was feeling. Could've gone out on the road as Donna Summer's lead guitarist at the height of her disco career, turned it down. Turned down Bonnie Raitt -- more on that one in a minute. Turned down lots of high-end coke-snorting producers who I didn't like or appreciate, as well as some others. At 34, I came to terms with the fact that I'd always love making music, and by that time, I'd even developed into a fairly decent songwriter, having co-written one of Laura Branigan's hits, Captain and Tennille recorded one of my tunes, my bands were now consistently performing tunes I'd written or co-written.

But tell you what. I truly hated going out on the road for weeks and months at a crack. It wasn't fun and fellow band members' antics would always take their toll on my sense of wellbeing at some point...and I sure as hell loathed being some star's kiss-ass side musician. Also, I'm essentially an introvert by nature and couldn't abide the particular sort of collective personality adopted by Hollywood culture and especially ones at every level of the grotesque music business. I no longer wanted to live for and/or with them.

I was coming to terms with the fact that I truly wanted to be a family man, a good husband and father. I knew I'd always come back to music in some way, shape or form, but for now, I wanted to create some heavy distance from its scene. I called Anne on the phone one afternoon while she was at work at Warner Bros. I told her I wanted to quit music, build the best-possible life with her, have some kids. Within a few weeks, she was pregnant with first baby, born in late '86. Another one followed 20 months later. I played Mr. Mom and raised babies while working on our fixer house and we learned together that we truly enjoy that sort of activity. She held down a Hollywood film-biz career that she no longer particularly loved with all of her heart -- she was growing out of that scene as well -- but stayed with it for quite a few years' longer as a means to an end so we could move forward in figuring out how to live the lifestyle we wanted. I've never regretted the decisions we made that favored family and home over Hollywood.

At that moment, I walked away from my music career, probably at the height of it. Once the kids were old enough to go to school, Anne and I discovered the real estate appraisal business. We liked it because it would allow us to work at home and call our own shots, so we could parent our own kids...and it put us into daily contact with houses, something we both found very interesting in many ways. I spent about a year learning how to appraise and opened our business, and when it started making enough money to support us, Anne was able to finally walk away from Hollywood after 20-ish years in it and join me.

But looking back over those years as a rock-and-roller, I think about how so many experiences within it took me back to my small-town upbringing in Carbondale. All of it was so nostalgic...and all of it managed to creep into everything I was doing in my LA music life.

Here's what I mean -- I'll give you a few examples. During my Carbondale-based, college-era music experience, I started listening to Bonnie Raitt's early albums. Since The Beatles and Eric Clapton (whom I modeled my playing style after), I'd never fixated on someone's songs, guitar playing and vocal chops as I did hers, and it was a big dose in a short span of time. Anne, who has always been a bit clairvoyant or something -- and being, more or less in her words, "the young, immature, love-smitten, possessive, downright paranoid type who'd developed radar-like tendencies for discovering, threatening, chasing off an endless burlesque show of beer-bar floozies who vied for your attention on a near-nightly basis," well, her antenna shot up to the ceiling while I intently fixated on Bonnie Raitt's records. She will tell you she'd never seen me go so balls-out crazy for a single body of musical work, especially from some rising female rocker type on the west coast. I sat in front of my cheap Magnavox speakers day after day in Carbondale, hanging on her every guitar riff and slobbering over every vocal lick.

Anne said just now that she was thinking at that time "Am I outa my mind? Is this Bonnie Raitt person also after the love of my life, just like the beer-bar females? I don't care if she's a stranger, a star, a female who's twelve hundred miles away. It's a minor point! She's trouble, I tell you! I see her coming... C'mon old Bonnie girl...I'm ready for ya...C'MON!!! "I will come face to face with her...and oh, please don't let me die of a broken heart. Yeah. I'm crazy, that's true. But I smelled her planned dissent on me from halfway across the country. Of course, I knew I was mad at a hatter…yes, outa my mind...so young and insecure."

Anne's Bonnie Raitt-driven anxiety was something she didn't talk about, except once when she bawled during a high-drama argument and hollered out her deep-seated worry to me. I concurred. Yes. She was indeed out of her mind. Bonnie Raitt was a total stranger. But I kept listening, copying, perfecting turns of my slide guitar to match hers, played them out at Bonaparte's Retreat, Merlin's, big nightclubs and dances in Champaign and Bloomington and St. Louis, the one-horse roadside bars in Benton, Tamms, Dongola and drove 'em wild with my newly acquired tools of the trade.

So flash forward about six years or so to West Hollywood -- several years of marriage happily yet tentatively placed under our belts. I was rising up through the ranks of hip rocker types within the LA music scene, and Anne was also rising up and finding her place within the ranks of film-biz execs, so we were rubbing elbows here in town with its happening elite. Just for fun and politics, I sometimes played out in a band at The Troubadour with some music luminaries of the time — I recall the Tower Of Power rhythm section coming and going, the Chicago horn section, guys who'd played with the Cars, Steely Dan, Jackson Browne, some others, whoever was either coming or going from any given tour. As a hot casual "fun" band of sorts with inside-trackers on board, we grew this buzz and following Hoot Night and always, always filled the house.

On this one particular evening in the front portion of a set, I stepped forward and played a particularly inspired blues solo. The Troubadour room went wild — was at one with the delivery of it — and it was a prideful and satisfying moment of creating music I love.

Then suddenly, a surprise. Like a devil child rising up out of a menacing fire (says Anne) and a Dream Come True (says I)… The cheering and adoring Bonnie Raitt jumped up out of a seat from a few tables away…ran up to the edge of the chin-high stage, elbows supporting an excited face with adoring eyes, excitedly unabashedly parked herself on the steps on my side of the stage — and hung on every note I played as though her own life depended on it — wildly bobbing her head in creative solidarity, deeply and visibly drinking in every sound and move as if to let the entire Troubadour audience know, without question, that she supported my arrival to the inside-track scene. Anne's heart stopped. Bonnie remained there throughout the long duration of the set. It ended. Scads of friends, acquaintances, strangers lined up to speak with the two of us.

On Anne's side across the room, she was receiving these greetings from friends: "Hey, big night for Chuck, Anne..." "Congratulations to you guys, Anne..." "She's someone who ALWAYS calls, Anne...get ready!" Little did they know, Anne had been ready for a very long time. "Wow, what a talent, Anne...he's going somewhere..."

The room cleared out to a stage of quiet emptiness. Overhead lights came on. Chairs up on tables, waiters sweeping. Alone, Anne was still sitting. Bonnie was excitedly laughing, comparing notes with me, two kindred souls. Chuck. Bonnie. Lots of empty square footage. Finally, Anne gathered up her wits, sanity, poise...and made her way over to us. After all, at this point there was nowhere else for her to go.

Bonnie Raitt was utterly gracious and charming to Anne and me, and Anne in turn behaved in that moment like a nonchalant sane person, a grown-up who was delighted to be in her presence. There was no visible trace of "Carbondale Anne" at that moment. Bonnie invited us to come along with her to an after-gig gathering at Jennifer Warne's Hollywood bungalow. Of course, we went. We sat cross-legged on Jennifer's dining room floor with Bonnie and her manager Gary. We smoked, we drank, we laughed and scratched. In my altered state of mind within a whirl of revelry, we sized her up for the moment as being a so-called "real" person just like us. And then in the spirit of the social moment, Anne disclosed to Bonnie her looneyville Carbondale story that had vexed her during that time of life. Bonnie laughed older-sophisticate-style recognition (she was, what, 28?)...she asked Anne "How old are you?" "23" "Oh! Hahahaha...23! You're so young! I wish I could remember 23...you're so cute!" She continued "Hey, don't worry about a thing...See Gary here, my manager? We're a couple...very serious about each other, you see? Please, just relax."

Six months later Bonnie did indeed call me, just as predicted by one of my fellow musician friends on that Troubadour evening. Also as others predicted, she asked me to become her regular touring guitarist — I would travel all over the world with her, playing the songs and arrangements I'd so carefully studied back in Carbondale from analyzing her records. So far, so good. Then she shared, quite pointedly, in a disarmingly aggressive tone "Oh...Gary? I want you to know that he and I broke up. I'm now single."

Much to my amazement, without waiting even a millisecond...I turned her down flat. She was my music idol, my favorite. But I said no. First of all, it was crystal clear to me that going out on the road with Bonnie Raitt would quickly turn into a rough ride in the marriage department. But an equally jarring truth that flashed before me during that telephoned invitation was that I didn't want to live as someone/anyone else's sideman, not even the great Bonnie Raitt's. I have never wanted to be owned, to be someone's puppet on a string...and her cavalier revealing of her now-single status just in case it mattered to me, well, I had to ask myself just how much I actually enjoyed her personality, and more importantly, it made me sick to my stomach to think of putting Anne in that untenable situation. At that moment, I was indeed my own person, for better or for worse.

That lead guitarist Bonnie hired and put into the gig she offered me? He's George Maranelli, who was a friend of mine at the time, and he's still there. He's the one who took that gig those many years ago and benefited from it, and good for him. And just the other day, I was driving in Santa Monica with a local oldies radio station playing in the background. A song suddenly played that I hadn't heard in years...one by David Lasley called "If I Had My Wish Tonight" where I was hired to sing backgrounds in David's studio session, singing a part on my own in a small vocal booth at A&M Records that was mixed in with scads of others via multiple tracks. But in the closing bars of the song before the fade out, one can clearly hear me singing a background duet with Bonnie Raitt, who was also brought in on a separate day to sing on the same record and then our tracks were mixed together. It's a ghostly thing to hear...instantly takes me back to Walnut Street and Oakland Avenue where I sat in the basement of my drummer's ramshackle white house and taught myself Bonnie's musical links and style. Flash forward all these 40-some-odd years later...and there we are, singing together in the same style I learned in Carbondale serenading me through my car's speakers.

Here's another Carbondale-based coincidence that appeared later in my music life. In the early '80s, I went out on tour with Kim Carnes and James Taylor. One late night in some dank bar outside of Baltimore, I sat with James at a table in the corner and he got pretty sideways on some Jack Daniels. As he slid into that frame of mind, he started singing with some soul his improvised rendition of "Thanks A Lot" by HankWilliams, replete with some tasty yodeling. Suddenly I was catapulted back to Tatum Heights and then Canterbury Street in Carbondale. "Thanks A Lot" was a song my father repeatedly sang as he drank, puttered around the house, went about his daily business. It was uncanny to be sitting there on my own with James Taylor while he sang the same song with practically identical licks to my Dad's. I had the presence of mind to whip out the Sony Walkman recorder I carried in my pocket, and many years later, I found the tape in my studio mess, imported his a capella vocal into ProTools and created a backing track behind it, just for my own enjoyment. Funny thing is, I'd listened to that performance on that cassette tape a hundred times or more and each time I thought I detected a flaw in James' delivery, which I chalked up to his being a mere mortal like the rest of us. And years later, once I'd built that backing track, I realized James Taylor's drunken delivery of my Dad's favorite song was spot-on perfect. I guess he is indeed an exalted creature just as everyone believes.

Typical Carbondale high school-era songs that provided the background music for any and all romances, heartbreaks and slow dances were ones like "Cherish" by The Association, and certainly "Make It With You," "If," "Baby Im-A Want You" and others by Bread. In my travels through groups of people who worked alongside me to chase unattainable record deals, showcases, demo recordings were the very creators of those romantic theme songs of my Carbondale youth -- Barry Devorzon, who produced and probably wrote "Cherish" and got very rich from its royalties (not so for the band), and for years I worked very closely with Robb Royer from Bread as well as others from that band -- James Griffin, David Gates (to a lesser degree because of defunct Bread's in-fighting between members), Mike Botts, Larry Knechtel, who also played the famous piano part on "Bridge Over Troubled Water."

Carbondale band life also found me learning the hits of early-era Steely Dan. And then In the late '70s, I received a call to come join a band called Wha-Koo that was signed to ABC Records and was undergoing some personnel changes, and was already enjoying significant success in Australia and Canada, but hadn't yet broken into the U.S. market in any noteworthy way. The lead singer of Wha-Koo was a fellow by the name of David Palmer. I recognized the name...and yes, just as I thought, he used to be the lead singer of Steely Dan back when I resided in C'dale, and most notably sang their hit "Dirty Work." Along with David and other seasoned musicians in that band, we toured all over Australia where we were treated like The Beatles. We played outside the Sydney Opera House to a hundred thousand and did countless radio interviews and TV appearances. Then our fast-talking manager Leonard "Lenny" Stogle, who was also the promoter behind The Canada Jam, booked us into that event to play on the same bill as The Doobie Brothers, Commodores, Dave Mason, others. We played that day to an audience of 110,000 people, delivered to the venue backstage via helicopter. Lenny was on a roll, using The Canada Jam and a following east-coast tour to build us up for recording and marketing a new album that was intended to launch us in the U.S. market. We made one of the first-ever/pioneering rock videos for newly established MTV on a soundstage at SIR in Hollywood. The video "Fabulous Dancer" still plays on YouTube, and it's funny to see and hear the now-dated fashion and music trends of the time that we adopted. The production values were considered to be so forward-thinking at the time, but now look trite and jokester-ish. Although I never truly liked Wha-Koo's music, I was excited to be a key performer in a project that appeared to be actually leaving the ground and succeeding. And then...on May 25, 1979, the American Airlines flight #191 on which Lenny was a passenger crashed upon takeoff from Chicago O'Hare airport. Everyone on that flight perished. Ironically, Lenny was terrified to fly, didn't do it too much because his own parents died in a nearly identical American crash back in the '60s. Lenny's sudden death marked the end of Wha-Koo's anticipated upward trajectory.

And related to Wha-Koo...two more of my Carbondale-era music idols were Elvin Bishop, from whom I learned so many blues chops and developed my own version of that style, as well as Jerry Garcia and The Grateful Dead. I have a vivid memory of sitting in that aforementioned basement on Walnut Street and Oakland Avenue in C'dale, intently learning the Dead's licks and songs to play out at Merlin's, especially "Truckin'." I imagined in my mind's eye that I'd someday play music just like those folks...never once imagining I'd play with them. Art follows life and vice versa, so they say. During one of the Wha-Koo tours, we had a warm up date at a Santa Cruz bar where I met and jammed with my boy Elvin Bishop. He called me "Cochran!" in a barky but loving voice, and he immediately took a big liking to my style as a lead guitarist and singer -- after all, a portion of my Carbondale days were spent studying his style -- and then it was discovered that all of us would be playing together on the same ticket the next afternoon at a 20,000-person big concert on the football field at UC-Santa Barbara, along with The Grateful Dead and Warren Zevon. So Wha-Koo played (we were the low men on the ticket), at some point prior to Elvin's band coming to the stage, Bishop, Palmer and I worked out vocal harmonies to "Right Now Is The Hour" I still have a "board mix" recording of the actual performance of it living somewhere in my aforementioned studio mess. So his set started and when it was time for me to play, I strapped on my guitar, he introduced me and I walked out, plugged in, stepped up to the mike, poised to sing the part we'd rehearsed...and then he announced an additional surprise player...and he brought out Jerry Garcia to play with us. The crowd, of course, went hog wild -- and so did my insides. As the top-billed band, The Dead hadn't yet played. So Jerry and I traded guitar solos on a long rendition of "Right Now Is The Hour." I won't lie. It was a thrilling moment. My mind jumped back and forth from "Hey, watch what you're doing here..." to "Pour It On" to "Oh my

God, these guys were in my Carbondale life on Oakland and Walnut."
When the song ended, all guest players unplugged and left the stage for
Elvin to finish his set and Jerry complimented me on my playing. Pretty
thrilling moment for a guy who sat in front of a cheap record player
during a frigid Carbondale winter, copying Jerry Garcia's licks.

In the Carbondale period I was also crazy about Loggins and
Messina's music in their early years, turning up their hits on my van's
radio whenever KXOK played them. And then years later, I found
myself in a Santa Barbara studio for about a month's-worth of recording
with Jimmy Messina on his "One More Mile" album. A few weeks ago
while driving Anne home from her hip-replacement surgery, I turned on
the radio and what do you know? Playing through our Prius speakers was
me singing duet-style background vocals with Jimmy on the song "I Got
Radio" from that album. So ironic...I learned Jimmy's music in my youth
from hearing them on the radio. I was listening to the car radio now. I
was now hearing me sing "I Got Radio" with Jimmy Messina on my car
radio.

And fast forward to our kids' elementary school years in Los
Angeles. By that time, I'd long left the music business and just played
around with it for fun and for teaching my own kids to experience its
joys. Like everyone else in Carbondale during the late '60s and into the
'70s, music from Creedence Clearwater Revival played in the
background of everything we did. And then when our kids landed at
LA's Berkeley Hall School, it turned out John Fogerty was a fellow
parent there. I often produced the school's yearly so-called Variety Show
in its outside amphitheater as well as in its auditorium. John Fogerty was
always generous with his time and money, and practically every year he
brought his band to the show and performed for all of our families. After
the Fogerty and Cochran families' kids left Berkeley Hall to attend
nearby high schools, Berkeley Hall acquired an even bigger idol of mine
as a dad who commonly performed at subsequent BHS Variety Shows,
but alas, I never met him...he was Stevie Wonder.

I went through a period of time in being called to sing various TV
shows' and movies' theme songs...and they always seemed to represent
near misses of one sort or another. I was hired by Lorimar TV to sing the
theme song for the show "Married: The First Year," which immediately
bombed, but the recording is still alive on YouTube. And most notably in
that vein, I was hired to sing the rock song that ran over the end credits
of the movie "Loving Couples" starring Shirley MacLaine and Jason
Robards. I recorded the lead vocal, all was well, Anne and I attended the
cast & crew screening at 20th Century Fox just prior to the domestic
release, the end credits rolled, there was my name and there was my lead

vocal, all was well. Then a marketing/distribution exec decided an opportunity was being missed by not having a star sing that same song...and at the last moment my lead vocal track was shit canned, and one from Burton Cummings was added, and he copied my every lick. After all, he was a known entity that mattered in cross-collateralization and I was a nobody. But hey, back to life in Carbondale. How many times did I spin the record "These Eyes" by Guess Who, and I learned Burton Cummings' vocal delivery style, copying every lick and trying them out at Bonaparte's, etc. to deliver that hit song of his creation to the drunken college-bar hordes. The thrill of that one was now Burton Cummings was copying me.

You know, as I look back over my years in the LA music scene, I laugh at the realization that my career consisted of "near misses." I nearly missed a career of playing with Bonnie Raitt. I nearly missed having a major motion picture under my belt where I sang the end-credits song. I was in a band that nearly missed a first-class launch from a tried-and-true manager/promoter type...and then lost him in a flash to a tragic accident. I nearly missed scoring any number of record deals that went south for one reason or another.

But I don't regret a single thing that's happened because I've loved every moment of my life since that time. I loved being a good dad and the kids are grown up and gone. I still love being a good husband. I still have so much fun. I'm building a great recording studio and garden. Anne and I have a gas at the high school she started. I teach kids there to play and write rock and roll. Welcome to Hollywood!

LIFE LESSONS LEARNED IN THE 1960'S
IN CARBONDALE, ILLINOIS

By Col. Tom Blase

Input offered for the 50th Reunion of CCHS Class of '69
Non-graduate – but a Grateful Friend

I offer the following input to the book project of short stories for the CCHS 50th Reunion of the Class of 1969, with a humble and grateful heart for the many in the Class of '69 who had an impact upon my life. I lived in Carbondale in the early to mid '60's, as my father was in the military (U. S. Air Force Colonel) and the head of the Reserved Officer Training Corps (ROTC) … the Professor of Aerospace Science at Southern Illinois University. In the military community, we moved as a family every 3 years on the average. So when we were stationed at Carbondale for five years with my Dad on staff at S.I.U., I felt as if we won the lottery. We got to live in the same place, make friends and memories, and enjoy life in a college town. I didn't realize until later years in life (even to this day) how good life was then!

During those years, I was in the 3rd thru the 7th grade and had the privilege to meet a lot of great people at Winkler Elementary School and Lincoln Jr. High. I was not fortunate to graduate from Carbondale Community (due to my father's military transfer), but I knew a lot of the people in the Classes of '68 and '69. My life was impacted by so many friends, teachers / administrators and family members in Carbondale that I took life lessons with me to other moves within the military… as a child and then in my adult life and military career. After my Dad retired from the military, we moved to St. Louis, and I was able to renew friendships with C'dale friends during 1967-69 and beyond.

The lifetime influence of many in the list below (although I know that I will unintentionally miss or forget the impact of some not mentioned) touched me and shaped me for the man, son, husband, Christian, military officer, pastor and the citizen in society that I have had the privilege to experience. In no particular order, I am grateful for the following and others not mentioned, due to my 68 year old memory: Ms. Acks (my 3rd grade teacher and whose son played football at CCHS and later at Univ. of IL, I believe), Ms. Wiggins (my 4th grade teacher), Mr. Mendenhall (my sixth grade teacher and elementary basketball coach), Mr. Martin (our principal at Winkler Elementary), Bruce Fohr, Dick LeFevre, Wally and Bob Crane, Terry Etherton, Mike Cochran, Doug Woolard, Bob Pankey, Tom and Denny Pankey (Bob's brothers), John Wham, Steve Waller, Eric Beyler, John "Old Boy" and Betty Jo Fohr (Bruce's parents), Bruce's brother (Johnny), Harry and Mary Pankey (Bob's parents), Coach Larry Drake (Lincoln Jr. High), Coach Stevenson (Lincoln Jr. High), Charles Horst (teacher & scorekeeper at BBall games at Lincoln Jr. High), Tim and Mike Higgins (neighbors who lived across the street & attended University High), many athletic opponents from other elementary schools in C'dale...Brush & other grade schools (Bob Westburg, Jim Martin, Steve Thompson, etc.) and my family...Mom and Dad (George and Ferne Blase), older brother & younger sister (George "Sparky" & Melinda "Lindy") and younger brothers (Roger & Mike). Life was good in the early to mid '60's, my best childhood memories... C'dale was the place!

Family, Faith, and Friends

As I view family, I feel that all those mentioned above are a community of support and should be considered "a family of support and encouragement". But the primary human source of encouragement and development for me in my life was (and is) my immediate, biological family. I do realize that there are many in society, and perhaps some in the CCHS Class of '69, whose biological family are not a positive influence in their lives. To that end, I'd encourage those persons to consider their closest friends or their positive role models within their extended family, even their spiritual / faith understanding of a Heavenly Father or spiritual mentor, to be a source of encouragement, accountability, inspiration, and guidance. Perhaps some of those in the CCHS Class of '69 can (or already) serve in that capacity.

My Mom & Dad and siblings, and now my children and grandchildren, serve as my second greatest source of guidance, encouragement, and inspiration… only behind my faith and spiritual journey with my Heavenly Father, who has revealed himself in the person of the Lord Jesus Christ. Although I am passionate about my Christian faith ever since I repented from my sinful nature and asked Jesus to forgive my sins and be in relationship with me as my personal Savior and Lord of life (back in May, 1977), I fully respect all persons of different faiths or those with no faith allegiance. Life is too short for us not to love and respect all people, and we are all called to reach out to others in kindness and hope.

My Mom and Dad lived a life in the active duty military, with moves to many locations, cities, and also foreign locations. My Dad retired in August, 1967, and we moved to St. Louis, where I finished high school in the northern part of the city and then entered the US Air Force Academy in late June, 1969. I followed in their footsteps as a military man and family….and now some of my children and grandchildren are continuing in their career pursuits in a similar fashion. More about that later. The military journey is not an easy life because of family separations, sacrifices, challenges and some heartaches; but the military also has its joys, adventures, meaningful relationships and rich experiences.

Some of those joys and meaningful relationships came in my life in southern Illinois. My Dad and Mom (and our family of five children) moved to Carbondale, IL in 1959 from the Washington, D.C. area, where my Dad was finishing up his second tour at the Pentagon. Earlier in 1951, I was born at Scott Air Force Base, IL (near Belleville and Ofallon, IL). We lived in various places in my early life, including time in Tokyo, Japan, as my Dad was involved in senior leadership in the post-Korean Conflict and other strategies in the Pacific region of the world. My Dad and my wife's (Beth's) Dad were both WW2 bomber pilots, and they served courageously with great achievements alongside their patriotic colleagues. Where would we be today in our nation without the self-sacrifices and contributions of the "Greatest Generation"? My wife's Dad and mine were highly decorated war heroes, as Beth's Dad helped plan and execute the air cover for D-Day at Normandy and Omaha Beaches in France. My Dad also served in the European Theater, receiving the Silver Star and numerous Distinguished Flying Crosses for his leadership in combat missions. Through all our moves as a military family, I was not a great fan (especially as a child and a teen) in moving often when I was doing it ….but, later in reflection, I am a better person for it and more appreciative of diverse cultures and traditions in our country and abroad. My Father and Mother and their military experiences (and the service of my in-laws) definitely inspired me and contributed to my calling to serve our country in my career of over 37 years of military service… to include 30 years of active duty and over 7 years of Air Force Reserve service.

When we saw the house on 2.5 acres of land on Chautauqua Ave. that the University (S.I.U.) provided to our family, my siblings and I were elated. I believe that house is used now for SIU Alumni Affairs, or at least it primarily was used in that capacity (when I revisited the property in 1995 in between military moves for my family from FL to OK). In those early days at Chautauqua, we didn't have much to watch on TV (or even very many stations that had any programming, and we only had one TV). Nor did we have video games or other sedentary types of entertainment, so a big yard with many trees to climb and a driveway for a basketball goal and half-court were a joy unspeakable. And the best part of our home was a huge backyard that my older brother (Spark) and I turned into a full baseball field with homerun fences, etc. ….that also doubled as a football field in the different seasons of sport life. Plus my Dad later purchased a couple of horses that were boarded about 1 to 2 miles down Chautauqua, heading west. Now our home and yard and fields were not the "Field of Dreams", but you could have fooled my brother and me and our many friends who came to play.

My Dad and Mom met in Columbia, MO, back in the 1930s, where my Dad went to the University of Missouri and played football and baseball in those days. I believe that my Dad's love for Mizzou (as well as my brother's and my love for MU) perhaps had some impact on Bob Pankey selecting that scholarship to play for the Tigers, when he was recruited by quite of few quality Division 1 programs. Bob told me later that after his Dad, Harry, had passed away during his high school years that my Dad, George, was one of the voices from which he sought counsel. My Mom went to Stephens College in Columbia, as she was raised in Harrisburg, IL (where her Dad was a Fire Chief). I still have great memories playing catch in our backyard with my Mom's Dad (Grandpa Ray). He died way too young in 1960. To this day, I have a huge respect and gratitude for my Father, who chose to take a job at SIU with the ROTC Detachment, versus staying in DC for another Pentagon assignment and hoping to make the rank of General. He served selflessly during his whole career in his active duty assignments before retirement as a Colonel. We lived in Carbondale… about 40 miles from Harrisburg, IL and about 100 miles from St. Louis, where my Dad's Father lived. We were in a great place in between both sets of grandparents, although my Grandma Eva on my Dad's side had died when we were stationed in Japan. While in Carbondale in our great home / yard and schools, my older brother and I (and my family) developed a great joy for sports (including my lifelong following of the St. Louis Cardinals) and other professional and college teams. My love for sports and desire to achieve academically would impact my future pursuits and career interests (to be addressed later).

It was in those early 60's in Carbondale and my love for the simple things of life in mid-America that my interests in matters of faith also began to take root. The church life in our neighborhood church near Winkler Elementary School is where I saw faithfulness in my folks, and it is where I had other interests begin to catch my joy, like enjoying Boy Scouts. My faith journey did not take full bloom until later in 1977, but the beginning of my searching began in Carbondale, as influenced and encouraged by my loving folks and those in the community of faith. Later in life, after a few years as a Christian in my faith walk (in 1979-80), I felt the call of our Lord into full-time Christian ministry. It was also in those early years in the '60s that I saw the great value of friends and the special connections at school.

School Connections

When we moved to Carbondale and found out that we would attend Winkler Elementary, I was encouraged that we could ride our bicycles to school. My older brother, George (Sparky), who I grew later in life to affectionately call "Spark" (and he dubbed my nickname as "Bud") helped pave the way for me in many respects... athletically and academically. We were different and confident in our own respective abilities, but we also had common school friends through the years... like Bob and Wally Crane (who lived around the corner from us), Mike Cochran, Bruce Fohr, and Bob Pankey, as well as others. I have vivid memories of academic challenges and accomplishments at Winkler School. I recall a poor progress report that I got in 4th grade from Ms. Wiggins in Science Class. My Mother and Dad helped me realize that I needed to spend more time in reading and comprehension. I was able to pull the grade up, and it served as an eye-opener for me early in my academic life. I do admit that I enjoyed the athletic and recess realm much better than the books in those days... trying to out-run Wally Crane and Eric Beyler and others in speed races on the athletic / recess fields or during Field Day events.

My life met a small challenge during those years during one recess period. Terry Etherton, with whom I have no ill feelings and do not hold responsible, and I collided while running and playing tag on a crowded playground. My upper lip was split open, later became infected with a staff-infection, and I found out later from my parents that the infection became very serious during my hospitalization. Although it was a scare, I have some good memories of my hospital stay due to the ice cream and different jellos that I got to eat. Terry and I have had a few laughs about the event in later years, when I visited him, Bruce Fohr and John Wham in Tucson, Arizona. Wow, Terry has done quite well and has a beautiful art gallery and collections in his distinguished career. In reflection, I am sure it was my inattention that caused the collision, as I was likely trying to outrun or avoid the pursuit of the speedy Wally Crane or others.

It was during those Winkler days that my brother's skills and my athletic skills and interests increased in our backyard and driveway games of baseball, football, and basketball. School friends would come over and spend full days in the heat of the summer. We loved the sandlot games, as we only took a break for lemonade or water breaks or when my Mom would bring out lunch sandwiches. Only the dark hours or a periodical injury would stop the play for any significant time period. We all got a scare when my youngest brother, Mike (as an 18 month to 2 year-old, I recall), had wandered out onto our baseball area and got hit in the head with a player's warm-up bat swing. It knocked him out cold, and the same doc (who saw me through my hospitalized staff-infection from my schoolyard collision accident) made a home visit and calmed everyone's worst fears. I still can't remember to this day who swung the bat (it really doesn't matter), and my brother's hard head has served him well in life as a family man, school counselor, teacher, coach, man of faith, and now working in his Grandpa years as a Social Service worker in Hannibal, MO... helping the less fortunate find sustainable work.

In my sixth grade year, I met a new friend who moved to Carbondale, when his Dad was transferred as a Professor and Department Head at SIU. Bruce Fohr and I hit it off immediately in that 6th grade year, and as the Bible says, we became "iron sharpening iron" immediately. Yes, I admit that we had some mischief thru the years, but we became each other's "Best Man" at our weddings in 1977 (Bruce with Janet in June in Minneapolis, MN) and (my vows with Beth in November in Montgomery, AL). Bruce and my friendship continued into 7th grade at Lincoln Jr. High in Mr. Charles Horst's room and during other school activities. Bruce and I are dear friends to this day, along with others from our Lincoln Jr. High days. We had some laughs and great learning in the classroom with Mr. Horst's eccentric teaching style, but what a motivator Charles Horst was ... for each of us. His sponsored train trips to St. Louis to see the Cardinals and the great meals at the Forum Cafeteria downtown were great highlights. I cannot fully remember who all went on those trips with me, but I think it was Bruce Fohr, Bob Pankey, John Wham, Terry Etherton, Wally Crane, Dick LeFevre, and I'm sure others. Great Times!

I also have fond memories of the formative years in my love for sports that were birthed in our Chautauqua home field and driveway. My baseball skills were honed and lived out in the youth baseball league on the ball fields near CCHS and the CCHS football field. The basketball competition in the elementary schools against players like Bob Pankey, Bob Westburg, Jim Martin, Steve Thompson, and others sharpened our abilities…while Dick LeFevre, Wally Crane, and Terry Etherton joined me and others, like Eric Beyler, I believe, on our Winkler team. Most of us transitioned into the Jr. High classrooms and fields/courts at Lincoln Jr. High and continued our development in character, academics and athletics. My time playing on teams under Coaches Stevenson and Drake with guys like Bob Pankey, Doug Woolard, Mike Cochran, Bob and Wally Crane, Chuck Taylor, Bob Westburg, my brother (Spark) and others helped form me & others for what was to come in the future years of collegiate competition.

A Generation of Focus & Forever Friends

What I see as a common denominator in my Carbondale friends is an appreciation for our heritage during the time in which we were raised as "Baby Boomers". I know that the generational groups that followed after the "boomers" may see life and opportunities a bit different from the Class of '69 and other "boomers". I realize that the current generation of Gen Z youth (those born in 1996 or later), as well as the Gen X (1965-79 births) and Millenials / Gen Y (1980-95 births) youth, are wired differently from "Baby Boomers" (1946-64 births). I see our "Boomer" generation as individuals who can focus and develop lasting friendships. We seemed to use our friendship time to develop close bonds, and, yes, we had fun; but our work ethic, goal setting, and perseverance seemed to set us apart, for the most part… at least for the C'dale friends that I knew then and now. The friendships that I formed in those days have served me well to this day.

A few examples… when Bruce Fohr moved to C'dale with his Professor Dad, I saw a potential friend in the 6th grade, and he has become a lifetime great friend. Not only did we become each other's "best man" in our weddings to our brides, but the untimely tragic death of his brother, Johnny, in a car accident in AZ in the early '80's helped me deal with my brother's death (tragically from AIDS) about 6 years later. We both had remembered the heartache from our common good friend, Bob Pankey, when his Father, Harry, died way too soon…while Bob and Bruce were in high school at CCHS. I had moved back to the general area (when my Dad retired from the Air Force and returned to St. Louis, MO), so I was able to travel down to C'dale and be with my two friends and the Pankey family in their time of loss of the Pankey Patriarch. We had nurtured our friendship in the mid '60s, when my Dad left C'dale and SIU and was transferred in the Air Force to Montgomery, AL. I stayed in touch with my C'dale buddies, with us even making trips to see each other. When I resettled in St. Louis, after my Dad's USAF retirement, I made numerous trips back to C'dale, and even traveled to Cahokia, IL to see the CCHS Terriers play and win 25-20 in their road game against a quality opponent on their way to an undefeated season in '68. Through the years, Bob and Bruce also got to know some of my St Louis close high school friends, and they continue in friendship to this day… friends like John "Moe" Siemers, Bob Brooks, Ray Finke and others. All of us were saddened when Bob Pankey's brother, Tom, died of a brain tumor years later. And when my two friends' mothers, Mary (Bob's Mom) and Betty Jo (Bruce's Mom), left this earth for their eternal home, we all shared in that time of grief, as well. Friends like that are uncommon, as we shared in life's joys and heartaches. These friends should be kept forever, and I sense that there are a lot of CCHS Class of '69 friends who fit that "forever" category.

C'dale Roots, Career Pursuits and Legacies Left

When I reflect upon my C'dale roots, as the best childhood days and place to live in my entire life (even with multiple military moves), I realize we had an idyllic setting with great friends. I know that the '60's were some challenging times in our nation, with the assassination of President JFK, the Civil Rights struggles, the Vietnam War conflict and manner in which our society dealt with those dynamics and disrespected our military servicemen, the Beatles and other rock groups, the hippie movement, and later the tragic assassinations in '68 of MLK, Jr. and RFK. However, in C'dale there seemed to be a calm, focus on the simple matters of life, and many traditional life experiences. I do recall the personal impact and feelings, when Bruce Fohr's brother, Johnny, went to Vietnam as a medic, and later in life how I realized that Johnny's time in the jungles of Vietnam changed him for life. I'm sure it helped my friend Bruce grow up more quickly, and we were all saddened by Johnny's untimely car accident and death in the early '80's. Life has a way with up turns and down turns, but our friends help make our paths and our journey smoother.

Granted that C'dale was not just filled with "Leave it to Beaver" or "My Three Sons" families, but our time of growing up in southern Illinois (with good role models and concerned / effective teachers and coaches) helped set us up for success. With the academic and athletic achievements of CCHS friends, and even how my brother Spark and I were able to make the most of our military moves and multiple schools, our circle of friends from C'dale (and those friends who I later met) were able to make some significant transitions to our college years and beyond. My brother Spark applied for and was accepted at the U. S. Air Force Academy and their first-class education & training (fully paid scholarship). He, like me, saw the great experiences and the adventures of our Father's full military career. Since Spark was already at the Academy, it made it easier for my friend Bruce Fohr and me to consider also going out to Colorado Springs to the Academy. Like Spark, Bruce and I also had the high school academic achievements, sports and leadership credentials, and interest to attend the rigorous training. I was also fortunate to be recruited by the AF Academy to play Division 1 basketball (which was a life goal of mine). I realized that all the games in our C'dale Chautauqua driveway and the years of sweat and hardwood play that followed in Alabama and St. Louis had paid off. I found out later that CCHS graduate Steve Waller also became a Class of '73 AF Academy classmate of Bruce and mine, and Steve made us proud as a player on the Air Force football team. And when I heard that Bob Pankey had accepted a full football scholarship to University of Missouri (my Dad's alma mater and where my brother and I later went to Mizzou for our Master's Degrees), I was elated. Furthermore, when Bruce and Pank shared with me the many different schools where some of CCHS friends and the undefeated Terriers teammates received scholarships, I wasn't surprised that so many from our C'dale friends were set up for success in career pursuits and life.

As our college years unfolded, my brother (Spark) and good friend (Bruce) did not finish their education at the Academy (although they both were fully capable). They both left to follow other pursuits. Spark got his multiple degrees in business and education and had a very successful career in corporate business, teaching / coaching, sports administration, and college and high school officiating. Bruce went back to S.I.U. for his undergraduate and Master's in Business, and then to Mizzou for his advanced degree in Journalism. And his career in corporate business, worldwide media research, and as an entrepreneur is nothing short of remarkable. With Bob Pankey going on to receive his PhD and become a dynamic college professor after his football playing days at Mizzou, I further saw vivid examples of C'dale roots setting friends up for success. One interesting side note from my brother's and my time in C'dale was how my brother later re-connected with an old teammate from our Lincoln Jr. High days (Doug Woolard), as Spark officiated games for Doug in later years in C'dale, when Doug was in Sports Administration. We live in a small, yet connected world... where friends reconnect and remain friends forever.

As for me and how my life unfolded from the seeds planted in C'dale, I finished my education at the AF Academy and served as captain of our basketball team, later attended Mizzou on a NCAA Postgraduate Scholarship and went on to serve over 37 years in the Air Force. I started my Air Force career as a graduate assistant basketball coach for Air Force and then served as a management engineer. During my engineer years (doing manpower studies on AF medical centers and hospitals), I became a Christian and soon thereafter felt called into full-time Christian service in pastoral ministry. After much prayer and counsel, I resigned my regular commission in the Air Force, took a reserve commission, and moved my young family from Alabama (where Beth & I married) back to Missouri (Kansas City) to study theology and other pastoral skills at seminary.

During those seminary years, my wife worked as a teacher and a registered nurse and I pastored a small inner-city Baptist church. Finances were tight in those years, and we were so grateful for "forever friends", like Bruce and Janet Fohr who graciously provided not only prayer, but financial support. Later after graduation and pastoral experience, our family moved across the state to serve in mission work in the St. Louis area, where I was able to enjoy proximity to my biological family for about 5 years…until I re-entered the Air Force as an active duty chaplain and served for the next 22 + years until my AF retirement. When my family celebrated our retirement from the Air Force in late 2010, I was blessed to retire at the same rank (Colonel) as my Father, but I never felt that I could sincerely be compared to my Dad and his sacrificial service of WW2 and beyond. I did have the privilege, like my Mom and Dad, to meet many great people throughout our country and around the world in Air Force assignments and deployments to distant places (even combat zones), but few people compared to the friends that I had met in Carbondale back in the '60s. Two of those C'dale friends from the '60s were at my retirement festivities and luncheon in 2010… Bruce Fohr and Bob Pankey. Thanks!!!

Yes, the roots in C'dale had set me up for success in life, and as I now look at life as a 68 year- old, I am interested in "passing on the baton" to my 4 children and 12 grandchildren. I am blessed beyond what I deserve. I had a wonderful family growing up and even so now. Some of my children and my oldest grandson, at the time of this writing, have followed in my folks' and my wife's parents', and my wife and my career footsteps. Three of four of my children have served or are currently serving our country in the military family. I sense my oldest son would have also served in the military, if he didn't have some medical challenges with his asthma. Nevertheless, he has done quite well in the corporate world with his strong work ethic and sincere dedication. My daughter is married to an AF pilot, and she has served sacrificially as a spouse and mother of seven military children. My middle son and his wife both are Marine Corps veterans and now serve in public service as law enforcement officers. My youngest son and his wife are currently in South Korea, where he serves our nation as an AF F-16 pilot. My oldest grandson (son of my daughter) just started his freshman year at the AF Academy. It is a joy that my AF Academy Class of '73 is the Legacy Class (50 years prior) for my grandson's Class of '23. All of Beth and my children and our grandchildren are our heroes, as I believe they understand the greater purpose and calling in life. They continue to mature in their character development and career pursuits, but I believe they already have an understanding that life is bigger than each of them and that their humble and selfless service and love for others will please their Heavenly Father as they live a life of faith. Yes, it will also make my wife and me proud, but I am grateful for their hearts' desire is to please Almighty God.

Summary Thoughts and Lessons Paid Forward

As I now continue to serve in ministry with an international parachurch non-profit organization with the military, I have the privilege to assist military chaplains and chapel staffs on military installations. I partner with dedicated and faithful volunteers and team members in my role as a Local Director for a military ministry, supporting ministry of military chaplains and chapel staffs. As our ministry team shares the gospel of our Lord Jesus Christ with a younger generation of primarily "Millenials and Gen Z" military service members, we recognize that we currently live in a digital age with much more of a consumeristic, secular & humanistic society. Traditional values, family traditions, patriotic service, and lifelong friendships (built on face-to-face relationships) may not be now what they used to be in our development as "Boomers" in the '60s. Yet we have lessons learned that we should "pay forward" to the next generation and beyond… maybe more important now than ever.

I know that there were plenty in our C'dale days and beyond who helped ("paid forward") with lessons for the Class of '69 with their inspiration, encouragement, and examples, as we chased our dreams and goals. People have made a difference in our lives…individuals like Denny Pankey, Johnny Fohr, Mike Cochran, Doug Woolard, Tim and Mike Higgins, George (Spark) Blase, our parents, our siblings, our classmates, and the list goes on. I close my stories with some enduring principles that continue to serve us and will empower others in years to come. Perhaps these statements will resonate with you (please add more): Love well, offer and receive forgiveness, and be trustworthy; Live a life of thanksgiving with a heart of gratitude and love / service to others; Know your faith and life priorities and don't be distracted by detours, minor irritants, or major bumps; Perseverance and dedication will help you triumph over adversity; Find and keep a balance in the following dimensions of human wellness – spiritual, physical, social and emotional; Nurture others and care for those with needs; It's not about you, and there is no "I" in team; Be a person of hope and kindness; Believe in yourself and others, but know your limitations; Be accountable, learn from your mistakes, and take responsibility; Strive for excellence and be a person of integrity, with transparency; Know yourself and don't take yourself too seriously; Be humble and don't think too highly of yourself; Slow down, be inspired in order to inspire others; Value others and serve them with intentionality.

I know that each of us in the Class of '69, whether graduates from CCHS or elsewhere (like me), have experienced life with challenges, joys, heartaches, and achievements, but I believe that all of us can collectively share that we are better people with lifelong lessons from our days in Carbondale in the 1960's. I am grateful for the opportunity to offer an input to your CCHS Class of '69 book project for the 50th Reunion. I sincerely appreciate the invite of Bob Pankey to share my stories. God bless you, CCHS '69 members, families and friends !!!

Made in the USA
Las Vegas, NV
05 January 2022

40361185R00144